The Handbook of
RIDING

Mary Gordon-Watson

Foreword by
Captain Mark Phillips

D0279019

Pelham Books

The Handbook of Riding was conceived, edited and designed by
Dorling Kindersley Limited, 9 Henrietta Street, London WC2E 8PS

Project editor   Susan Berry
Art editors   Polly Dawes
Bob Gordon
Editors   Miren Lopategui
Ann Kramer
Designer   Gillian Della Casa
Technical consultant   Jenny MacArthur

Managing editor   Jackie Douglas
Art director   Roger Bristow

PELHAM BOOKS

Published by the Penguin Group
27 Wrights Lane, London W8 5TZ, England
Penguin USA, 375 Hudson Street, New York, NY 10014, USA
Penguin Books Australia Ltd, Ringwood, Victoria, Australia
Penguin Books Canada Ltd, 10 Alcorn Avenue, Toronto, Ontario,
Canada, M4V 3B2
Penguin Books (NZ) Ltd, 182-190 Wairau Road, Auckland 10,
New Zealand

Penguin Books Ltd, Registered Offices:
Harmondsworth, Middlesex, England

First published 1982
Reprinted 1991,1993,1995

Printed in Hong Kong by Wing King Tong Co. Ltd

ISBN 0 7207 1998 4

Contents

Foreword

Mary Gordon-Watson and I were exact contemporaries when we embarked on adult horse trials. Her generosity in allowing Richard Meade to ride her great horse, Cornishman V, in the Mexico Olympics was to be amply rewarded in the years to follow, when she had the unique run of winning the individual European and world titles in 1969 and 1970, followed by being placed fourth in the European Championships in 1971 and fourth in the Olympic Games in 1972 in Munich. It has to be said that Cornishman made the major contribution to those five team gold medals, with Mary riding him on the last four occasions. This record has never been equalled and will surely never be bettered, and it was achieved because Mary created a remarkable partnership with her horse. Her understanding and sensitive approach brought out the very best in Cornishman, an attitude which forms the basis of her teaching in *The Handbook of Riding*.

I wish I had possessed such a book when I was a novice in the riding world – both Mary and I had to learn by our mistakes. I remember only too well my own early years and, knowing what I do today, when I think of some of the things I tried to do in those days, I get a cold shiver down my spine. Mary, too, suffered many disappointments before she came back to the top of the sport for those four golden years. The lessons she learned the hard way have been set out in this book for today's aspiring riders.

There can be no doubt that standards have improved dramatically over the last decade. Every year the international competitions seem to get harder and harder to win, as competitors get better and better. I'm sure the reason for this is that the level of knowledge about the horse is being improved all the time, as are standards of training.

The young of today, if they want to learn, are very fortunate to have so much information so readily available. Mary has made a handsome contribution to this fund of information, and I am sure that all who aspire to follow in her footsteps will be helped enormously by reading this excellent and authoritative book.

Mark Phillips

Captain Mark Phillips on the young horse, Out and About

Preface

My own experiences as a young rider were the main influence on my later competitive career, and on the approach I have taken to this book.

My early riding days had not been particularly promising. An inability to control a wilful but talented Connemara mare led me, at the age of 14, to have lessons from the late Captain Ben Jones, who taught me within one week more than I had learnt in six years of struggling on my own. This apparently miraculous transformation and the successes which followed so impressed and inspired me, that riding suddenly became my obsession.

This experience also gave me the confidence, enthusiasm, and ability later on to train my father's immature, 17hh, near-thoroughbred hunter/racehorse, for eventing. Cornishman's strong character and powerful physique – qualities that later combined to make him such an outstanding event horse – made the progress towards a partnership far from smooth at times.

The problems and setbacks that I experienced as a young rider, and with Cornishman, have made me very aware that *all* riders, whether novice or more experienced, need consistent and expert tuition.

I hope that this book will help to provide this, and will prove an inspiration to all riders, at whatever level of experience.

Finally, I would like to thank all those who have helped to produce this book. In particular, I would like to single out my "stable manager", Julia Baxter; the riders who demonstrated techniques for the camera (and who also very unselfishly produced errors on demand!); Jenny MacArthur and Christine Dodwell for their invaluable comments on my text; and the team of editors, designers, photographers and illustrators who helped to turn the original manuscript into the finished book.

Above, Captain Ben Jones, who did so much to further the career of Cornishman, riding him at Burghley Horse Trials in 1968.

Right, Mary Gordon-Watson, also on Cornishman, at Badminton in 1969. They went on to win the Individual Gold Medal in the European Championships in France the same year.

Mary Gordon-Watson

8

Riding today

The explosion of interest in riding that has taken place in the last forty years may seem astonishing alongside the rapid progress of mechanization, but on reflection the reasons for it are easy enough to understand. The attractive nature of the horse and his versatility have appealed to man for longer, probably, than history relates. For centuries the horse was the principal means of transport but now the emphasis has moved from utility to pleasure. Gradually different breeds of horses and ponies have been selected, developed and improved to suit a wide variety of equestrian activities, and those lucky enough to have enjoyed contact with horses realize that they have much more to offer than faster, noisier and lifeless alternatives.

Horses deserve their popularity. If well treated they are willing to please, bold yet calm, and trusting. They are easy to train and unusually adaptable – the same horse can be successful in eventing, show jumping, dressage, racing, team chasing, and can also travel up to 150km (93 miles) in a day.

One of the greatest attractions of riding is that it can be enjoyed at every level, according to skill and experience. More and more people of all ages and backgrounds are discovering this pastime and deriving unlimited pleasure from it, either as active participants or interested spectators. This development owes a great deal to the guidance and encouragement of dedicated organizations such as the Pony Club and riding clubs which have sprung up all over the world. The standard of teaching has steadily

Trail riding, Western-style, above, offers plenty of scope for healthy outdoor exercise and can be enjoyed by riders of all standards. Young riders who prefer a challenge can enter for Pony Club events, right, which provide excitement as well as valuable all-round experience.

KKIO2468

improved while easier communication and travel have brought new instruction, rivalry and competition, leading to better horses, and improved horse management and training facilities. A greater selection of useful books and films is spreading knowledge still further, while progressive examinations in every branch of equitation, set by the governing national organizations, ensure that standards are maintained.

It is never too late to become involved with horses. A "mature" or elderly rider, who may perhaps have lost some dash, but has great enthusiasm and knowledge, can enjoy riding as much as the keen, brave young rider who has many years of learning ahead before his skill matches his courage.

No time spent in the saddle is wasted; as you learn to communicate with the horse and appreciate what he can do for you, it will add a fascinating new dimension to your life. Even just "sitting" on a horse provides some rewards, but most riders would agree that some investment in good instruction proves invaluable as it makes riding more comfortable and more fun.

Riding for pleasure

Those who want to ride occasionally, just for pleasure, can go hacking or trekking, or take a riding holiday. These are enormously popular and demand little skill. They are usually supervised and provide an excellent opportunity for healthy physical exercise while enabling you to see the countryside in the company of others, and improve your riding at the same time.

Riding can be a leisurely activity or a demanding one. Above, a group of young riders being taken for a quiet hack and, right, the thrill and excitement of top-level show jumping, as Nick Skelton and Lastic clear a huge fence at Olympia.

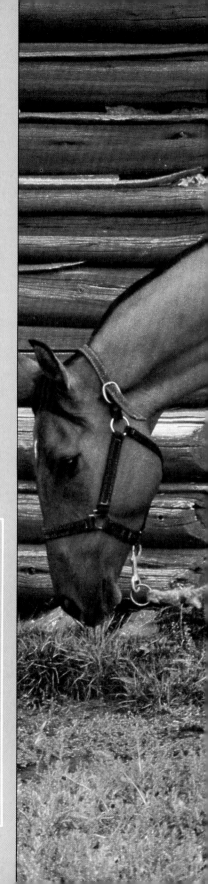

INTRODUCTION

For the more ambitious, long-distance or endurance riding offer a greater challenge and require greater skill. They are physically demanding and can be hazardous, as you and your horse must cross difficult terrain. This form of riding has developed into an international competitive sport, with ultimate tests of up to 160km (100 miles) in one day. Most of the popular official pleasure rides and team relay rides are 16–32km (10–20 miles) long, with the emphasis on maintaining an average speed, rather than racing. Any rider of any age, riding any sort of horse, can take part, provided they are fit.

Recent years have also seen a strong revival in side-saddle riding – a return to elegance and grace – while Western riding, too, has won popular interest and is spreading rapidly across the world. An important recent development too has been the organization of riding for the disabled, recognized as excellent therapy as well as an enormous source of pleasure.

Most riders are non-competitive, attracted mainly by a love of horses and the enjoyment they can give, and by their closeness to the more natural pace of life, too often elusive in modern times. But for those who love excitement and speed, and the challenge of competition, there are many opportunities. Sports such as hunting, cross-country riding, racing and polo have never been more popular. These exhilarating activities are often expensive and can be dangerous; to minimize the risks you must be a competent rider. Other popular activities include hunter trials, orienteering, gymkhana events, showing, musical rides, and quadrilles.

Different styles have been developed in riding. Christine Stückelberger and Granat, above, demonstrate the art of classical dressage at Grand Prix level, while a rider, right, prepares his horse in Western tack for an informal trail ride.

Competitive riding

The greatest ambition for many riders is to compete with success in dressage, show jumping or one- and three-day events, sports which have earned their own places in the Olympic Games. In these, the rider's skill and dedication become paramount. The training will be long and arduous and often painfully frustrating, but the rewards can be thrilling. Luck, too, plays a part; you must have the right horse at the right time to reach the heights. Horses are increasingly expensive to buy, keep and transport, and although their owners and riders are prepared to forgo most other pleasures to continue in their chosen sport, many have found escalating costs too high, and have been forced to seek sponsorship to maintain high standards. Despite financial depression, many sponsors have been forthcoming, which is in itself a strong tribute to the horse. Certainly there is little to equal the thrill of aiming for, and competing at, the top level, displaying a harmony with your horse that is both beautiful to watch and fulfilling to achieve.

Dressage

Essentially dressage is the "art" of riding, its aim being to improve the horse's balance and physique and to achieve complete harmony between horse and rider. Its origins go back over the centuries, although formal principles date first from sixteenth-century Italy and subsequently from France, and from such great riding masters as François de la Guerinière. Until recently, dressage, whether as an art or a training technique, remained fairly exclusive to

Right, jumping down over the third of a series of steps on a cross country course at a three-day event. This is just one of the many gruelling obstacles that competitors have to tackle.

Above, jumping up out of water. Such obstacles are often included in the cross-country phase of a three-day event, in which the all-round training of horse and rider is tested.

Steeplechasing, above, attracts those riders that enjoy the challenge and risk of jumping at speed. As with all forms of racing, it is extremely popular with spectators, who are attracted by the thrills and drama of the sport.

Above, a young competitor and his horse clearing a fence in effortless style. Patient and careful training is needed to negotiate solid obstacles at high speed.

Europe; riding in Britain, for example, being influenced more by such pursuits as fox hunting and steeplechasing. But today dressage is enjoying world-wide interest, and competitions are held not only at Olympic level but also at local and Pony Club level. Competitions vary considerably depending on the level required – from a basic test of riding and training at walk, trot, canter and halt, to the extremely demanding Grand Prix dressage test which includes such movements as the pirouette and piaffe.

Ultimately, however, dressage is perhaps most valuable as a fundamental preparation for all other forms of riding.

Owning your own horse

Every young rider dreams of having and training their own horse or pony. But before buying one, consider carefully whether you have gained the necessary experience, and whether it is really practical. Owning a horse is not only a long-term and full-time commitment but it is also expensive – you need somewhere to keep the horse, and will have numerous costs such as veterinary and farrier's bills, feed, equipment, and the expense of transport. Horses are valuable and sensitive animals; they need constant attention including grooming, exercising and feeding. To keep a horse happy and in good healthy condition demands time, knowledge, some dedication, and the necessary financial means. Decide, therefore, how much time you have available, especially if you are working or at school, before making the final commitment.

The satisfactory owner or trainer must make every effort to learn as much as possible about every aspect of horses

Above, horse and rider descending the steep Derby Bank at Hickstead – probably one of the most notorious obstacles in show jumping.

Right, a member of the world-famous French equestrian school, the Cadre Noir, performs the spectacular capriole.

and their care. Young riders will find that the best way to do this is to join a local branch of the Pony Club. This well-known organization was founded in England in 1928 with the initial aim of helping farmers' children with their ponies. Gradually it was extended to include all young people interested in riding. The idea was enormously successful and today the Pony Club has world-wide membership with branches in some 22 different countries.

The chief aims of the Pony Club are to encourage young people to ride, to instruct them in all aspects of horsemanship, and to encourage sportsmanship. Membership is open to all young people under the age of 21, and the club runs proficiency tests for its members that are recognized throughout the world. The Pony Club also organizes "working rallies", summer camps, film shows, lectures, and gymkhanas; the most successful members can represent their club teams in eventing, show jumping dressage, polo or pentathlon events. In this way, the Pony Club offers not only a high standard of instruction but also provides considerable fun and entertainment.

Each year thousands of children and ponies take part in gymkhanas, competing against each other in the most improbable contests. Events such as the sack race and the potato race are immensely popular, not only as entertainment but also as a chance to compete and compare your skills with rivals and friends.

For many children a gymkhana pony is the first that they own, and provides an excellent opportunity to gain experience in stable management and training. Ideally a gymkhana pony should be small, active and fast and must

Among his many needs, the horse must be shod regularly – the farrier above is shaping a shoe on the anvil. The rider will have to spend time on the horse's general care – for example, right, putting on protective clothing such as travelling boots or stable bandages.

20

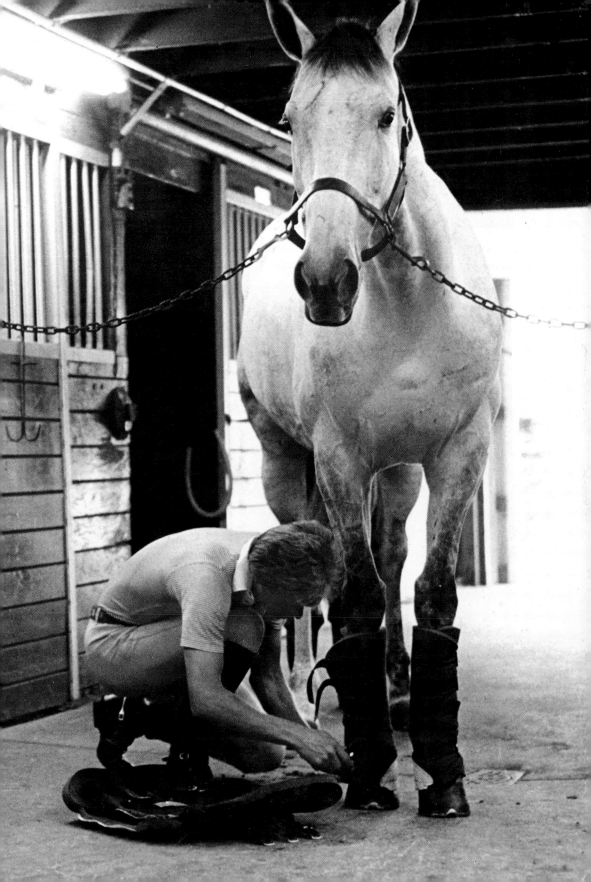

accept unusual noise and excitement, and strange sights such as balloons or fancy dress. Mounted games can be controversial as some feel that the ponies are handled too roughly and that the events themselves have little to do with good horsemanship. Against this claim, gymkhanas provide an invaluable opportunity for young people to learn to ride with balance and accuracy at speed, and the importance of establishing a good rapport and understanding with the horse. Gymkhanas have the advantage of being open to everyone since practically any pony can be trained for mounted games which adds enormously to their popularity and value. Nevertheless to excel at them, proper training is essential.

Training the horse

Training a horse is an even greater responsibility than owning one, requiring considerably more knowledge, time and skill. If in doubt, do not attempt it. If you buy a young horse and hope to ride it in competitions eventually, seek advice and assistance. If none is available, send your horse away to be schooled by an expert. It may be expensive, but probably less so than trying to do it yourself and failing.

It will save time and effort as well as expense if you can avoid many of the unnecessary mistakes which will cause setbacks, and if you learn how to overcome those which are inevitable. By understanding how your horse thinks, feels and reacts you will be able to influence him, physically and mentally, to produce his best possible performance. The partnership is rewarding beyond belief.

Young people are often attracted to riding. Above, a young rider and her pony make a speedy turn in the Pony Club mounted games competition at the Horse of the Year Show and, right, a group of young riders enjoying a leisurely trek over open moorland in summer.

Milton, one of the most brilliant and best
loved of modern show jumpers,
displaying the superb movement,
strength and style that have contributed
to his success.

Learning to ride

Preparation for riding

Anyone who would like to learn to ride is faced with the question: "How do I start?". There are various choices: you can go to an established riding school and be taught on a school horse, you can learn to ride on a friend's or relative's horse, or you can learn on a horse of your own. For most beginners, the first or second choice is the more likely; it would be foolish to buy a horse before you knew for sure that you would enjoy riding.

The riding school

First, you need to find a reputable riding school where the instructors are properly qualified. Preferably it should be recommended by someone you know and whose opinion you value, because a bad riding school could put you off riding for ever, whereas, if you are fortunate enough to find good instruction, you may discover a lifetime of pleasure in the saddle. When selecting a school, certain aspects will soon tell you whether or not it is well organized and run. The yard should look and smell clean, and the buildings should be in a safe condition with good drainage. There should be plenty of clean bedding in the stables and the horses themselves should have been groomed and cared for, with a well-fed, contented appearance. Look in the tack room: it should be orderly; inspect the tack itself to see if it is in good repair, and supple, not stiff or dirty. It is no pleasure to learn to ride on over-worked, thin, reluctant horses wearing worn-out, dirty tack. It also shows a lack of regard for the horse which is likely to influence the beginner's attitude.

In most countries, riding schools are graded by official inspectors. The schools are then checked periodically and will be downgraded if there is a decline in standards, or promoted to a higher category if the standards and facilities improve.

The instructor

Instructors, too, are graded through examination. However, certificates alone do not make good instructors. The instructor must be able to give confidence and pleasure to the rider and must be both sympathetic and patient. The pace of the lessons must be varied so that the pupil does not get bored, but the instructor should be strong-minded enough to insist on the correct use of the seat, legs and hands so that the rider acquires a solid foundation for his future riding.

A good instructor teaches the pupil not only the elements of riding but also how the horse behaves, mentally and physically. Lessons in stable management are invaluable, too, even for non horse owners, as they help you to get to know more about the nature and behaviour of the horse, which will, in turn, improve your riding. A good instructor always gives logical explanations supported if necessary by demonstration. If able to support the theory with practical proof, the instructor will gain vital respect from the pupil.

The lessons

The better riding schools provide an enclosed schooling area with a good level surface. The first lessons can be given on the lungeing rein so that the pupil is able to concentrate on establishing a good seat. Some establishments also have an indoor school where lessons can be given at any hour, regardless of the weather. Most riding schools offer group lessons (the number of pupils should not exceed six in one class if they are to derive any real benefit). Although group lessons are cheaper than private ones, the latter may be more economical in the long run, since the rate of progress is likely to be faster.

Riding is a two-way communication between horse and rider, and, like any language, it can develop to a high degree of refinement. Even if you do not aspire to great heights of equestrian achievement you will soon realize that bad riding gives little pleasure to either yourself or your mount. Not everyone can become an excellent rider, but very few are incapable of acquiring the balanced seat which is the foundation of all good riding.

A good riding establishment will take the trouble to teach you on the lunge on a well-schooled quiet and obedient horse until you become secure enough in the saddle to control him yourself, through the use of simple aids. You will not progress to this stage if you are nervous, tense and stiff. It is vitally important, therefore, that the rider gains enough confidence to relax and feel comfortable in the saddle. Riding is as much about "feel" and "influence" as it is about acquired technique, and a rider who is nervous will be unable to communicate with his horse. Although the correct position is crucial to good communication, no amount of physical force will produce it. Instructions like "sit up", "sit straight", "toes up", and "knees in" are far more likely to cause rigidity and discomfort than to produce the required position.

The rider

A rider of medium height and build will encounter fewer problems than one who is very short or very tall, very bulky or very thin and weak. Someone who has long slender legs will find it easier to establish a good deep seat on a horse than a rider with short fleshy legs. However, you have only

to look at the extraordinary diversity in physique of some of the top riders in equestrian events to see what can be achieved with the most unlikely conformation! Naturally, it is an advantage if you are agile and reasonably fit. It will help, therefore, if you do some exercises at home before riding to stretch and exercise the particular muscles you are going to use (see page 280). You are certain to feel stiff after your first lesson, so keep these early lessons short.

It is important to be comfortable while riding, so your clothes should help you rather than hinder you. There is no need to buy any expensive clothing or equipment to begin with, but you should obey the rules of common sense about what to wear (see pages 28–9).

Although riding attracts a wide range of people, those with a patient and sensitive attitude are more likely to succeed at the sport, even if nervous at first, than those who have a more impulsive approach. For your riding to be rewarding, as well as fun, you must be capable of forming a proper relationship with your horse.

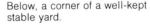
Left, riders returning to the school after a lesson.

Below, a corner of a well-kept stable yard.

Rider's equipment

Riding clothes have varied little over the years, not so much from tradition, but because they have generally fulfilled the needs of safety and efficiency. The rider should also feel comfortable, and not be impeded in any way from communicating with his horse.

Breeches or jodhpurs are far more practical than jeans or trousers, since they fit closely, have reinforced protection at the inside of the knee and thigh area, and do not chafe. Loose trousers will pinch your legs, rubbing against the stirrup leathers and creasing or riding up uncomfortably.

The most essential item of the rider's equipment, however, is a hard hat. An approved standard riding hat, secured with a safety harness, can be used for most riding activities, but for maximum shock absorption it is best to wear a skull cap (also called a crash helmet). This, too, must be of the legally approved standard design. It is constructed so that the shell or outer casing, not the rider's head, will absorb the force of an impact. The cap's rim is lined with spongy foam, and four webbing straps can be adjusted inside the cap to protect the top of the head from hitting the hard outer casing. A skull cap should be light and comfortable to wear, as well as strong, and of course it must fit the rider's head snugly.

Casual wear

Formal wear

Clothing

A selection of suitable clothes for riding is shown right. A hard hat or crash helmet, and a suitable pair of boots or shoes, are essential.

Jacket
A jacket is practical in cold weather, and is always used for formal riding, like showing, dressage or show jumping. It should be made of good-quality woollen cloth, well-lined, and should fit you properly so that it does not restrict your movements. It will need a vent at the back so that it lies smoothly over the cantle of the saddle.

Breeches
Well-cut breeches, left, or jodhpurs (similar, but ending just below the ankle) are the most comfortable for riding. Light-coloured breeches are traditional and smart, especially for formal competition wear, but for everyday use, darker breeches in an easy-to-wash stretch fabric are more practical. They must fit closely to your inside leg, so as not to crease and chafe. Reinforcement at the inner knee and thigh increases comfort and makes them more durable.

A peak can provide shade from rain or sun, and some protection to the face in the case of a fall. It should never be fixed or too rigid since, if you fall from the horse on to it, the impact could cause concussion or a broken nose.

You also need proper footwear. Strong shoes, provided they have no buckles which might catch on a projection or the stirrup, can be worn, but they give little protection to your ankles. Boots, either rubber or leather, are best, provided they are close-fitting and have plain, unridged soles. A small heel is essential to stop the stirrup from sliding back too far towards your ankle.

You will need a well-fitting shirt or sweater and an equally well-fitting jacket that does not restrict your movement. You will also need gloves. They keep your hands clean, and prevent your fingers from chafing on the reins or from slipping on them, if the reins become slippery with rain or the horse's sweat. Although a whip is not essential, it is a good idea to get used to carrying one, even as a beginner.

You should always aim to look neat and tidy. Female riders should tie their hair back or cover it with a net. Remove any jewellery before riding, and make sure that you have no dangling scarves, or long hair, which could catch on an obstruction and cause an injury.

When schooling a young horse over jumps or riding cross country, for example, it is advisable to wear a crash helmet, which will afford greater protection than the standard hard hat.

Hard Hat
Buy the best and safest riding hat you can afford. It must fit snugly and its design must meet approved safety standards. It must also have a chin strap.

Crash helmet
Stronger and tougher than a hard hat, it is designed to absorb great pressure – as when falling at speed. A silk covering with a flexible peak is usually added to make it look more attractive. Modern designs offer the best protection.

Boots
Boots or shoes can be worn. Calf-length rubber or leather boots are normally worn with breeches; elastic-sided ankle boots are worn with jodhpurs.

Gloves
Gloves should fit well and allow a sensitive feel on the reins. String gloves are ideal as they will not slip when the reins are wet.

The horse

The horse is surprisingly well disposed towards man, considering that we use and often abuse him in ways that nature never intended.

Whether or not he was meant to carry a rider, we take every possible advantage of his ability and willingness to do so, and it must be our duty, therefore, to do our best to aid his task. We need to be aware of the horse's general character and sensitivity to gain his confidence and cooperation, and to make a relationship between horse and rider possible. We must learn how he reacts, feels and works, both physically and mentally. It is as important to realize the limitations of a horse's brain as to know his physical capacity. To overtax his brain or his body will cause fear, stress or resistance. A horse is not ill-tempered or stubborn by nature – most of his "vices" are, in fact, man-made, and it is our responsibility to prevent their development, using tact and understanding. Hence the importance of sympathetic handling from birth, and the need for careful, expert schooling.

A horse obeys his instincts, but has few reasoning powers. Some of his natural instincts are subdued through training, but others can be used to develop a relationship. However, the horse must be taught obedience: he is a powerful animal and, in a battle of strength, will win every time. He much prefers to cooperate provided he understands what is required. He responds best to quiet, firm handling and needs to know what is expected of him. If he is allowed to get out of control, he becomes insecure, knowing he cannot trust or depend on his rider for direction.

Of the horse's natural abilities, his memory is one of the most useful. It allows his training to be simplified by means of reward and punishment. If rewarded by praise for doing what we ask, he will be eager to cooperate the next time; if sharply corrected by voice or hand when he misbehaves, he will remember what displeased us and will learn to respect our authority.

The herd instinct is present in every horse to some degree and, again, is useful during training. He follows his companions happily, making it easier to introduce him to situations which might otherwise frighten him, such as riding on the roads, and to jumping. He will jump obstacles much more readily in company with other horses, tackling bigger fences when out hunting, for example, than he would alone in the practice ring.

The horse is much more sensitive than is generally realized. Apart from the obvious sensations of smell, touch, sight, hearing and taste, he is very conscious of atmosphere and can take time to adjust to new surroundings with different people around him. He will often show his anxiety by going off his food and walking nervously about his box. He usually senses a rider's feelings of timidity, hesitation or anger, and will react similarly. Equally, he senses a rider's courage and confidence, and will draw from them.

His sense of touch is well developed, and he is afraid of pain, instinctively trying to escape from anything which suggests it. His sensitivity to touch should be respected in his schooling and when riding him, and used to his and our advantage.

His sense of hearing is highly developed and is an important aid in training. He can be taught to respond to individual words of command, and can be soothed and reprimanded most effectively by words and tones. If we watch his ears, they reveal his feelings. Laid back, they show he is unhappy; pricked forward, they indicate that he is alert and interested, but probably not in his rider. Flickering constantly, they show that he is being attentive to the rider's wishes.

The horse's sense of smell is not particularly helpful in his training, although he can smell fear in a rider. He often dislikes particular odours – and can associate them with unpleasant experiences.

If a successful partnership is to be established between horse and rider, the horse must feel secure. He has a great love for his stable or field, and his life revolves around his food. Unless his "home life" is unhappy, the horse will normally be keen to return to his stable or field (he is not a natural worker – pre-domestication, horses wandered around in herds, grazing), and his love of comfort can be used in training, to reward him after work well done. In particular, he will look forward to eating, so it is best to keep to a routine or he may become agitated and develop bad stable habits out of frustration.

Although timid by nature, the horse will summon up tremendous courage to please us. It should never be abused by expecting too much of him. He is acting against his instincts of self-preservation when asked to cross boggy land, or jump into the unknown. He wants to rely on us, and trust us; in turn, we must respect his faith and not let him down.

Suitable horses for beginners

There are numerous breeds of horse and pony suitable for riding (see page 243). The ideal type for a beginner has good strong conformation (build) and a quiet, calm temperament. He should be big enough to carry the rider's weight without difficulty, but not so big as to be intimidating.

As a novice rider you do not need a detailed knowledge of the horse's anatomy but it will improve your ability to learn if you understand how the horse moves at all his paces (overleaf). You also need to know the correct names for the different parts of the horse (below), as these will be referred to in your lessons.

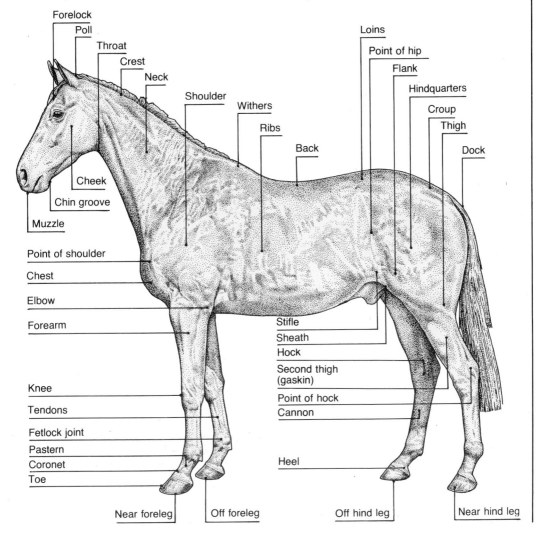

Forelock
Poll
Throat
Crest
Neck
Shoulder
Withers
Ribs
Back
Cheek
Chin groove
Muzzle
Point of shoulder
Chest
Elbow
Forearm
Knee
Tendons
Fetlock joint
Pastern
Coronet
Toe

Loins
Point of hip
Flank
Hindquarters
Croup
Thigh
Dock

Stifle
Sheath
Hock
Second thigh (gaskin)
Point of hock
Cannon
Heel

Near foreleg
Off foreleg
Off hind leg
Near hind leg

The paces

The horse has four basic gaits or paces: the walk (a four-time movement); the trot (a two-time movement); the canter (a three-time movement) and the gallop (a four-time movement).

The walk is a regular marching pace in which each footfall can be heard separately. At least two legs are always on the ground simultaneously, so the horse is never in suspension, which makes the walk a level, comfortable gait for the rider. A "good" walk has lively, rhythmical steps, with the hind feet overlapping the imprints of the forefeet ("tracking up"). The walk may be free, ordinary, collected or extended.

The trot is a regular two-time movement in which each diagonal pair of legs strikes the ground alternately in a swinging gait. The pace should be unhurried with free, even strides, and there is a moment of suspension as one pair of legs leaves the

Sequence of legs

As the horse changes pace, he will also alter the sequence in which each of his feet strikes the ground.

At the walk, the sequence will be near-fore, off-hind, off-fore, near-hind. In the collected, extended or free walk, this sequence remains the same but the length of stride will vary.

At the trot, the horse's legs move in diagonal pairs: the near-fore with the off-hind, and then the off-fore with the near-hind. This gait may also show collected or extended variations in the length of stride.

At the canter, a three-beat gait, the horse moves in bounds, each one followed by a moment of suspension. In the illustration below right, the horse is leading with the off-foreleg. The sequence will be: near-hind, off-hind and near-fore together, and off-fore (then a moment of suspension). To lead on the opposite foreleg, the near-fore, this sequence is reversed. The canter too may be collected or extended.

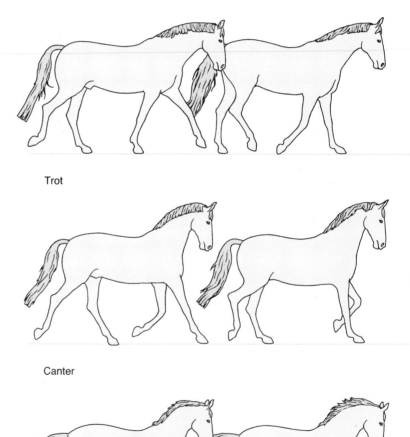

Walk

Trot

Canter

ground and the other pair rejoins it. The trot pace can be ordinary ("working"), collected or extended.

The canter is a rocking, three-time movement in which either the near-fore and near-hind leg lead, or the off-fore and off-hind leg lead. There is a moment of suspension when all four legs are in the air, before the sequence begins again. The canter, like the trot, can be ordinary ("working"), extended or collected.

The gallop is the fastest pace, and the strides are more extended than at the canter. There is a longer moment of suspension when the horse appears to be flying through the air. Although similar to the canter, the gallop is a four-time movement and the sequence of legs, with the near-fore leg leading, is: near-hind, off-hind, near-fore, off-fore. When the off-fore leads, the sequence is: off-hind, near-hind, off-fore and near-fore.

The basic tack

When you have your first riding lesson you may not be expected to tack up your horse yourself. Nevertheless, you will need to know about the equipment the horse needs (known as the tack) and understand how it works. Ask to be shown how to saddle and bridle the horse correctly; after watching once or twice, you should be capable of tacking up the horse yourself (see pages 38–9). As a horse or pony owner, of course, you will have to know not only how to put on the tack, but what equipment to buy, and how to make sure that it fits properly (see pages 274–8).

The equipment shown on these pages is that normally required for most horses or ponies used by beginners. Some additional equipment may be needed, such as boots or bandages to protect the horse's legs (see page 278), a different type of bit, or an alternative form of girth. The snaffle bridle fitted with a single loose ring or an eggbutt snaffle bit, and a general purpose saddle

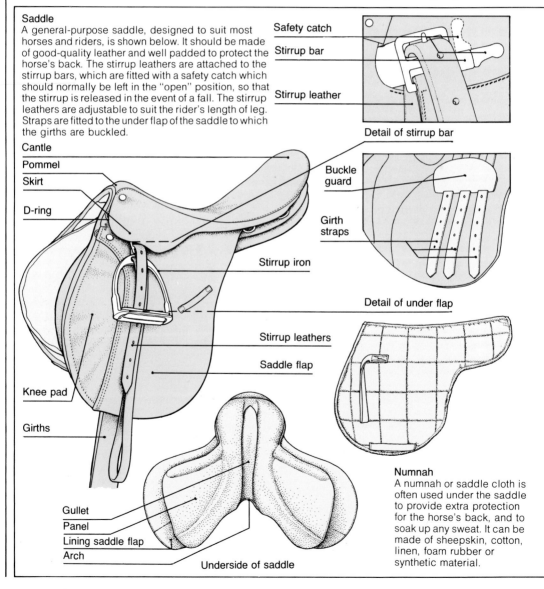

Saddle
A general-purpose saddle, designed to suit most horses and riders, is shown below. It should be made of good-quality leather and well padded to protect the horse's back. The stirrup leathers are attached to the stirrup bars, which are fitted with a safety catch which should normally be left in the "open" position, so that the stirrup is released in the event of a fall. The stirrup leathers are adjustable to suit the rider's length of leg. Straps are fitted to the under flap of the saddle to which the girths are buckled.

Safety catch
Stirrup bar
Stirrup leather

Detail of stirrup bar

Cantle
Pommel
Skirt
D-ring

Buckle guard

Girth straps

Stirrup iron

Detail of under flap

Stirrup leathers
Saddle flap

Knee pad

Girths

Gullet
Panel
Lining saddle flap
Arch

Underside of saddle

Numnah
A numnah or saddle cloth is often used under the saddle to provide extra protection for the horse's back, and to soak up any sweat. It can be made of sheepskin, cotton, linen, foam rubber or synthetic material.

are the most commonly used (see also page 275 for information about other types).

If the horse you are given to ride at a school has extra gadgets, you have good reason to suspect that he may be unsuitable for a novice rider. However, even well-schooled horses may need the occasional piece of corrective equipment, which does not mean that they are dangerous or difficult rides. For example, a martingale may be used to prevent the horse from throwing his head up or a dropped noseband may be used if he persistently opens his mouth.

Most saddlery is made of leather, which requires regular cleaning. It has to be soft and supple so that it is comfortable for the horse to wear and the rider to use. Dirty, stiff and hard tack will make the horse suffer, and you will have a difficult ride as a result. Tack which looks neglected, dry and brittle indicates that the riding stable is not being run well, and you should look around for an alternative establishment.

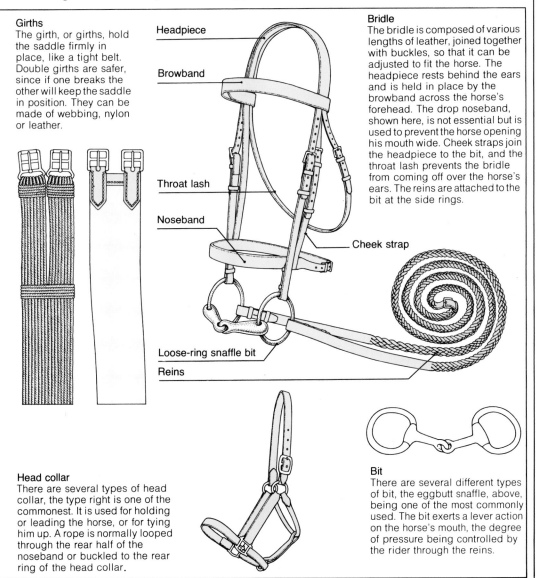

Girths
The girth, or girths, hold the saddle firmly in place, like a tight belt. Double girths are safer, since if one breaks the other will keep the saddle in position. They can be made of webbing, nylon or leather.

Headpiece

Browband

Throat lash

Noseband

Loose-ring snaffle bit

Reins

Bridle
The bridle is composed of various lengths of leather, joined together with buckles, so that it can be adjusted to fit the horse. The headpiece rests behind the ears and is held in place by the browband across the horse's forehead. The drop noseband, shown here, is not essential but is used to prevent the horse opening his mouth wide. Cheek straps join the headpiece to the bit, and the throat lash prevents the bridle from coming off over the horse's ears. The reins are attached to the bit at the side rings.

Cheek strap

Head collar
There are several types of head collar, the type right is one of the commonest. It is used for holding or leading the horse, or for tying him up. A rope is normally looped through the rear half of the noseband or buckled to the rear ring of the head collar.

Bit
There are several different types of bit, the eggbutt snaffle, above, being one of the most commonly used. The bit exerts a lever action on the horse's mouth, the degree of pressure being controlled by the rider through the reins.

Getting to know the horse

Before learning to ride, you should get used to handling horses and know how to communicate with them, from the ground. When you are at ease together, the horse will allow you to catch him and lead him without anxiety. Always remember that a horse can be startled easily by any sudden or unexpected movements. Never rush towards him, therefore, but walk quietly and confidently. Talk to him in a friendly voice and always approach him from the front or side so that he can see you; never from behind – he may be taken by surprise and kick out at you. Never touch his rear end without warning – he could react sharply with his heels.

If you think he may prove difficult to catch, take a pocketful of his favourite food with you and hold a morsel on the flat palm of your outstretched hand, to entice him. Be patient: any hasty move could easily deter him from approaching.

A horse is particularly sensitive to noise, smell and strange sights so never shout at or threaten him. Never take unruly dogs with you, or wear rustling, flapping garments, and don't carry anything which may alarm him.

A rider getting to know her horse. Building up a good relationship with your horse from an early stage is an important part of the learning process.

Catching the horse

When catching a horse, it is best to use a head collar with a rope attached. Do not brandish it, particularly if he is difficult to catch, or he will most likely avoid you. Don't carry the saddle and bridle with you either. In any event, you will need both hands free to catch him. Walk towards him naturally, holding out a handful of food with one hand, while keeping the halter and rope behind your back with the other. Allow him to nibble the food while you slip the rope around his neck, near to his head, as shown. Once caught, he will usually stand quietly.

1 Approach the horse with the head collar and rope behind your back, holding the food in your outstretched hand.

2 Having slipped the rope over the horse's neck, hold the end of the rope securely, and calmly put the head collar over his head.

3 Buckle the cheek strap of the head collar to secure it.

Leading in hand

When led in hand correctly, the horse should move freely. Never try to drag the horse along by force, but stand beside him, looking forwards, and ask him to move on as you move forwards; if your intentions are clear, he will follow. If he hesitates, click with your tongue or use a firm tone – you may have to resort to tapping his flank lightly with the end of the rope or with a whip. If he still refuses to move, push him sideways, away from you, or turn him towards you. If your horse pulls ahead of you, stay in front of his shoulder and lean against it, at the same time using your voice and jerking on the head collar with the rope. The correct method of leading in hand with a halter is shown, right. Once inside the stable, secure the horse to the wall with a quick-release knot (see below).

Lead the horse with the rope held in both hands – nearest hand about 15cm (6in) behind his chin, and the other hand holding the slack end.

Securing the horse

Three kinds of knot may be used to secure your horse. A simple knot, right, tied in a rope halter will fasten it securely. A stop knot, far right, tied at the end of a lead rope will prevent it from slipping through your fingers if the horse pulls. A quick-release knot, below, is used to tie the horse to a wall. A small loop of string should always be used to attach the rope to the ring.

Using a rope halter
Tie the knot where the rope runs through the loops in the noseband. It must always be tied on the leading side of the halter.

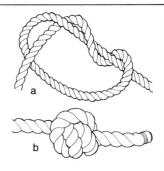

The stop knot
Pass the free end of the rope twice through the standing part (a) and pull it through (b). Untie the knot by pulling the twists apart.

The quick-release knot
1 Form a loop through the loop of string with the free end of the rope, as shown.

2 Make another loop in the free end and pass the second loop through the first loop, as shown. Pull the end to release the knot.

3 If you wish, you can put the end of the rope through the loop to ensure that the horse does not pull the knot loose.

Saddling up

It is important that the saddlery should fit the horse correctly, and be clean, supple and properly adjusted. If the horse is to enjoy being ridden, he must be comfortable: he will be no pleasure to ride if not.

Before saddling up, check the leather and stitching – particularly on the girths, stirrup leathers and reins – for signs of wear, and check that the buckles are functioning properly – many accidents are caused by broken saddlery.

To tack up the horse you will need the saddle, with stirrup leathers, irons and girth, and a bridle. You may also need a numnah or saddle cloth, to protect the horse's back. Occasionally, the horse will need bandages or boots, for example, or a martingale (see page 274–8).

The saddle should fit so that the rider can sit in the middle, as near as possible to the horse's centre of gravity. It should not produce any pressure on the horse's spine, and a passage of light should be plainly visible along the arch and gullet of the saddle, when it is placed on the horse's back. The withers must be free, in front of the saddle, and not pinched. The shoulder blades should also be free to move, unimpeded by the saddle flaps. If the saddle fits properly, the rider's weight should be on the hard muscle along the upper part of the horse's ribs, not on the tender loins, and it should be evenly distributed over the entire bearing surface of the saddle's under part, not dipped to the front or the rear. If a numnah is used it should be pulled up into the arch of the saddle when put on, not stretched across the horse's back when the girths are tightened. The girths must not pinch the horse's skin, and the stirrup irons should be large enough to allow the rider's foot to slide easily in and out.

The fit of the bridle is very important. The bit should be wide enough to avoid rubbing the sides of the horse's mouth, but not so wide that it moves sideways in his mouth. It should be high enough in the mouth to keep it still, just wrinkling the corners. If the bit is too low, it may bang against the horse's teeth, or he might want to put his tongue over the bit, to avoid the pressure.

Further information is given on pages 274–8 about choosing saddlery and equipment and fitting them correctly.

The horse should always be groomed or at least brushed over, including the mane and tail, before being saddled. Once he is tacked up, he should not be left loose in the stable. Put a headcollar or halter over the bridle, and leave the stirrups run up to the top of the leathers and the reins hooked over the irons on both sides, to prevent the horse from lowering his head to the ground and treading on the reins. A rug should be thrown over the saddle, if he normally wears one.

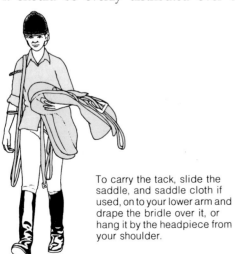

To carry the tack, slide the saddle, and saddle cloth if used, on to your lower arm and drape the bridle over it, or hang it by the headpiece from your shoulder.

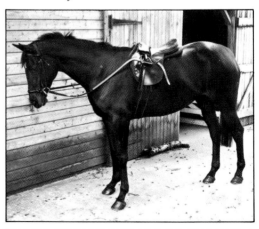

The horse, saddled up and ready to ride; the reins have been drawn over the stirrup irons which have been run up to the top of the leathers.

Putting on the saddle

1 Standing on the near side of your horse, lift the saddle on to the horse's back, high up on the withers.

2 Ease the saddle back into place so that the centre of the saddle rests on the lowest part of the horse's back.

3 Drop the girth down and check that it lies flat. On the near side, reach under the horse for the girth.

4 Buckle the girth to the saddle. Pass your hand between the girth and the horse's belly to check that it does not pinch anywhere. It will need to be tightened before you mount (see page 40).

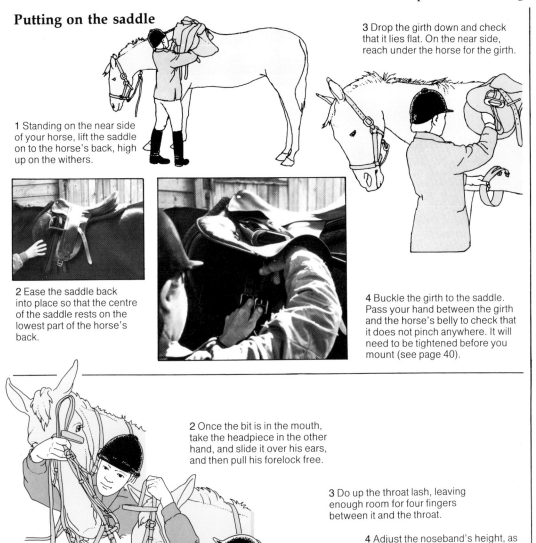

2 Once the bit is in the mouth, take the headpiece in the other hand, and slide it over his ears, and then pull his forelock free.

3 Do up the throat lash, leaving enough room for four fingers between it and the throat.

4 Adjust the noseband's height, as necessary, and do it up, not too loose or too tight.

Putting on the bridle

1 With the headpiece in your right hand, draw it up the horse's head and slip the bit into his mouth with your left hand. If he does not take the bit easily, press gently against the bars of his mouth with your thumb until he does.

Mounting

Before getting on, you should check that the girths are tight enough to prevent the saddle from slipping round when you put your weight in the stirrup. If you cannot tighten them enough, ask someone to hold the offside stirrup while you mount. You can then tighten the girth once mounted (see page 52).

Sometimes a badly trained horse will try to move off as he is being mounted. If no help is available, lead him to a wall or gate so that he stands facing it. Alternatively, if there is someone there to lend a hand, ask him to hold the offside rein while you are getting on.

The standard method of mounting is shown right. If you find it difficult to raise your leg high enough to put your foot into the stirrup, lengthen the nearside leather accordingly. If you lengthen it too much, however, you may find it difficult to swing your right leg over the horse's back. You will, of course, have to readjust it to the correct length once mounted (see page 45). Alternatively, you can ask someone to give you a leg up, or you can use a mounting block (opposite).

Right, tighten the girths before trying to mount, remembering to keep hold of the reins while doing so.

Below, pull the stirrup irons down the leathers before mounting, if necessary lengthening the leathers a little to enable you to mount.

Traditional method

You should stand near the horse's nearside shoulder, facing backwards, and put your reins and whip in your left hand, resting it on the withers or on the pommel of the saddle. Keep a contact on the reins to prevent the horse from moving off, and make sure that the offside rein is slightly shorter, to keep the horse's head straight, and to prevent him nipping you.

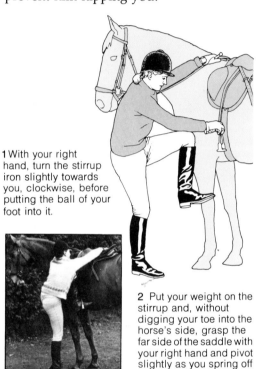

1 With your right hand, turn the stirrup iron slightly towards you, clockwise, before putting the ball of your foot into it.

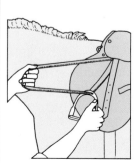

2 Put your weight on the stirrup and, without digging your toe into the horse's side, grasp the far side of the saddle with your right hand and pivot slightly as you spring off the ground.

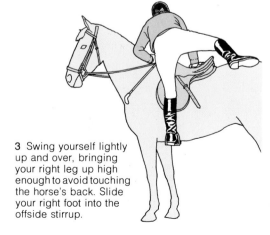

3 Swing yourself lightly up and over, bringing your right leg up high enough to avoid touching the horse's back. Slide your right foot into the offside stirrup.

Alternative methods

If you prefer, you can mount in the traditional way, but facing forwards, putting your left foot into the stirrup first, below. Alternatively, you can mount from the off side, in which case your right foot is put in the stirrup first.

Using a mounting block

If your horse is too tall for you to be able to reach the stirrup iron, or if you are not particularly agile, you can mount from a solid block or similar raised platform. Lead the horse over to the block and position him so that his forelegs are level with its leading edge. Then, standing on the block, raise your left leg and put your foot into the stirrup in the usual way, or, if you prefer, you can mount facing forwards.

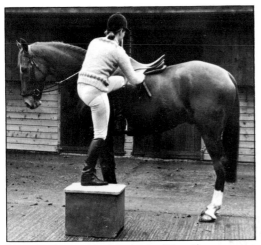

Mounting from a block in the traditional manner

Leg up

An alternative to using a mounting block is to have the service of someone to give you a leg up. Provided they know what to do, it is a quick and easy method of getting on – jockeys are given a leg up when mounting before a race.

Hold the reins in the usual way and stand facing the withers. Bend your left knee, with your lower leg at right angles to your thigh. The helper should cup your lower leg in both hands. On an agreed signal, the helper lifts your left leg while you spring from the ground, your right hand supporting your weight to prevent a heavy landing in the saddle.

Vaulting

Only the most athletic can manage to vault on to a horse, although most children can usually succeed in doing so on to a pony. You should take the reins in your left hand, and put both hands on the withers in front of the saddle. Then you should bend your knees and spring, using your arms as a lever, to push yourself high enough off the ground to swing your right leg over the horse's back without kicking him.

The rider has just vaulted high enough to be able to clear the horse's back when he swings his leg over the saddle.

Dismounting

Although you normally dismount from the near side of the horse, it is worth practising dismounting from the off side as well, as it may be necessary on the side of a hill.

The safest and best way to dismount is to remove both feet from the stirrups first and then jump off, keeping hold of the reins, as shown below. There is then no danger of your being dragged along with your foot in the stirrup if the horse moves off unexpectedly. However, some riders prefer to keep the nearside foot in the stirrup until the right foot is on the ground, so that, if the horse moves off, they can swing back into the saddle again. Once dismounted, run the stirrup irons up the leathers, and slacken off the girth, if you are not likely to be unsaddling the horse immediately.

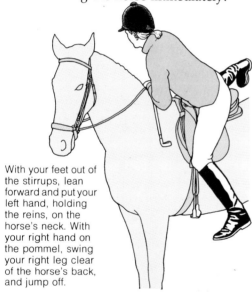

With your feet out of the stirrups, lean forward and put your left hand, holding the reins, on the horse's neck. With your right hand on the pommel, swing your right leg clear of the horse's back, and jump off.

Fault
Although some people dismount by swinging a leg casually forward over the pommel, right, it is a bad habit to acquire. You will have to let go of the reins and so you will be unable to control your horse if he moves off suddenly.

Unsaddling

The instructions here are for removing a saddle and bridle only. If the horse is fitted with other saddlery, see pages 274–8.

If your horse is likely to escape while being unsaddled, make sure you have a halter or rope to hand which you can slip over his head before removing the bridle. If you are unsaddling your own horse you will have to attend to his needs after exercise to make sure that he is comfortable (see page 261).

Above, run the stirrup irons up the leathers and then tuck the leathers through the stirrups.

Right, having undone the girth buckles on the near side, slide your arm under the arch of the saddle and pull it gently off the horse's back, folding the girths over the saddle as you do so.

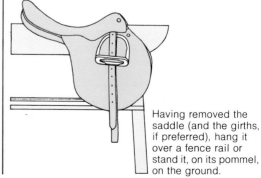

Having removed the saddle (and the girths, if preferred), hang it over a fence rail or stand it, on its pommel, on the ground.

Taking off the saddle

You should normally take the saddle off first and then the bridle. If it is raining, try to unsaddle the horse under cover, to prevent the saddle getting wet. Run the stirrup irons up the leathers, if you have not already done so, and, taking the reins over the horse's head, slip them over your left arm. Raise the saddle flap and undo the girths on the near side, letting them drop. With one hand on the front arch, and the other on the cantle, slide the saddle off towards you and on to your forearm, with the front arch resting in the crook of your elbow. Take hold of the girths with the right hand, as you draw the saddle off the horse's back, and fold them over the seat of the saddle, with the underside of the girths facing the saddle. Then, without letting go of the reins, rest the saddle gently on its pommel on the ground, or hang it over a fence rail, if there is one.

Taking off the bridle

Standing on the near side, undo the noseband and the throat lash. Slip the headpiece over his ears with your right hand, and ease the bit out of the horse's mouth slowly and gently, keeping his head still, if necessary, with your left hand.

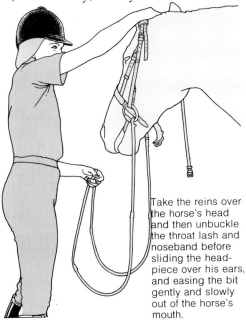

Take the reins over the horse's head and then unbuckle the throat lash and noseband before sliding the head-piece over his ears, and easing the bit gently and slowly out of the horse's mouth.

Storing the tack

The tack is expensive and should be looked after properly to make it last. If you have your own horse, you will have to take care of the tack yourself (see page 276). Whether you own the horse or not, you should always look after the equipment while handling it. The saddle should be rested on the pommel when left on the ground, with the girth folded under it to serve as protection. The greasy underside of the girth will do the saddle no harm, but the muddy side could easily scratch it, so always fold the underside on to the saddle's surface or detach the girth altogether. Make sure you hold the saddle firmly when carrying it – if you drop it you may damage the tree. All the tack should be stored in a dry atmosphere. Hang up the saddle and bridle as shown below, having rinsed off the bit, and wiped any parts of the saddlery that have been in contact with the horse's skin.

A well-ordered tack room with the bridles and saddles neatly hung up. (See also page 276).

The classical seat

The classical seat is not only elegant but practical, both for controlling the horse and for allowing the maximum use, with the minimum effort, of the natural aids: the body, seat, legs and hands. It requires you to be straight but not stiff, supple but not slack. Any stiffness or tension in the rider usually sets off a similar reaction in the horse, while a slack position makes it difficult for the rider to give clear, concise aids (see page 51), and is also insecure. Suppleness is important if you are to be able to remain in harmony with the horse's movement, and to encourage the horse to use himself efficiently.

To develop a good seat you must have the largest possible bearing area of your seat and legs in contact with the saddle and the horse's sides so that you are in a position to feel and influence the horse with the greatest possible ease. Your seat bones – the flat bones of the thighs (not the buttocks and soft, round parts) – must be on the saddle, with the result that the knees are against the saddle flaps. The upper part of the body should be tall and straight, with the shoulders square and level. The head should be erect with the spine and neck in a natural line, neither curved nor bent. The legs have to be long and straight to secure as deep a seat as possible, and the knees and ankles should be supple: stiff joints will cause loss of overall elasticity making it difficult to move with the horse. The legs should be still, firmly against the horse's sides, but not tightly gripping. The lower half of the leg, just below the knee, must be far enough back to be able to apply the aids behind the girth without having to move the leg to do so. The stirrup leathers must

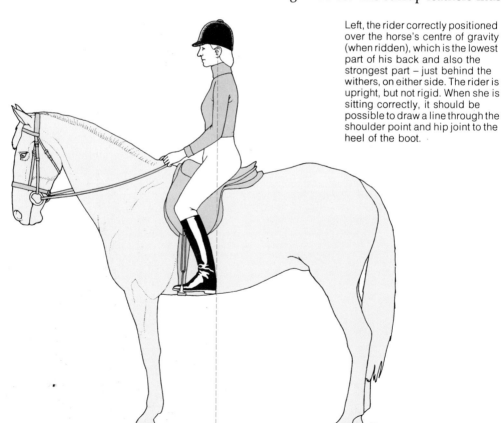

Left, the rider correctly positioned over the horse's centre of gravity (when ridden), which is the lowest part of his back and also the strongest part – just behind the withers, on either side. The rider is upright, but not rigid. When she is sitting correctly, it should be possible to draw a line through the shoulder point and hip joint to the heel of the boot.

hang vertically. If the leg slides forward – a common fault – it will cause loss of balance and displacement of the upper body, as well as less flexion in the ankle joints. Communication problems between horse and rider are often the result of faulty position. It is crucial to your eventual success to be taught to sit properly; many experienced riders regret their lack of basic training as faults are often difficult to cure.

To maintain the correct position in the classical seat, your stirrup leathers must be neither too long nor too short (see Fault, below right). Properly adjusted, they should allow your legs to be in close contact with your horse's sides, with the thigh stretched down and flat, the knee in and low, and in a vertical line with your ankle joint, which coincides with your horse's centre of gravity. The heel should be down and the ball of the foot should rest on the stirrup iron.

Adjusting the leathers
To gauge the length of your leathers before mounting, face the saddle, and, with the knuckles of your right hand against the stirrup bar, measure the length of leather and iron against your arm. When the iron reaches up under your arm, as shown, the leathers should be approximately the right length.

Final adjustments can be made when mounted. Use the nearest hand, and practise adjusting the leathers until you can do it quickly, without looking down. You can also check the length by taking your foot out of the stirrup. If the iron reaches just to your ankle, the leathers are the right length.

Right, the rider's legs should fit snugly to the horse's sides, so that it is not possible to see daylight between them and the saddle. The legs should not grip so tightly that the muscles tense and stiffen.

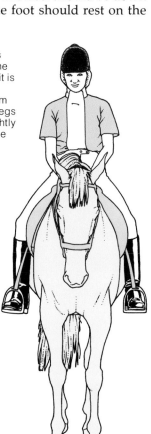

Fault
The rider below is making the common error of riding too short, and gripping with her knees, so that she rises out of the saddle, instead of sitting deep in it. Her balance and security in the saddle will be adversely affected.

Position at the walk

The most effective way to acquire an independent seat (that is, not dependent on the hands for maintaining balance or influencing the horse) is to remove any contact with the horse's mouth until your seat is well established. It is best, therefore, to learn to sit at the walk on a quiet, sensible horse, on the lunge. You can then also concentrate on establishing the correct seat without gripping with your knees and legs.

While you become accustomed to the feel of the walk – a four-time beat (see pages 32–3) – you should keep your feet in the stirrups. Then, once you have found your balance and can keep still in the saddle, you should remove the stirrups or cross them over in front of the saddle.

Your position at the walk remains the same as when standing still – that is, with a straight line from your ear, through your shoulder point and hip, to the heel of your boot (as shown on page 44). Among the common faults to avoid are a rounded back; a "chair" seat – slouching with the legs sliding forwards; or sitting too much on your fork, with your legs too far back and your weight inclined forward. Any of these faults will spoil your balance and weaken your effectiveness as a rider. To strengthen your position in the saddle, you should practise the exercises opposite. Once you are balanced over the horse's centre of gravity, with a deep, secure position, you can start to relax, in harmony with your horse's movement. Gripping should never, in fact,

be necessary to maintain your balance. To make sure that you are sitting correctly in the saddle, and have the deepest possible seat, take your feet out of the stirrups (if you have not already done so) and let your toes and ankles hang down naturally. Find the lowest part of the saddle by easing yourself downwards, as deep as you can get. Stretch your legs as long and straight as they will allow, and then ease the fleshy part of your inner thigh to the rear, so that the flat bone lies against the saddle. Ease downwards on your seat bones, through which you will be able to feel the action of the horse's back. Your position is now set up. The lower you can sit, the stronger will be your position as the largest proportion of your body is in contact with the horse.

When you take back the stirrups, you may find they need to be lengthened by a hole or two as you will be sitting deeper in the saddle by this time.

Above, horse fitted with lungeing equipment

Left, on the lunge at the walk; under the scrutiny of the instructor, who is in control of the horse, the rider is free to concentrate on establishing her position correctly.

Mounted exercises at the walk

Mounted exercises will improve your suppleness and balance, helping you to develop a firm, deep seat. They will also develop your reflexes, and an increased and independent control of your limbs and body, with the ultimate aim of turning you into a relaxed and effective rider. The exercises should be practised on a quiet school horse, and never for too long at a stretch. Before trying out the exercises below, at the walk, loosen yourself up as much as you can by rotating your wrists, ankles, head and shoulders, while sitting on the stationary horse. Remember that throughout all the exercises below your legs must remain firmly in the correct position.

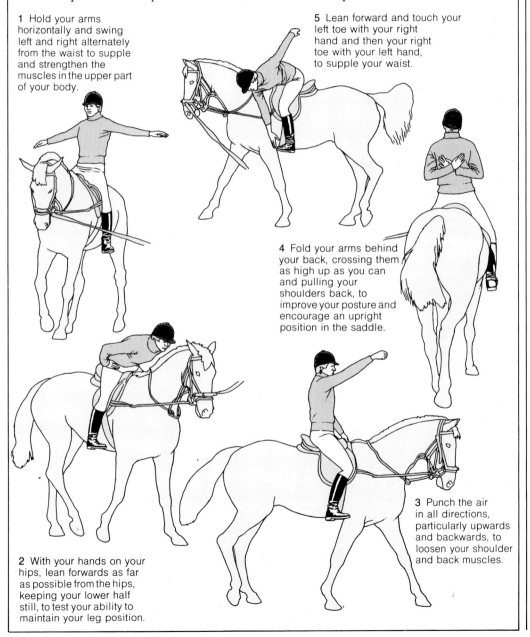

1 Hold your arms horizontally and swing left and right alternately from the waist to supple and strengthen the muscles in the upper part of your body.

5 Lean forward and touch your left toe with your right hand and then your right toe with your left hand, to supple your waist.

4 Fold your arms behind your back, crossing them as high up as you can and pulling your shoulders back, to improve your posture and encourage an upright position in the saddle.

3 Punch the air in all directions, particularly upwards and backwards, to loosen your shoulder and back muscles.

2 With your hands on your hips, lean forwards as far as possible from the hips, keeping your lower half still, to test your ability to maintain your leg position.

Position at the trot

Once you have learned to sit comfortably and well at the walk, you can learn to rise to the trot. Trotting is a diagonal two-time movement of the horse's legs in which diagonal pairs strike the ground alternately. It is an uncomfortable pace for a beginner, particularly on a horse with a very "bouncy" movement. If possible, you should learn on a horse with a smooth, level and fairly slow trot.

Although you can learn to trot while controlling the horse yourself with the reins, it will be much easier for you, and less hard on the horse, if you learn on the lunge. Insecure beginners usually hang on by the reins to keep their balance. No horse will enjoy having his mouth jerked, however unintentional it may be.

To begin with, keep your stirrups so that your ankles can absorb as much of the movement as possible, saving you from bumping about in the saddle, which is very uncomfortable for both you and your horse.

Rising trot
As one diagonal pair of legs leaves the ground you will be pushed upwards out of the saddle, and you sit down again as the same pair of legs hits the ground.

Rising trot

The stirrups should be adjusted to a length which allows you to keep a firm, strong seat which is both deep in the saddle and also allows you to rise slightly from it as the horse's movement throws you upwards. If you learn to rise to the trot using the reins there should be a neck strap on the horse, which you can hold with one or both hands if you feel insecure.

The rising trot will test your balance and will quickly prove to you how secure you really are in the saddle. As the horse's diagonal pair of legs leaves the ground, you will bounce up a little. Allow yourself to be pushed up and forward slightly – you will have to incline slightly into the movement or you will get left behind (fall behind the horse's centre of balance) on rejoining the

Sitting trot
When you sit to the trot you should not leave the saddle. Your back should be upright, but relaxed enough to absorb the motion smoothly, and your leg position must remain constant.

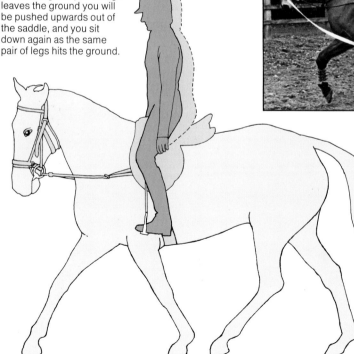

saddle. As the same pair of legs returns to the ground, so you gently return to the saddle, to rise upwards again, in rhythm, as the action is repeated. If you count aloud, "one-two-one-two", in time with the horse's movement, it will help you not to lose the rhythm as you rise with every other count. Once the knack of rising to the trot is learned you will find it surprisingly easy and natural.

At all times your leg position must remain constant. Your hips, knees and ankle joints should absorb the vertical movement, and avoid any jerkiness. They should be loose enough to allow you to move up and down smoothly and rhythmically without extra effort, while remaining controlled enough to allow you to maintain the correct position. Your back remains straight but not stiff, and you should avoid a stiff, hollow back with your stomach pushed forward and your seat stuck out behind – a common fault.

Sitting trot

Gradually, as you get used to the feel of the movement, you can learn to sit to it. Your position remains much the same as for the walk, upright but not stiff. The more relaxed you are, in fact, the less you will tend to bump up and down, as hard, tense muscles cannot absorb movement. The more elastic and responsive your muscular action, the greater the degree of communication will be between you and your horse – the correct balance between muscular action and relaxation comes with practice. It will help to repeat the exercises you did at the walk, but at the sitting trot this time.

Once you can sit comfortably to the trot, you can practise without stirrups to strengthen your position.

Exercises at the trot

You will find that your position in the saddle at the trot is improved if you practise the exercises for the walk, on page 47, at the sitting trot. You should keep your leg position constant throughout, first with the stirrups and then without them.

Additional exercises can be used to help improve your balance – particularly helpful for maintaining your position at the rising trot – and for increasing the strength of your thigh muscles.

More experienced riders sometimes practise the rising trot without stirrups. It is not easy, so you may not succeed at first.

Above, try to remain standing in the stirrups on both up and down beats of the trot – it will improve your balance.

Right, once you become proficient at the rising trot with stirrups, you can try to rise without them – it will strengthen your thigh muscles.

Riding off the lunge

Your first lessons off the lunge should be within an enclosed area, such as a small paddock or indoor school, to avoid distractions. Unless your horse is suitably quiet and reliable, it is a wise precaution to have an assistant ready to take hold of the reins in case you lose control. Having mounted, check the length of your stirrup leathers (see page 45) and tighten the girths if necessary (see page 52).

Using the reins

The sensitivity of your hands is all-important because they are in direct contact, through the reins, with your horse's mouth, which is naturally vulnerable. Your hands must be controlled independently from the rest of your body's movements to preserve this delicate contact, so that you never allow them to jerk his mouth – hence the importance of first acquiring a secure and balanced seat on the lunge.

Hold the reins as shown below, keeping your wrists supple to allow an elastic feeling between your hands and the horse's mouth. Your hands should never be stiff or they will not stay in harmony with the natural movement of the horse.

Although it is a natural instinct to want to use your hands more than any other part of your body, they are nearly always too active. They must never be used alone, but always in combination with leg and seat aids (opposite). A rider with "good hands" is one who hardly uses them. They should be steady, light and sensitive.

To shorten the reins, draw the free end of each rein through the hand by the required amount, using the forefinger and thumb of the other hand, and without letting go of the reins. The reins should always be of equal length.

To increase or decrease contact on the reins, see The hands, opposite (below).

Holding the reins
Take up the reins, passing them between the little and third fingers of each hand, through the palm and out between the thumb and first finger. Keep your fingers supple yet firm, with the thumbs upwards and the fist closed but not clenched (see far below). Your wrists should remain supple. The reins should form a straight line through to your elbows, which hang naturally by your sides.

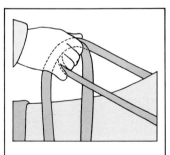

Holding the reins in one hand
To hold both reins in your right hand, transfer the left rein into your right hand, so that it lies flat on the right rein, between your thumb and forefinger, the free end down through your palm.

The aids

A well-schooled horse has been trained to understand and to respond to pressure from the rider's legs, seat and hands. The application and relaxation of this pressure, known as the aids, is the means by which you control your horse's movements, indicating to him any change of pace or direction that you may require.

The legs

Your legs are used to create and regulate the forward movement (impulsion) of the horse. They also guide the hindquarters. In their normal position your legs lie against the horse's sides, with the heel just behind the girth. To increase pace or impulsion, squeeze your legs inwards, the calves pressing against the sides of your horse. The leg position remains constant, unless a hard kick is necessary. To move the hindquarters to one side, or to straighten the horse, it may be necessary to take one leg back a little – never as far as his flank. Each leg must act independently of the other, yet in coordination. Always release any pressure as soon as the horse responds to the aid.

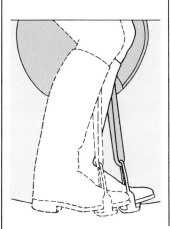

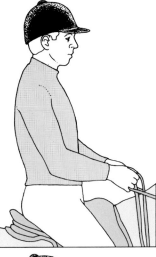

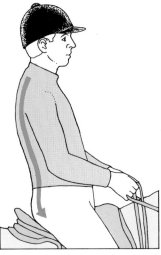

Seat and weight

You can feel the movement of the horse through your seat, and therefore you should strive to use the entire bearing area that is in contact with the horse to maximum effect. By using the distribution of your weight and by the bracing of certain muscles (your back, thigh and pelvic muscles) you can influence the horse's actions.

A braced back is used to warn the horse of any change of pace or direction. Without leaning forwards, push down with your pelvis, allowing it to tilt as shown, left, so that your spine is straightened and the bearing area of your seat becomes more effective.

This action is momentary and should never be prolonged, but it can be repeated as often as necessary, using stronger or lighter emphasis, depending on the response obtained. This response, in turn, will depend on the horse's sensitivity, and on how well he has been trained.

The hands

Your hands direct the horse's forehand, and regulate the forward movement created by the seat and legs. They must always work in coordination with the other aids – seat and legs – yet they should be particularly sensitive to the horse's mouth. To give with the reins, stretch your arms forward slightly, without losing your balanced seat or, more subtly, merely loosen the wrists and fingers. To take with the reins, do not pull back on them, but use a momentary resistance to slow the horse down or gain submission. Use an elastic action on the reins, always in conjunction with the other aids.

The voice

Your voice can be used as a supplementary aid if your horse fails to respond to regular aids. The tone is most important; it can be varied according to your message: to scold or praise, to encourage, to warn, to steady and halt or to urge forward – clicking your tongue is also effective in the last case.

Using the aids

All the aids – seat, legs and hands – are used in every transition of pace, to turn and to halt. Only the intensity varies with which each or all of these influences is applied. For instance, a transition from walk to halt will need a considerably lighter application of the aids than a transition from canter to halt. You should also use the aids to keep your horse attentive at all times ("on the aids"). No aid should ever be prolonged – it should be a momentary action which can be repeated more than once and more strongly if necessary, depending on the response of the horse and on what you want him to do.

It is important to use the aids carefully and with consistency so that your horse remains sensitive to them. He will become confused if he receives variable or indistinct messages. To make precise aids, your body must always be still and your hands quiet so that you move no more than necessary.

If the horse is sluggish, you will have to sharpen up his responses by using strong driving aids (see page 122).

As well as the natural aids already mentioned, there are various artificial aids which can be used to supplement them. A whip, for example, is often carried and is used to reinforce a leg aid (below). However, it should never be used to punish the horse, particularly in the hands of an inexperienced rider. Spurs are used to gain greater response to the leg aids (see page 131) but should never be worn by beginners since complete control of all leg movements is essential if the spurs are not to hurt the horse and destroy his trust.

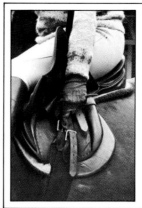

Tightening the girth once mounted
Before moving off, check that the girth is tight enough to keep the saddle securely in place. Move your leg forward and lift the saddle flap. Then tighten the girth firmly, taking care not to pinch the horse's skin.

Moving off

Before moving off, make sure that your horse is receptive to the aids by bracing your back and making contact with your legs and hands, preparing him to go forward smoothly and willingly when asked.

To move off, apply light pressure with both legs equally, relaxing it as soon as he responds by moving forward. Maintain a light steady contact with his mouth without restricting his forward movement or straightness. Keep your hands and body still but relaxed, not tense, so that there is minimum movement. To maintain a regular active walk it may be necessary sometimes to re-apply the aids. The horse must be responsive to your seat, legs and hands at all paces (on the aids) if you are to remain in control.

To turn

A horse can flex his neck to left and right (laterally) much more than he can bend the rest of his body since the lateral flexion along his spine is limited. A highly trained horse, whose muscles are developed to their maximum extent, can bend throughout his length around a circle as small as 8m (25ft) in diameter. A typical riding school horse, however, would be unable to achieve such a tight turn and you should not try to pull him around by using the reins alone.

Although it is a natural instinct just to pull the right rein to turn right, unless your outside hand has at least as much influence as your inside one, the horse's shoulder

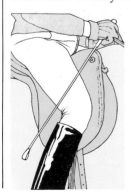

Using a whip
If you carry a whip, hold it at the angle shown. To use a short whip, hold both reins in one hand and the whip in the other, and apply the whip just behind the girth, flat against the horse's side. However, a schooling whip can be used without taking your hand off the rein.

will move outwards, throwing him off balance. To turn correctly, the entire horse should follow a continuous arc, and the neck should not bend more than the rest of the body.

The horse has been taught that equal pressure from both legs, supported by an equal feel on both reins, means that he must go forward and straight. When turning, each of your legs and hands has a separate role. Your inside leg creates forward movement (known as impulsion) while your outside leg controls the horse's hindquarters. Your inside hand asks him to bend and guides his direction, while the outside hand must regulate the amount of bend and the direction, and must also control the impulsion.

To halt

To prepare to halt, first brace your back and then, sitting deep in the saddle, apply light leg pressure, with feel on both reins (by closing your hands). Relax your legs and yield with your hands immediately the halt is achieved to prevent further movement or resistance. You can use your voice as well, by saying "whoa", if the horse is unresponsive. Your aim should be to halt squarely, as shown. Never pull the horse back to correct an untidy halt, but ask him to go forward a step.

To move off
Apply light pressure with both legs equally, relaxing it as soon as the horse moves forward. Allow your hands to follow the movement of his head, while still maintaining light steady contact with his mouth.

To turn
Use your inside leg for impulsion and your outside leg just behind the girth to control the horse's hindquarters. Feel on the inside rein to ask him to bend, but do not pull or he may resist. The outside rein is used to regulate the amount of bend, and impulsion, and by doing so supports the horse on the turn.

To halt
Left, brace your back to prepare the horse and then, sitting deep in the saddle, apply light pressure with both legs equally, and close your hands to feel on both reins. Relax your legs and hands immediately the halt is achieved, above.

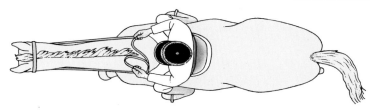

Practice off the lunge

When you can control your horse at the walk, turn him and halt him, you can learn how to make transitions of pace, and to canter and gallop.

Transition to trot

To ask the horse to trot on from the walk, squeeze his sides with both calves equally, your legs remaining in their usual position. The strength of your leg aids will vary according to the sensitivity of the horse. A light squeeze should be enough, but if not, use a stronger leg aid, or kick. As soon as the horse responds by moving forward into a trot, relax the pressure. Remain sitting down in the saddle until you feel a definite rhythm, then start to rise. By this time, you should be able to keep your legs still at the trot. If they move about, you will not only disturb the horse's rhythm and pace, but any aids you give will be confusing, and eventually the horse will cease to respond. Practice on the lunge will help to improve your leg position.

At the trot

At the trot the horse moves his legs in diagonal pairs (see page 32). The off-fore and the near-hind move together, known as the "Right Diagonal". The near-fore and the off-hind move together, known as the "Left Diagonal". When you are rising to the trot, and your seat returns to the saddle as the off-fore and near-hind legs touch the ground, you are on the "Right Diagonal". You should use the "Right Diagonal" on a left-handed circle, and the "Left Diagonal" on a right-handed circle. This distributes your weight more comfortably for the horse, as it is in the saddle when the inside hind leg is on the ground, and off the inside shoulder when the inside foreleg touches the ground.

To change from one diagonal to the other, sit in the saddle for an extra beat, before rising again. Make it a habit to change diagonals whenever you change direction. Eventually it will become automatic and you will feel uncomfortable riding around a circle on the wrong diagonal. When out hacking, it will be more comfortable for the horse if you remember to change diagonals at regular intervals.

Left, the rider is practising the sitting trot without stirrups on a correct left bend.

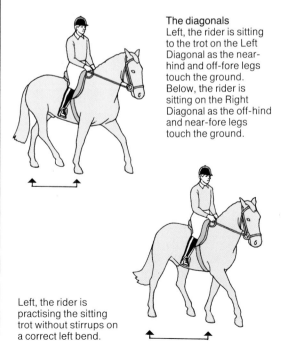

The diagonals
Left, the rider is sitting to the trot on the Left Diagonal as the near-hind and off-fore legs touch the ground. Below, the rider is sitting on the Right Diagonal as the off-hind and near-fore legs touch the ground.

The canter

The canter has a three-time beat, and is normally a comfortable, rocking, rhythmic movement. Your position at the canter remains the same as for the walk, upright but not stiff, and supple enough to absorb any movement, particularly through your lower back and your joints. If your muscles are tense, you will bump against the saddle instead of relaxing down into it. Avoid leaning forward, which will unbalance your horse, although it may be your natural instinct to do so to avoid getting "left behind" the movement.

Many riding school horses cannot canter on the lunge or within a limited space because they cannot bring their hindquarters under sufficiently to support themselves and they tend to go fast to counteract the lack of balance. You may find it easier to make your horse canter when hacking out than in the schooling area.

A willing horse will need no strong driving aids once cantering but may need some encouragement to maintain impulsion. Use your inside leg, balanced by an elastic contact through the reins. If you find your horse is increasing his speed, do not pull at his mouth. Instead, brace your back and apply leg pressure, alternating it with smooth, rhythmic resistance from your hands, until he returns to a slower canter.

When cantering on a bend the horse's inside pair of legs must lead, moving in advance of the outside pair of legs (see below). If the outside legs lead, the turn will feel awkward and unbalanced.

Transition to canter

You will find it easier to strike off on the correct lead if you ask for the transition on a bend. To canter to the left, first engage your horse's attention by sitting down in the saddle at the trot and bracing your back muscles – he should not quicken or lengthen his stride. Bend him slightly to the left and, in the stride following the preparatory action, increase the leg pressure, controlling the extra impulsion thus created with a relative feel on the reins. Release pressure from both hands and legs as soon as the transition is made correctly.

Left, cantering to the left on the correct lead, that is with the near-fore and near-hind legs leading. Far left, cantering to the right on the correct lead, with the off-fore and off-hind legs leading.

Faults
Left, this rider's reins are too long and she is leaning back, trying to stop the horse. Right, the rider is sitting on the back of the saddle and her legs are pushed too far forward. If you give the wrong aids the horse may strike off on the wrong leg or canter disunited. In the latter case, return to the trot and repeat the transition correctly.

The gallop

This is the horse's fastest and most "extended" pace, with a definite moment of suspension when all four legs are in the air (see pages 32–3).

It is exhilarating to move at this speed, but if your horse gets over-excited and takes charge, it could be dangerous, so never gallop unless you are in control of your horse. Before a gallop you should shorten your stirrup leathers two or three holes to bring your seat slightly above the saddle, and to allow you to lean forward slightly from the hips. This will prevent your getting "behind the movement", since the horse's centre of gravity moves forward when he is moving fast.

Transition to gallop

To make the transition from canter to gallop, incline your body forward, shorten the reins and squeeze with your legs. A lazy horse may need urging forward. If so, sit down in the saddle and drive him on with your seat and legs. Once he is galloping, adopt the forward seat.

The gallop
The rider has shortened her stirrups, and is leaning forward to stay with the horse's movement, keeping a firm but sensitive contact on the reins.

At the gallop

Your hips, knees and ankle joints must be flexible enough to absorb the horse's movement, and your thigh muscles and ankles will bear most of your weight. Too much movement will upset the horse's balance and will be tiring and uncomfortable for both of you. Keep your back straight, but not stiff: there should be a flowing line from your elbow to the bit. Keep a firm yet sensitive contact with the horse's mouth, but do not pull.

To make a turn at the gallop, you will have to slow down slightly before the bend so that the horse does not over-balance. Never pull up suddenly at the gallop – it puts a strain on the horse's forelegs.

Decreasing pace

The aids to decrease pace are always the same, only the strength with which you apply them varies according to the speed, and the horse's obedience. Never pull on the reins continuously to slow down, and always keep your legs against the horse's sides in readiness to control his impulsion, direction and balance.

To slow down, first brace your back muscles and tighten your seat before increasing the feel on the reins using a rhythmic "give and take" action. When the horse responds, yield to him with your hands without losing contact.

If you do not get an immediate response or if the horse does not slow down to the required pace, increase the strength of all the aids, in the same order as before, relaxing the pressure as soon as he responds.

Never ask the horse to stop suddenly when galloping. Slow down gradually, and sit more upright, using your legs and weight to bring his hindquarters under him. You will find it easier to reduce speed while turning because the horse will find it difficult to set his neck and spine against you. You can use your voice too, calmly and firmly, to emphasize your aids.

To go from a canter to a trot, and from a trot to a walk, apply the same aids as before, sitting to the trot during the transitions. The aids to halt, from walk, have already been given (see page 53).

School figures

The object of school exercises is to improve your balance, sense of rhythm and timing, and your control of the horse. The exercises also help to sharpen your reflexes, refine your use of the aids, and develop a better understanding of how the horse thinks, moves and reacts. They are usually performed in a standard sized arena of 40 x 20m (130 x 66ft) with a good level surface which is neither so hard that it jars the horse's legs, nor so soft that it strains them. A corner of a field will do, provided it has a good surface and straight sides.

The following figures and exercises are most useful:

Changing the rein: This means to turn from one direction to the opposite one (from right to left rein, and vice versa). It can be done diagonally across the arena or directly across the centre (below left). Be careful to turn in good time so that you do not overshoot the line, and be as accurate as possible because, if you veer off-course, it may be difficult to straighten the horse again. When turning, do not go too deeply into the corners of the arena or the horse will lose balance and rhythm.

Transitions of pace: The instructor may ask for a halt or change of pace at a certain marker. To begin with you will find it easier to do along the side of the arena, but as you gain experience you will be able to halt, for example, without the help of a guiding fence or wall.

Simple turns and circles: The large circle (below centre) – usually 20m (66ft) in diameter – is a recognized school figure used to test the pupil's control and use of the aids at the walk and trot (and, when more experienced, at the canter). A truly round circle touches the sides of the arena for only two or three strides at the walk or trot. It is not easy to achieve as the rider must apply effective aids, and it is a common fault to follow the sides of the track for too long, making the circle more square than round.

To change from a left circle to a right one, you will have to go straight for a stride or two while you change the aids to ask for the opposite bend or direction.

Serpentines: You can also practise changing bend and direction with two or three serpentine loops (below right). You will need to plan ahead or you may find the space available too small, and will thus lose balance and rhythm. You should practise the serpentines first at the walk and then at the trot.

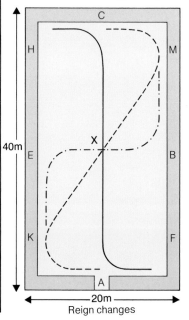

Reign changes

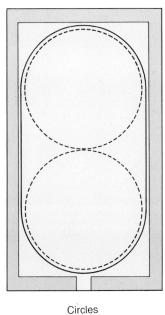

Circles

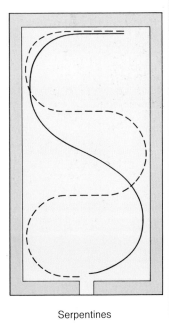

Serpentines

Riding out

Riding out (also known as hacking) can be more exhilarating than any other equestrian activity: the freedom of riding in the open, over moors, downland or farmland, can give unlimited pleasure. Since you will probably be more relaxed than you are when under instruction in the school, your seat and balance may well improve, increasing your security in the saddle, and your confidence, as a result.

If you have little experience of riding in the countryside, you should go with a reliable companion and follow his example. If you go alone, tell someone at the stables exactly where you will be going and at what time you expect to return, in case you have an accident.

Plan a ride that will take about 40 minutes to one hour, and which will include some trotting, and a canter or two. You can expect to cover three to four miles per hour, depending on your pace and the type of terrain. Later you may progress to longer rides of up to two hours or more, if both you and your horse are fit enough (see Trekking, pages 99–103). Your horse should always be treated with consideration. When trotting, use the rising rather than the sitting trot, as it is more comfortable for you both.

Always be aware of your surroundings and of any possible hazards. Watch your horse's behaviour and that of your companions. When crossing public or private property, respect other people's rights. There is a great temptation to ride at speed, once away from the confines of the riding school but beware of upsetting other animals or people who may be startled if you suddenly rush past them. If they are, they could, in turn, possibly frighten or excite your own horse.

If you are not familiar with the area, study a map and then keep to the authorized tracks or bridle paths, always asking permission first before riding on private land. Leave the countryside as you find it: even if you do not mind seeing litter lying about, others do. Close any gates that were shut when you came to them. When approaching a gate, if you are not going to jump it, go slowly so that the horse is not confused as to your intentions. Opening and closing a gate without dismounting are shown opposite; if you are not sufficiently experienced or if the horse is not well trained, dismount and lead him through, closing the gate afterwards.

If you are crossing farmland, you must be able to tell the difference between young wheat and stubble, or between new grass

Cantering over a stretch of open grass is always enjoyable, but you should take care to vary the pace on a ride, and should canter for short periods only.

Opening and closing a gate

If the gate you want to open is well-hung, so that it swings easily, and if it has a simple form of latch, you may be able to open it without dismounting. If you are riding in a group, the first one to reach the gate should open it for the others and wait until they have gone through before riding through himself, and closing it. If the gate is awkwardly placed, or leaning, or has a complicated fastening, he will probably have to dismount, and lead the horse through, closing the gate afterwards. The other riders should wait until he is back in the saddle before moving off.

1 Approach the gate at a walk and position your horse with his shoulder near the latch. Hold the reins in your outside hand and unfasten the latch with the other, pulling the gate open.

2 Pull the gate open wider, and avoid hitting it against your horse. If you do, he may become gate-shy.

3 Keeping the gate open with one hand, ride through slowly, putting your hand on it to prevent it from swinging.

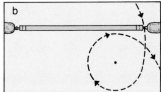

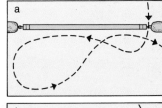

4 Turn the horse around, using either of the methods shown, far right, depending on your level of experience, and bring him alongside the gate.

5 Position the horse with his shoulder near the latch, and close the gate, fastening the latch securely.

An inexperienced rider will have to make a complete turn (a) after going through the gate, whereas a more experienced rider can execute a turn on the forehand (b) – see also page 126.

and old pasture. You will be in trouble, rightly, if you trespass on growing crops. Avoid deep, heavy ground, such as ploughed fields, where the horse may strain his legs pulling them out of the mud, or may pull off a shoe.

When out on a ride take care not to disturb any farm animals, particularly cows in calf, or sheep in lamb. If you have to go through a field of livestock, give them a wide berth, and go no faster than a walk. If you have to pass under any overhanging branches, duck down low on your horse's neck, but keep hold of the reins to guide him. Never gallop up behind another horse; he may kick out at you in fright, or take flight. When you see another rider approaching, slow down to a walk; if you dash past, you may excite the other horse.

When going for a canter or gallop, choose level ground which is neither soft nor hard, avoiding sharp stones, holes or ruts. Your horse's legs and feet are always vulnerable, and a strained or pulled tendon could result in a year's enforced rest. However familiar the land may be to you, inspect it before cantering over it. Do not always break into a canter when you reach a stretch of grass, or the horse may make a habit of it, which you could find difficult to control.

Going uphill
Keep your weight forward, inclining your body over the horse's centre of gravity, leaving his loins and hindquarters free. Do not interfere with the horse's mouth but allow him to balance himself with a free use of his head and neck, while you keep a light contact on the reins.

Going downhill
Avoid sitting so far back that you are over the horse's loins. Remain vertical in the saddle so that you are "going with" your horse. Maintain a steady, light contact on the reins to keep him on the right track, but allow him to use his neck to balance as he moves down the slope.

Slow down when you get to rough or uneven ground and let your pony pick his way carefully.

Your horse may not be particularly fit, so do not charge up steep hills or tire him unnecessarily. A horse can climb slopes quite easily when free, but your presence on his back will make it very difficult for him if you do not distribute your weight correctly. It is natural, but wrong, to get "left behind" by sliding back towards his loins and clinging on to the reins, thereby interfering with his mouth. Your horse's ability to climb energetically would therefore be restricted and the steeper the slope, the faster he will want to go to summon enough energy to reach the top. You must free your weight from his loins and hindquarters by leaning forward over his centre of gravity, keeping the minimum of contact with his mouth, for guidance only.

Before going downhill, particularly on a steep slope, choose the best place for your horse to descend, avoiding any rough, uneven or slippery ground. He will normally have the sense to walk very cautiously downhill. The steeper the slope, the slower he will want to go, lowering his hindquarters until he is almost sitting down and sliding. Although your instinct may well be to lean right back and brace your legs and feet against the stirrups, the horse would find it uncomfortable. You should stay forward instead, keeping just enough rein contact to guide him, so that he can stretch out his neck and head to pick his way down the slope. Take him down straight, as a slip sideways could result in his falling.

You may meet a river or stream which you have to ford; if so, choose a suitable crossing place with a hard, sound and fairly level bottom. Select a bank where the descent to the river is gradual so that your horse does not drop suddenly into deep water, and try to avoid a fast-running current. Always cross water slowly, no faster than a slow trot, even if the water is very shallow. If your horse stops and begins to paw the water, he may be intending to roll; keep him moving, using your voice and whip, if necessary, to prevent him from doing so.

Crossing a river
When wading through deep water, raise your knees up high. The horse will find it hard work, so keep him walking on straight – if he stops he may find it difficult to start moving again.

If you wish to jump (see pages 66–75), you should always get permission from the landowner first, and jump only if you see that the obstacle is within your capabilities, and if you are accompanied, so that someone is at hand in the event of an accident. First make sure that the landing area on the far side of the jump is suitable. If you break a fence or gate, you should report it as soon as possible to the owner, having first done your best to patch up the gaps.

If you come across a ditch, you should not try to jump it if at all uncertain. However, if you have a companion with you who is more experienced, and you wish to try, ask him to give you a lead; your horse will almost certainly follow.

Hazards

When riding out in the country you may, very occasionally, have to deal with an unexpected problem. However, some mishaps – such as the horse losing a shoe – are more common than others, and you should learn how to deal with them. Others are unpredictable, and you will have to use your common sense, while trying not to pass on to the horse any anxiety that you may feel.

If the horse loses a shoe he may go lame. A lost front shoe is more serious than a lost hind one, since the forefeet of the horse take most of his weight. If he should lose a front shoe, return to the stable at the walk, keeping to soft ground, and avoiding any stony areas or hard roads. If you have no choice but to travel on hard or rough ground, dismount and lead the horse. Sometimes a shoe can be wrenched out of position (known as "spread") which can be dangerous as the jutting edges may cut him. Try to remove the shoe if you can, taking care not to damage the hoof. If you fail, get help from a blacksmith or from

Falling off

Beginners used to be told that they should have at least a dozen falls before they could claim to be able to ride. Of course this is not true – no-one benefits from a fall, and you should do your best to avoid one. Apart from the risk of physical injury, you could lose your confidence which would hinder your riding progress.

To prevent falls, the first essential is a firm balanced seat, giving you the ability to manage your horse, in all circumstances, normal or unexpected. You must stay alert, anticipating any possible trouble and always ride with your horse "on the aids". Try to avoid any unnecessary provocation – for example, a horse that is obviously fresh should be lunged first until his excess energy has been expended, or he should be taken to a quiet spot and made to trot or canter quietly until he feels more settled and obedient. You should also try to avoid obvious hazards such as noisy machinery, flapping objects (washing lines or plastic bags, for instance) or any other animals, such as pigs or dogs.

If you can hold on to the reins when you fall, then do so rather than allowing the horse to gallop off. Remount quickly, having checked over the horse for injury and adjusted your saddlery, if necessary. If he has been frightened, talk to him soothingly.

However angry or humiliated you feel, never punish him. It will not remove the cause of your fall, and will only make him nervous and wary in future. If riding in company, the other riders should stand still until horse and rider are reunited.

If the horse gets loose and escapes, he may injure himself or someone else. In an overexcited state, he may not want to be caught and you may need help to drive him slowly and quietly into a corner. Make sure no-one moves suddenly or shouts. If he should get loose on the road, try to alert any traffic and then attempt to get in front of the horse, if possible, and head him away from the road. If he slows up, you may be able to catch him, but do not try to grab him if he does not; you may get dragged, or trampled upon. Try to avoid frightening him, and prevent others from doing so. If he escapes completely, call the police and then collect as many helpers as you can, armed with headcollars and ropes if possible, to search for him.

If a fall is serious, and you or your companion(s) injured, then someone should ride for help, leading the loose horse. Common sense will govern your actions following a serious accident, but some horse sense and a basic knowledge of first aid are of great advantage.

someone else who knows how to remove the shoe and who has the appropriate equipment (a buffer and hammer will normally be needed).

Provided tack is checked regularly, it should not break. However, a broken rein, when you are going fast, could result in complete loss of control. If possible, you should try to turn your horse in a circle with the remaining rein, and reach forward to catch hold of the bit with your other hand. Be careful not to grip harder with your legs while doing so, or you will simply urge him to go faster. Do not panic; your horse will slow down eventually.

A broken girth usually results in your falling off, but if you realize that it has become detached while you are still in the saddle, quickly dismount, carry the saddle (if necessary), and lead the horse back to the stable.

If the stirrup leather breaks, you can remove the broken leather and the stirrup iron, and carry them, riding slowly without stirrups, or with just the one. If you feel insecure, dismount and lead the horse. In any emergency, always do your utmost to keep hold of the reins, even if you fall, to prevent him getting loose.

If by any chance your horse should get "cast" (stuck) in a ditch, and if you cannot get him out by pulling on the reins, remove the saddle, if possible. Your companion (if you have one) should pull on the reins while you urge your horse to struggle out, encouraging him from the rear, and using a whip if necessary. If the horse clearly cannot extricate himself, get help.

Leading from another horse

As a beginner you will be busy enough controlling your own horse, without trying to lead another as well. But in an emergency you may have to. Run the stirrup irons up on the saddle of the horse to be led, and secure them so that they do not flap at his sides. Take the reins over his head, and line him up on the near side of your horse so that he is on the inside when you are on the road. Hold his reins in your

Left, a rider leading a pony from his horse. The pony is lined up correctly on the near side, the reins held in the rider's left hand.

63

left hand, flat against those of your own horse. If he is excitable, hold him on a short rein with your hand nearest to him, while controlling your own horse with your other hand. If the led horse attempts to pull away, try to get him under control by using a "give and take" action on the reins.

Bolting

A horse that might run away with you is obviously unsuitable, but even a normally quiet animal can bolt if something frightens him. If the horse is pulling, it may make you grip too hard in your attempts to restrain him, causing him to go even faster, instead of slowing down. To regain control, try to turn him, by pulling hard on one rein, by using your voice and bracing your legs forward, not against his sides. If you cannot turn because you are on a road or path, use your voice, and try to bend his head and neck to the near side so that he cannot set them and thus pull harder. It is better to use a "give and take" action on the reins, rather than a constant tug which will only cause him to resist more strongly. A stronger bit might help but it is seldom the right solution for a horse that pulls (see page 223) and you will need experience and skill, rather than force or strength, to keep him under control. If you find great difficulty controlling the horse, it is better to get off and lead him.

Riding in a group

When riding in a group across country, the standard of training of riders and horses may vary, so be considerate to those who are less experienced. You should always keep at least a horse's length away from the one in front, and never suddenly break into a trot or canter, without ample warning. If you want to canter, and your companion(s) do not, you risk upsetting the horses left behind. If the whole group wishes to canter but suspects that the horses may excite each other and become out of control, it is advisable to break up, and go singly, or in pairs. It is often wise to canter in opposite directions, round the outside of a field for instance, so that there is a better chance of being able to keep the horses under proper control.

Once the horse is out of control he can be hard to stop. The rider has tried to turn him, but the bit has slipped through his mouth. By standing up and gripping with her legs, she is urging him on even faster.

Riding on the road

You should know the highway code, and obey it at all times. You must remember that motorists are generally unused to horses, and often drive past too fast or too close, or both. Firstly, your horse must be used to traffic; if he has been frightened or is fresh and excitable, avoid riding on the road until he is calmer, or choose quieter roads with a sound, wide grass verge. You should always wear light, bright colours so that you can easily be spotted. If you are riding on the side of the road, keep slightly out from the kerb to give yourself room to manoeuvre if the horse is alarmed. Remember that sudden noises – dogs barking and children shouting – may startle him, as may unexpected strange or flapping objects.

Keep alert, with your horse on the aids, and don't allow him to "slop" along on a loose rein. A walk or a slow trot are the best paces to use – never canter on the road, you risk losing control, and the hard surface will jar his legs. It is best not to canter along the grass verge either – he may get over-excited or he may injure himself on litter, or by stumbling over a ditch.

When riding in a group on the road, you should put the quietest horse at the front to set a good example, and the best trained

When turning right at a busy road junction, indicate your intentions clearly, in plenty of time.

horse at the rear so that the rider is able to keep an eye on the horses ahead. The leader should make any necessary signals to traffic, and should make sure the group does not become separated. Courtesy to drivers is vital for all-round safety and for cooperation of motorists in the future. Always thank a motorist who slows down.

It is never advisable to ride at night or in fog, particularly on the road. If you must, wear strong stirrup lights, white in front and red at the rear, and wear a fluorescent jacket.

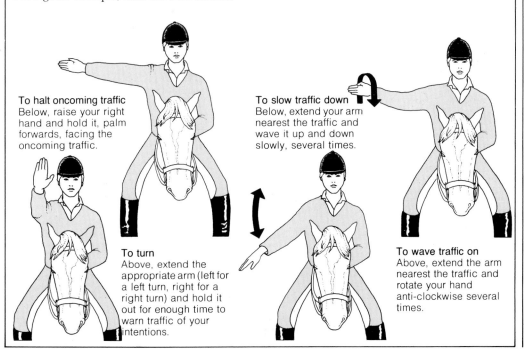

To halt oncoming traffic
Below, raise your right hand and hold it, palm forwards, facing the oncoming traffic.

To turn
Above, extend the appropriate arm (left for a left turn, right for a right turn) and hold it out for enough time to warn traffic of your intentions.

To slow traffic down
Below, extend your arm nearest the traffic and wave it up and down slowly, several times.

To wave traffic on
Above, extend the arm nearest the traffic and rotate your hand anti-clockwise several times.

Jumping

Once you have acquired a secure seat and you can control your horse, you will be ready for preliminary jumping exercises. Find a good instructor and, if possible, a willing, experienced horse. You must learn the correct way to jump, otherwise you will interfere too much with the horse's natural style of jumping so that he no longer enjoys it and may refuse to jump altogether.

Most riders find jumping difficult at first. Although you will need a lot of practical experience and patience to become an expert, it is worth taking the time and trouble from the start to acquire a good jumping style. You will appreciate the benefits of this sound foundation work when jumping suddenly seems easy, and you no longer have to concentrate on what you should be doing, but can give all your attention to making it as easy as possible for your horse.

The key to successful jumping is in making a correct approach to the jump. The rider must inspire confidence: any lack of resolve will be felt by the horse, affecting his concentration, which could cause him to refuse. The slightest hesitation could also upset his balance and may well cause him to jump badly. You must begin by practising over small jumps; only when you can handle these confidently should you progress to larger and more difficult ones (see also pages 162–3).

Understanding the mechanics of how a horse jumps will help you to solve any problems which may arise.

Below, a horse and rider jumping in perfect style, with the horse displaying free use of his neck, back and loins as he rounds over the fence. His forelegs are neatly folded, and his rider is well balanced to follow the horse's flight.

How the horse jumps

It is generally accepted that horses are not natural jumpers. Very few, when turned loose in a field, will jump out over the surrounding fence. However, when they have been trained with a rider, many horses appear to find it easy and enjoyable.

Some horses barely seem to rise when jumping; their legs simply fold up, closing under their bodies in a smooth, economical movement (bascule). This is ideal for it uses little energy, is comfortable for the rider, and imposes the minimum strain on the horse.

Since the secret of successful jumping lies in the approach, if the horse arrives at the point of take-off correctly balanced and with enough impulsion, the jump itself will rarely be a problem. Only an experienced rider should try to influence the horse's correct take-off point (see page 149). The obstacle should be approached with impulsion, not just speed. If the horse approaches the jump too fast, he may become unbalanced, and will find it difficult to lift himself to clear the obstacle. The take-off, flight, and landing phases of a jump are shown below.

Phases of the jump

During the approach, the horse will have extended his stride and lowered his head as he brings his hindquarters underneath him to balance himself. Just before take-off his neck shortens as he prepares to spring. He flexes his hind legs under him, and a powerful thrust with his hocks pushes him up and forwards. One or both forelegs will take off either a fraction before or just as his hind legs immediately straighten again, propelling him through the air, his neck and head now reaching forwards at full stretch, maintaining balance and following the arc of the jump.

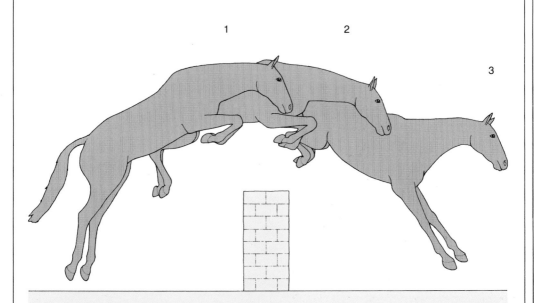

The horse's shoulders and elbows act as a hinge, to lift his forearm and bend his knees, enabling him to tuck his feet up close to his body (1). His hind legs also begin to fold under him (2). The horse lands on one forefoot a fraction before the other (3), so that for an instant his whole weight is over one delicate hoof – it must therefore be a light landing! As his hind legs land, his forelegs start to move forward again. The horse will slightly raise his head, so as to relieve his forehand, thus minimizing the shock of the landing and enabling him to re-establish his pace and balance.

Preliminary exercises over poles

By trotting over a succession of poles laid on the ground, you will learn to keep in a well-balanced position, in harmony with your horse. You may use either the rising or sitting trot – you are closer to your horse at the sitting trot, but if you bounce heavily on his back, he may tense against you, in which case rising trot would be better. To start with, place the poles at random and practise first walking over them, then trotting, from different directions, to get the feel of the horse as he picks up each foot to clear them. Eventually, you will learn to judge the distance and length of stride between the poles, and you can vary the angles of your approach. Then line up a row of three evenly spaced poles: the poles should be approximately 1m 30cm (4ft) apart to suit the trot stride of a normal-sized horse, but slightly further apart for a long-striding horse, and closer together for a pony. The horse should be able to maintain a rhythmic stride and pace, his feet touching the ground mid-way between each bar. Increase the number of poles to four, then five, and make sure a helper is there to check the distance between.

As you gain confidence, you can raise the poles above the ground to a height of about 15–20cm (6–9in) or you can replace them with cavalletti (see page 230) turned to their lowest height: if they are higher than 20cm (8in) the horse will be obliged to hop over them, instead of picking up his legs one by one. You can practise trotting over poles without stirrups to improve your balance and strengthen your seat – your security in the saddle will provide a sound basis for further progress. Some instructors may ask you to drop your reins as you negotiate the poles until your position is secure enough not to disturb your horse's mouth.

Above, the horse is bending his knees and hocks with exaggerated action over the trotting poles, displaying athletic power, rhythm and balance.

Below, a horse picking his way over a line of poles, with energetic steps. His rider encourages him to lower his head and neck.

The jumping position

Just as the rider has to depend on his horse to jump an obstacle, a horse depends on its rider to make this task as easy as possible. The rider can do this by keeping his position and balance in harmony with the horse's movement. When jumping, it is most practical to adopt the forward seat. Begin by shortening your stirrup leathers by about two holes: this will allow you to bring your weight forward, raising you slightly in the saddle so that you can stay over the horse's centre of balance throughout the jump, with the minimum of movement. Your security depends largely on a firm leg position. With your weight concentrated more over your stirrups, through your thighs and knees, and less heavily on the horse's back, you will be able to adapt easily to each phase of the jump, and yet readily sit deeper and more upright in the saddle if you need to apply stronger driving aids or half-halts to adjust the horse's speed or balance. You should practise the forward seat at the trot and canter "on the flat", before attempting to jump.

When your seat is too far out of the saddle, you will not be able to feel your horse's back or influence him with half-halts as easily as when you are sitting in the saddle. Equally, many riders find it difficult to use their legs effectively if they have to grip hard to keep their balance. Against this, if you sit down heavily you may restrict the horse's freedom of movement in the back. The sensible solution is to sit lightly, inclining slightly forward into the horse's movement. In the forward seat, whether sitting down on the saddle or slightly raised, your leg position must remain constant, with your toes up and ankles flexed to act as shock absorbers, and your knees pressed firmly into the saddle. As your position will be further forward, you will need to hold your hands further up the reins, making a flowing line from your horse's mouth, through the reins and your hands to your elbows. Keep your head up, always looking in the direction that you want to go. If you look down, you may topple too far forwards and thus upset the vital equilibrium so necessary for successful jumping.

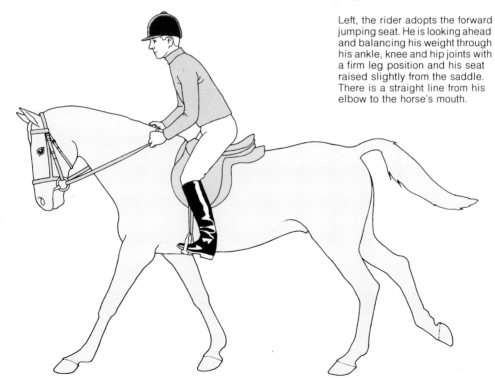

Left, the rider adopts the forward jumping seat. He is looking ahead and balancing his weight through his ankle, knee and hip joints with a firm leg position and his seat raised slightly from the saddle. There is a straight line from his elbow to the horse's mouth.

Preliminary jumping

Once you can negotiate trotting poles or cavalletti and have learned the correct forward seat, you can put a small obstacle or raised cavalletti (about 60cm – approx. 2ft high) at the end of the line of poles, about 3m (9–10ft) after the last cavalletti or trotting pole. (Cavalletti can be used as trotting poles by turning them to their lowest height.) Next, you can raise the height of the jump, and place it 5.5–6m (18–21ft) after the final pole. Your horse may canter one stride between the last trotting pole(s) and the jump. You will find it more comfortable jumping from a canter than a trot. The poles ensure a regular approach and accurate take-off point.

The small jump at the end of a line of cavalletti introduces you to the sensation of jumping without your having to plan the horse's approach yourself. A good instructor will correct faults in position and style during these preliminary exercises, which may also include cantering over grids made up of cavalletti, as shown below.

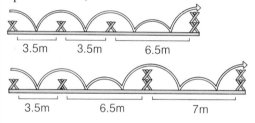

3.5m   3.5m   6.5m

3.5m   6.5m   7m

To stay in harmony with your horse while cantering over cavalletti, you must keep the forward seat. Practise by cantering around on a large circle, on both reins, outside the jumps. If your horse becomes excited when you adopt a forward seat, do not grip harder with your legs, but continue to trot and canter on a circle in the jumping position until he is less tense, then approach the cavalletti at a controlled canter. Keep contact with your horse, through the reins, but prepare to lean forward when he jumps, following through with your hands. If you find it difficult to lean forward and keep your balance, try holding on to the neck-strap (see over) or the mane, but never hang on to the reins, thus damaging your horse's mouth.

Phases of the jump

It is more difficult to jump an individual obstacle without the preparatory line of poles and cavalletti in front of it. You must now learn to approach and negotiate it with a rhythmic, controlled stride. You will not always arrive at the right spot for take-off, so a secure seat is most important to enable you to go "with" your horse in awkward circumstances. A beginner should adopt the forward position described, so as not to get "left behind" at any stage.

It is your aim to sit still, to avoid disturbing your horse's balance or concentration. Nevertheless, you must keep him always "on the aids" (see page 121) to control a straight, even approach with enough momentum to clear the jump easily.

Before riding towards a jump, decide on the best line of approach that allows you to arrive straight at a controlled pace. Then, adopting the jumping position described, canter around outside the jumps, settling into the pace and rhythm at which you will approach the obstacle.

At the approach, keep this position firmly, and maintain the same even pace, and rhythm, using your legs and hands to keep your horse balanced and straight. If you lean too far forwards, or backwards, it will affect your horse's balance.

At the take-off, do not come forward *before* your horse leaves the ground, which will overburden his forehand. With your weight absorbed through your ankle joints, and with your calves maintaining or increasing the impulsion as necessary, be ready to stretch your body forward on take-off, bending from the hips. As the horse's forehand rises, your body comes forward to stay over his centre of gravity and to allow your horse to use his neck, back and loins freely. There should be a straight line through your shoulder, knee and ankle, and your hands should keep light contact with his mouth.

During the flight, fold up close to your horse, to follow the bascule, your seat just clear of his back. Do not let your feet slide forward, pushing your body behind his centre of gravity, or you will find yourself hanging on by the reins and the horse may be forced to drop his hind legs on to the obstacle. Equally, do not get ahead of the movement, with your feet sliding back and your knees acting as a pivot: this is a weak and often insecure position. Your weight must not hinder your horse's muscular effort. Your hands must go forward and follow the stretch of his head and neck. Allow him all the freedom he needs. At the start of the descent from the jump, begin to straighten your body again.

On landing, you should straighten up, with your head up, and keep your weight just clear of his loins to allow his hindquarters to clear the fence. Absorb the slight shock on landing through supple hip, knee and ankle joints. Your legs should remain in the normal position, with your knees firmly on the saddle, so that you maintain your *own* balance as well as that of the horse. In this way you will not "collapse" on landing.

At the approach, left, you must keep straight and ride at the centre of the jump. Balance your horse between hand and leg by keeping a firm but sensitive contact, and do not interfere with his rhythm or pace, least of all during the last few strides. At the take-off, below left, you should go forwards with the horse as he leaves the ground, taking your weight through your thighs, knees and ankles, clear of his back; your hands should keep light contact with his mouth. Fold your body at the flight, below, and follow the natural arc of his jump, allowing him full use of his neck, back and loins. As the horse lands, far below, return to the vertical position without sitting heavily in the saddle, to reduce the weight over his forehand, yet staying clear of his loins.

Practising your jumping

When you have mastered the technique of jumping, you must strive to perfect this by practising over a variety of jumps.

There are two main types: uprights, such as walls and gates; and spreads, such as piles of logs, triple bars, and parallels (usually made up of several poles). They can be either "see through" or solid, and can be built as combinations of two or three obstacles, with suitable spacing for one or two strides between each element.

Even if you do not have access to a set of smart show jumps, it is not difficult to set up a variety of jumps with poles, barrels, oil-drums, straw bales, or car tyres. "Natural" obstacles such as small hedges, ditches, and piles of logs will provide even further variety.

Practice jumps need not be high; they are designed to improve your riding. If they are not more than 90cm (3ft) high,

they can be jumped from a trot as well as a canter. Solid fences are best because if the horse sees that the fence cannot be easily knocked down he will take more care to jump it properly. If he *does* hit the fence the first time he is unlikely to next time.

Choose the site for your jumps carefully: they must be on good ground – not too hard, boggy or rough. Look after the ground, keeping it in good order and well drained. Sand or shavings will improve most surfaces and will be easier on your horse's feet and legs.

Some jumps can be jumped from either direction, but there must always be a distinct ground-line, so that the horse can judge his take-off: a pole or branch on the ground is now considered dangerous as, if a horse refuses, he could get tangled in it. The correct take-off spot is approximately the same distance from the base of the fence as the actual height.

Left, straw bales or brush packed into simple wooden casings make an attractive solid spread for basic jumping practice. These fences can be adjusted to the height required. Right, a good home-made jump made with car tyres threaded on to poles, supported by stakes sunk into the ground. The poles can be raised to provide more of a challenge. Below right, horse and rider jumping over a "see-through" upright jump. Far right, a fallen tree trunk makes an excellent natural obstacle when learning to jump.

Vary the jumps by moving them around, or changing uprights into spreads, to prevent your horse from getting bored. To make a jump bigger it is better to increase its spread rather than its height: this will help to improve your jumping technique without overfacing the horse (see page 160).

To make simple "cups" (which hold the poles on the wings) use shaped blocks of wood, or cut out plastic or tyres and nail them to wooden stakes in level positions. Be careful that there are no sharp ends or nails projecting which could cause injury. The stakes which support the jumps should be sunk firmly in the ground.

Ditches can make very useful jumps. If you wish to dig one, make sure it has well-defined edges, and make it small at first. Once you can jump a ditch confidently, you can then fill it with water (this may surprise your horse when he first sees it, so sit down and ride with determination!).

When you have learned to jump correctly on flat ground, you can progress to jumping small obstacles placed on slopes. Below are some useful points to remember when practising your jumping.

Useful jumping tips
Although your preparations for practice jumping will depend on the facilities available to you, nevertheless there are certain important guidelines you can follow to avoid unnecessary problems and to make your jumping practice as easy and enjoyable as possible, both for you and, consequently, your horse.

Always have someone with you when practising your jumping: getting off to pick up fallen poles, or adjust the jumps, is difficult and disruptive, besides which a qualified person can give advice if things go wrong and can pick you up or catch your horse if you fall off.

To keep control of your horse when approaching small jumps, *trot* at them. It may be more comfortable to canter, but the horse is much less likely to get unbalanced or excited. Do not progress to cantering until you have negotiated all types of small obstacles, including up- and downhill fences, with a quiet, controlled approach. Whether trotting or cantering, your horse must be given every possible chance to arrive at the point of take-off balanced, with a controlled stride and rhythm. Having "set him up", you should allow him to jump freely through the air, so once he is airborne never restrict him with your hands, as you will damage his mouth.

Remember that the impulsion (see page 51) so necessary for jumping should not be confused with speed or sudden nervous energy produced near the fence.

Your horse may have his own individual style of jumping, such as a low or high head-carriage, or he may be very deliberate, or tend to quicken. You should not attempt to interfere with his natural way of jumping, particularly during the final strides approaching a fence. An advanced rider will try to perfect a horse's jumping technique with further schooling both on the flat and over practice fences, but at this stage it is not advisable for you to try to change your schoolmaster horse's style: he is likely to become confused or resentful, leading to further problems which you may not be able to overcome. If faults develop, however, they must be corrected, though you will need guidance to do this.

As a general rule, remember that different jumps have different requirements. For example, upright jumps have no projecting ground-line, and are therefore more difficult to jump accurately. The horse should be allowed to lower his head to judge the take-off and height. Spreads are easier to judge, especially when sloping. They are more inviting, and encourage a rounded jump, or bascule. The horse can take off quite close without hitting the jump, and from a faster approach on a longer stride than with vertical jumps.

Never jump an obstacle in the "wrong" direction, as there will be no ground-line. A horse that needs encouragement should not jump away from home. Some horses are inclined to rush when they see a line of fences ahead. To prevent this, approach the first jump on a circle, from both directions, so that he cannot anticipate so easily. This will also help to improve your judgement of distance and stride. Practise accuracy by jumping an exact spot on a fence, and when you can do this confidently you can approach from a slight angle, or vary the jumps slightly.

When jumping uphill, make sure you get well forward in the saddle. Downhill, you should be prepared to let the reins slip through your fingers, so that you do not catch his mouth on landing over the drop. You should brace your feet forwards slightly to absorb the impact.

Your attitude to jumping will be sensed immediately by your horse. A positive attitude, with an obvious desire to jump, will instil courage and confidence in the horse, but faint-heartedness or indecision will have a negative influence on him. Involuntarily, your feel on the reins or your position on his back may discourage him from jumping.

Sound, fit horses with a reasonable temperament do not refuse, unless badly prepared, badly ridden or over-jumped. Always choose obstacles that are within your capacity, not too big nor too difficult. Approach them at a controlled pace, with enough impulsion to clear them easily. Make sure your approach is straight. Your horse can then find his own point of take-off and will jump willingly. For correction of refusals, see page 160.

Never allow your horse to become bored or stale from constant repetition of the same jumps: a variety of solid and inviting fences will help to increase his enjoyment and interest.

End your jumping practice on a good note. If your horse has not jumped well, for whatever reason, do not leave him with unhappy memories, but try to restore his confidence and keenness by finishing up over a small, simple obstacle which he can enjoy. He will then be more eager to jump next time you practise.

Faults

Most jumping problems are caused by adopting an incorrect position, which will interfere with your horse's jumping. Your body should be supple, so that you are able to adapt to the horse throughout his jump without getting ahead of or behind him – upsetting his balance could result in a refusal. Common faults include stiffness in the shoulders, elbows and wrists, causing unyielding or insensitive hands. A stiff, hollowed or crooked back, or a "collapsed" hip will affect your suppleness and balance, and also that of your horse. To allow your arms and hands to follow your horse's head

and neck freely, do not let your elbows turn out, or your wrists turn under or up. Hands held too low or too high will result in a stiff position and possibly locked elbows, which will cause resistance in the horse and may unbalance you. Rough, uncontrolled hands will also provoke resistance. Do not let your legs swing backwards and forwards – they should be close against the horse's sides, and your knees must remain in firm contact with the saddle.

Refusals on the part of a horse can have many causes, but are due mostly to bad riding at the approach (see page 160).

Above, this rider is leaning back and holding on by his reins to save his balance, having got behind the horse's movement. Above right, this rider is too far forward and his tightly bent elbows are preventing the horse from stretching his head and neck. Right, this rider is severely hampering her horse; she had got left behind at the take-off and is hanging on by the reins. Below, this rider has allowed her pony to disobey her leg aids, and is refusing to jump.

Western riding

Although Western riding is now a universally popular activity, it derives from the practical stock and ranch work used in the plains of mid-Western and South America, where horses are the best – and often only – means of conveyance. The Western style of riding, with long stirrups and reins in one hand, makes it suitable for many ranching activities such as calf-roping, and cutting (opposite), and competition events such as barrel racing (see page 106) and rodeo riding, as well as pleasure riding. Western competitions have, in fact, become so popular that more Western horses are now trained for this purpose than for stock work. Apart from equitation classes, where the emphasis is on the rider's performance, there are many other popular contests, designed to test rider and horse.

Although the emphasis in Western-style events is on fun, you will only be successful if your horsemanship is competent, however well trained and talented your horse may be. Riding at speed will magnify any faults you may have, so you must learn to control your horse well.

Show classes

There are four main divisions in Western show classes: the Western Riding Horse, the Pleasure Horse, the Trail Horse and the Parade Horse.

In the Western Riding and Trail Horse classes, the horses are judged on both their behaviour and skills. The Western Riding Horse is required to show his paces, manners and suitability as an all-round conveyance; the Trail Horse must show his ability to negotiate a variety of obstacles and willingness to carry awkward objects.

In the Western Pleasure Horse division, the judges are looking for a well-turned-out combination of horse and rider which they regard as a perfect example of the well-trained partnership. The horse is required to perform at different paces according to the judge's preference, and is judged on performance and conformation.

The Parade Horse is required to display himself to music. He will be lavishly

"dressed", since his appearance is of primary importance. Attractive Palominos, Pintos, Appaloosas, Arabs, Morgans and walking horses are usually the most successful in these show classes. The horse will also be judged on conformation, paces, performance and manners.

Reining contests

There are many divisions at shows in which stock horses can demonstrate their reining skills. Any breed or cross-breed can enter these competitions if they are over 14.1 hands high, sound, and of working type. They are required to perform at the walk, trot and canter around the ring on both reins, at the judge's command. Each rider is then individually required to show his skills, which will include galloping on a straight line and a series of manoeuvres

which the rider will have learnt by heart beforehand. These vary in difficulty, and must all be performed at great speed.

Cutting

This contest, derived from ranching work, is probably the most popular with both riders and spectators. The horse must separate as many steers, one by one, as possible from a herd within a specified time and, with rapid, deft movements, prevent the steer from rejoining the others. The contest generally lasts two-and-a-half minutes per horse. A limited number of competitors, with the highest points in the first round, contest the final to decide the winner.

Although rider and horse participate, it is the horse's natural ability which is tested – the rider's task being to select a steer that is lively but not too fast, and which will show off his horse's skill to best advantage. When he has asserted his superiority over the steer, the horse returns to the herd to select another animal. He should not disturb or disperse the rest of the herd when singling out his "victim".

Gymkhana events, Western style

These, often known as Youth Activity Events, are most popular with children who can compete in Parade, Pleasure and Trail classes. They are similar to gymkhana in other parts of the world and include a great variety of events to suit all different abilities and temperaments, all designed to test the speed and agility of horse and rider. Popular examples are the walk and lead race, the sack race, tyre race, boot race, musical chairs, pole bending, the pony express, baton relay and wagon race, scoop shovel, and roping the sack (see also page 106). Barrel racing (see left) is also a popular competition and is often a part of rodeo entertainment, along with calf- and steer-roping, and steer-wrestling (see below).

Left, riders participating in a Parade Class. The saddles and bridles in these events can be extremely ornate, and are often encrusted with silver. Above, barrel racing – a popular Western gymkhana event. Right, steer-wrestling. As the rider catches hold of the steer's head and horns, he digs his feet into the ground to slow the animal down. He must then wrestle it to the ground until it is lying on its side. The fastest wins.

The Western horse

Despite the introduction of modern machinery and transport systems, horses are still much in use for stock work in ranches in many parts of the United States. A definite physical type is favoured for this type of work. The horses must, as a general rule, be small and strong, though not too small, since they must be capable of carrying their riders for long distances, and for long periods of time when working on a ranch; nor should they be so big that they tire out quickly when moving about on hard ground. They must also be nippy, able to turn and accelerate quickly as required. To some extent, their ability will depend on training, although innate temperament is also important.

Almost all light breeds of horse can be ridden with a Western saddle, and many breeds are becoming increasingly interchangeable, such as the Arab (see page 244): even the Thoroughbred (page 244), originally developed as a racing horse, is becoming popular for ranch work.

There are, however, many breeds which, though used for classical riding, have particularly close connections with the Western style of riding.

The American Quarter horse is the oldest surviving American breed, its name deriving from the fact that it was originally bred, by seventeenth-century Virginia settlers, for racing quarter-mile distances. A versatile horse, it is now used for riding, racing, ranch work and rodeo riding.

The Morgan (see page 245) is another of the old-established American breeds. It is a good all-round horse, its sturdy build making it ideal for trail and endurance riding.

The term "Palomino" – originally used as a description of a horse's golden colour – is now increasingly being used as the name of a breed, though it has not yet been officially

Five popular American breeds. Top, the Appaloosa. Originally developed by an American Indian tribe, it is now used as a pleasure and parade horse. Above, two Mustangs. These horses were the original cow ponies of the pioneer American West.

Right, a Quarter horse and a Pinto. Both make good ranch horses, though the Pinto is often a favourite in parades. Left, a palomino-coloured Tennessee Walking Horse. Its attractive golden colour makes a palomino horse ideal for parades.

recognized as such. Although it is used for riding and stock work, its attractive colour makes it ideal as a parade horse. The Pinto is another breed in which the name derives from the colour (black and white, or brown and white). Like the Palomino, it is used mainly as a parade horse.

Many of the popular Western breeds used today have close associations with the North American Indians. The Appaloosa, for example, was developed by the Nez Perce Indians from Oregon and Idaho, and is now used as a pleasure and parade horse. The same is also true of Mustangs, which were the original cow ponies in the pioneer days of the West. The Mustang is today on the decline, although government legislation is now ensuring its protection. It is used for riding, showing, trail and endurance riding, and also for competition and stock work.

Training

The Western horse will have many demands placed on him. He will be expected to start and stop in an instant, on command, which requires perfect balance and the ability to execute a sliding stop. He must also be able to turn at speed, using flying changes (see page 143). When necessary, he should be ready to stand still and calm in the midst of noisy, running cattle, and must learn not to react adversely to potentially frightening situations, such as a steer turning in his direction. In addition, he will need plenty of stamina, and must be able to conserve his energy so that he returns home in good condition from a long day's work. A great deal of work, patience and skill will be needed on the part of his trainer to achieve this state of efficiency.

The contemporary training of the Western horse is far removed from the bronco-busting methods of the Wild West, and now, for the most part, follows the system used for training horses for the classical style of riding (see pages 186–240), the main difference being that in Western riding, the horse will have to be trained for neck-reining (see page 89).

Wild horses are usually broken in and led as yearlings. They are then saddled, if reasonably mature physically, when they are at least three years old. A wild, untouched young horse will take much longer to train, since his instinctive fear of humans will have to be overcome before any training can even begin.

The Western horse is often used as a pack-horse, and must be used to having different objects placed on his back, at an early age. He must therefore be "sacked out" by having a sack or blanket draped over him. The next stage is to tie him up and introduce the saddle – the cinch will be tied loosely at first for the horse to get used to it.

The actual training of the horse will begin by lungeing in a confined area, to improve his muscular strength before being ridden. Gradual backing, without force or fuss, will pay off. He will then be introduced to the aids, still in an enclosed area.

The young horse will not, at first, understand neck-reining. At first, the trainer will use two hands on the reins for the first few weeks, as in classical riding, with a sideways feel on the inside rein, and the outside rein touching the horse's neck.

The horse is taught the paces in the normal way. At the walk, he should be brisk and free-moving with a rhythmic beat. The hind foot should overtrack the hoofprint of the forefoot it follows by 15cm (6in).

The trot, or jog, must also be economical and comfortable. There must be some degree of collection and engagement of the hocks, and a low, rounded outline.

The canter, or lope, must be straight with some collection to keep it balanced and smooth. The more the hocks come under the body, the better will be his balance, and the more controlled his gait. He will also be ready, thus "engaged", to increase or decrease speed suddenly, and to turn or stop as required.

Once the horse can perform all the Western paces correctly, he will be taught the flying change and also the rein back (see pages 134, 143).

At a more advanced stage of training, the Western horse is taught several more complicated manoeuvres such as the sliding stop, roll-back, pivot and spin. The sliding stop (in which the horse stops suddenly by "sliding" his hind legs under his body) is required in most Western activities, particularly calf-roping. It is taught progressively from the walk, the jog and the lope, before proceeding to the more spectacular gallop sliding halt. Since this imposes considerable strain on the horse's hindquarters and legs, it should never be taught to a young or inexperienced horse. Skid boots will protect his legs against injury, or bruising, and further protective measures must be taken by practising in indoor arenas or all-weather surfaces.

The roll-back should only be taught to a horse which can already rein back in a small circle. The horse is required to gallop on the left lead, stop and turn simultaneously to the right, and then to gallop forwards on the right lead.

Other advanced exercises are the pivot and spin, both of which, although often used to show off the horse's ability, are also of practical importance for the Western rider working on a cattle ranch. The pivot is a half-turn on the haunches (see page 126) performed at the canter or gallop. It depends on a light mouth and complete engagement of the hocks to enable the horse to lift his forehand off the ground while swinging around.

The spin is a pivot on a 360^{0} turn, similar to the canter pirouette (see page 144). In this manoeuvre the hind feet remain in one area, while the forefeet swing in bounding movements around them.

Roll-backs, flying changes, pivots and spins are natural movements to the cutting horse when working cattle. It usually takes several months or years to reach a high enough standard to be able to perfect these manoeuvres.

Left, a Quarter horse cutting cattle. To pick out a steer with this degree of accuracy requires years of training.

Western tack

Western tack can range from the very simple to the highly ornate, as used in show rings. It can also vary a great deal according to its use. The basic and more popular varieties of saddle, bridles and bit are illustrated below. Whatever type of tack you use, you should make sure that you keep any leather parts supple with the regular use of saddle soap.

There are two styles of Western bridle: the browband (see below), and the split ear variety (see page 84), of which the former is the most popular. The split ear bridle has a headpiece with a split in it on one side, through which the horse's ear passes. This anchors the bridle securely so that there is no need for a browband or throat lash. Two main types of rein are used: split

reins (that is, reins which are not joined together at their ends) and Californian reins, in which the ends are fastened together and finish in a romal (see page 86) – a long plaited thong which can, in turn, be used as a kind of riding whip. The horse is usually trained to halt and stand when one or both split reins are dropped to the ground in front of him, and therefore will not have to be tied up securely.

Western bridles are usually made from rawhide and latigo (soft, tanned leather), although nylon bridles are becoming increasingly popular for Timed Horse Events because they are more hard-wearing and easier to maintain. Popular bits include the ring snaffle and the full cheek snaffles as well as several varieties of curb, of which one of the most popular is

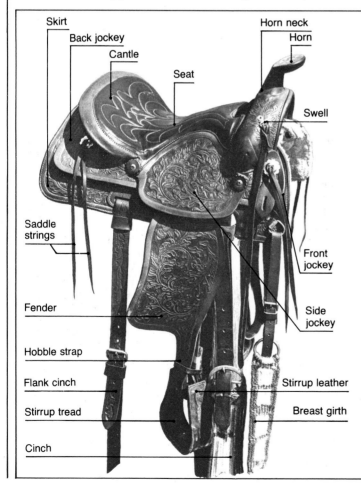

Skirt

Back jockey

Cantle

Seat

Horn neck

Horn

Swell

Saddle strings

Front jockey

Fender

Side jockey

Hobble strap

Flank cinch

Stirrup tread

Stirrup leather

Breast girth

Cinch

Left, a Western stock saddle with a wide fork, designed to help the rider maintain a secure and comfortable position. The breast girth is used partly for decoration but mostly for the practical purpose of keeping the saddle in place when under pressure, as when calf-roping or steer-roping. Most saddles have quilting (or some other type of padding) on the seat for comfort, but this is usually covered with suede or leather to prevent the padding from being worn away. The saddles vary in size to suit different riders and there are also several widths of tree, to suit various sizes of horse. Saddle blankets and pads should be used under the saddle, and should be regularly brushed, and kept dry and clean: horses can develop sore backs from dirty saddle blankets which are soaked in sweat. The stirrup leathers are combined with fenders – long narrow saddle flaps on each side of the horse which protect the rider's legs from sweat. The stirrups themselves are heavy and are made from curved oak. The treads are usually covered in leather.

illustrated below. The use of snaps (hooks) instead of buckles at the bit end of the bridle makes it easier to change bits over and to use the same bridle on different horses.

Nosebands are not generally used, with the exception of the bosal hackamore, which is a stiff, round noseband of varying sizes and weights. Its use is similar to the bitless bridle (see page 275), and it is used with mecate (plaited rope) reins to train the horse. Although it is a most useful item in skilled hands, it should never be used roughly, or by an inexperienced rider.

Today's Western saddle is based on the deep-seated saddle brought to America by the Spanish Conquistadores, and has largely retained its original shape, except that the pommel has become a tall, flat-topped horn, to which one end of the lasso is attached when calf-roping. It is kinder to the horse than the saddle used in classical riding because it enables the weight of saddle and rider to be distributed over a larger area of the horse's back and also because, though heavy, it holds the rider firmly in position: its traditional high cantle, deep seat and set-back stirrups help give the rider the characteristic, long-legged Western seat, making it extremely comfortable for long hours on horseback. Saddle blankets and pads should always be used under Western saddles, to protect the horse's back from the pressure of the saddle.

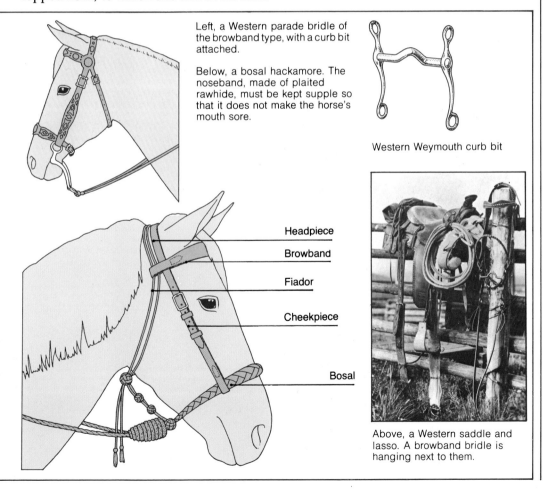

Left, a Western parade bridle of the browband type, with a curb bit attached.

Below, a bosal hackamore. The noseband, made of plaited rawhide, must be kept supple so that it does not make the horse's mouth sore.

Western Weymouth curb bit

Headpiece

Browband

Fiador

Cheekpiece

Bosal

Above, a Western saddle and lasso. A browband bridle is hanging next to them.

Tacking up

Put the pad and saddle blanket on to the horse, so that they are fairly far forward, showing 2.5–5cm (1–2in) in front of the saddle, then place the saddle gently on to the saddle pads, pushing the front edge of the pads up into the fork of the saddle to prevent them from being pressed down hard across the horse's withers. The flank, or rear, cinch (girth) should barely be in touch with the horse's body. It is linked to the front cinch with a short lace or strap. After cinching up, lift the horse's front feet and pull them slightly forward one at a time to remove any creases in the skin to prevent rubbing. The correct methods of saddling and bridling a Western horse are shown below. After saddling up the horse, fasten the breast girth as described.

Putting on the saddle
1 Put the pad and saddle blanket on the horse, and place the saddle over them.

2 Pull the cinch up through the buckle.

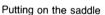

3 Slide your hand under the flank cinch to check that it is not fastened too tightly, and fasten the flank cinch to the front cinch with the connecting strap. Adjust the breast girth so that it fits correctly and is not too tight. It should lie just against the horse's chest.

Putting on the bridle
Above, put the reins over the horse's head, then open his mouth with the thumb of your left hand, and slip the bridle over his head. Holding your right hand in the position shown will prevent the horse from raising his head.

Left, correctly fitted split ear bridle.

Below, a fully tacked up Western horse. The saddle is equipped with good thick pads beneath and is set correctly on the horse – not too far back.

Mounting and dismounting

Mounting Western-style is basically as for mounting in the classical style (page 40), except for the position of the right hand. Face slightly towards the horse's offside quarters. Take up the reins in your left hand, which then rests on the horse's neck just in front of the saddle, and put your left foot into the stirrup in the usual way. You must then grasp the horn or offside swell of the saddle with your right hand as you swing your right leg over the horse's back.

To dismount, be sure your horse is standing square and still. Dismounting Western-style differs from the ordinary method in that the reins are kept in the left hand while the right hand holds the saddle horn, the right leg is swung over the horse's back, and the left foot is kept in the stirrups until the rider's right foot reaches the ground. The exceptions to this are children, novice riders and small adults.

Western clothes

There are certain basic dress requirements in Western riding, though the details may vary. Western-style hat, shirt and cowboy boots are compulsory in competitions, but spurs are optional. Although the choice of trousers is left to the individual, chaps are usually worn over them for extra protection. There are two varieties: shot-gun chaps, which are fairly narrow and zip up (see below), and the bat-wing variety, which are clipped together at the sides of the leg.

Left, a rider putting on shot-gun chaps. They should be buckled around the waist, then zipped up on each leg. Below, a rider wearing traditional Western clothes.

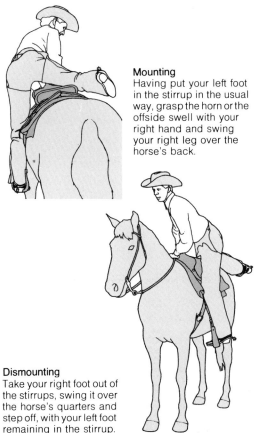

Mounting
Having put your left foot in the stirrup in the usual way, grasp the horn or the offside swell with your right hand and swing your right leg over the horse's back.

Dismounting
Take your right foot out of the stirrups, swing it over the horse's quarters and step off, with your left foot remaining in the stirrup.

The Western seat

The classical style of riding is based on the European military and artistic tradition, with the emphasis on discipline; the Western style is more relaxed, with the emphasis on suppleness. Both, however, aim for harmonious horsemanship with the rider's balance placed over the centre of the horse's gravity. A correct riding position is important, so bad habits must be avoided from the beginning; choose an experienced instructor who will insist on good posture and a correct position in the saddle. Start by riding an experienced horse which can cope with your mistakes and help you out. If you are a complete novice, it may be better if you use a felt saddle for your first lessons, rather than the substantial Western saddle, so that you are better able to feel your horse's movements. If you begin by using a felt saddle you will have to mount with a leg-up or by using a mounting block (see page 41).

With the Western seat you must sit in the centre of the saddle, with your head up and your shoulders square to the horse; your body straight, yet relaxed. When trying to maintain this position as a beginner you may be tense and rigid, and your insecurity in the saddle may cause you to topple forwards when the horse moves. You may, therefore, find it useful to hold on to the saddle horn to help you keep your balance. The stirrup leathers should be at a length which allows your legs to be straight, but with enough bend in your knees to allow you to clear the seat of the saddle by about 7.5cm (3in) when standing in the stirrups. Your heels should be lower than your toes, and your legs over the cinch, parallel to the horse's sides so that they can be readily used to give the required aids. The stirrup treads themselves should rest under the balls of the feet. The correct method of holding the reins is described opposite.

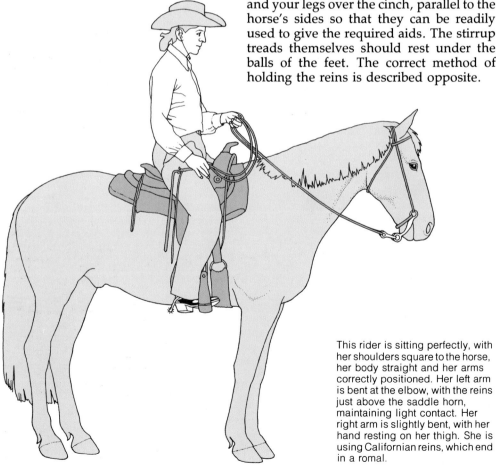

This rider is sitting perfectly, with her shoulders square to the horse, her body straight and her arms correctly positioned. Her left arm is bent at the elbow, with the reins just above the saddle horn, maintaining light contact. Her right arm is slightly bent, with her hand resting on her thigh. She is using Californian reins, which end in a romal.

Using the reins

In Western riding, the reins are held in one hand – usually the left, unless the rider is left-handed. The traditional basis for this was that the rider then had the other hand free for calf- or steer-roping. The choice of rein hand does not strictly matter, as long as it is not changed once the horse is in motion. The two methods of holding the reins are described below. Whichever you adopt, it is important that the reins are of equal length and that they are held as low as possible to the horse's neck.

A common fault made by many beginners is to allow the rein hand to go too far forwards. This will cause the opposite shoulder to move back, leading to a lop-sided and unbalanced position. A useful way of overcoming this problem, in the early stages of Western riding, is to practise maintaining your position at all paces, while holding the reins in both hands. (The horse should be quite used to the feel of this: although the reins are held in one hand when riding, it is standard practice to train Western horses holding the reins in both hands.) Once your position is secure, you can then progress to using one hand.

As in classical riding, it is important to maintain a light contact with the horse's mouth at all times. This contact must be even lighter if a severe bit is used. Since an inexperienced rider will, initially, have difficulty in maintaining this light contact, he should use a mild snaffle bit. The driving aids in Western riding are the same as in classical riding. The horse is turned by neck-reining (see page 89).

Holding the reins

There are two methods of holding the reins, depending on the type used. Split reins (below left) pass over the forefinger and come out of the heel of the hand; if preferred, the forefinger can be put between them. Californian reins (below right) are held with the reins coming up through the hand and out under the thumb and forefinger; the little finger may be between them. The spare ends of Californian reins lie under the rider's right hand on the thigh (unless the rider is left-handed, in which case the reins can be held in the right hand, with the spare ends in left hand). The length of rein between the right hand and the left hand should be about 40cm (16in). To shorten the reins, use your right hand to pull them through your left hand, always from *behind* the rein hand.

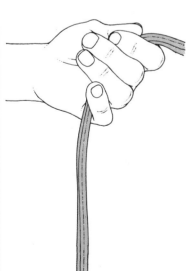

Split reins method

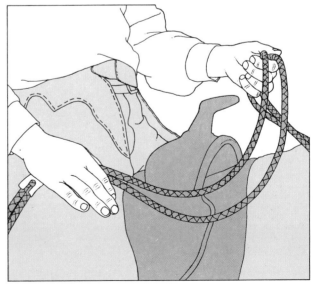

Californian reins method

Western techniques

The paces in Western riding are very similar to those in classical riding, as are the aids, the main differences being that the rider always sits to the jog (trot) and that the horse is turned by means of neck-reining (see opposite). As with classical riding, the novice rider should have his first lessons on the lunge, and should practise the usual suppling exercises as described on page 48. Initial lessons off the lunge should take place in a confined area, where you will learn first to walk and halt, and then the jog, lope and turn; you will find that practising the walk and jog alternately for about 20 yards at a time will be a good way of relaxing. Only when you have mastered all the paces should you go riding out in the open with other riders.

Moving off

To move off, make light contact by squeezing the horse's sides with your legs. Light pressure should be enough. Although stiff fenders on a Western saddle may make it difficult for you to feel your horse's sides with your legs, as a beginner you must never use the long – often rowelled – spurs which are standard Western equipment since they enable the rider to make contact with his horse.

Do not allow your balance to come forward when moving off, or twist your body, so that you are leaning towards your rein hand; it will disrupt your balance and proper use of the aids, so keep your shoulders square. Hold on to the horn to keep your balance if necessary – you should never hang on by the reins, thus hurting your horse's mouth.

Walk

The walk must be energetic and long-striding; your horse should be encouraged to move forward freely by the use of your legs, as in classical riding. He should have a rhythmic, swinging stride so, if the beat of his feet is uneven, he is not moving correctly. Keep a light contact on your reins and sit upright, to help his stride.

Halt

To stop the horse, close your lower legs against his sides, on the cinch, and feel the reins. Do not pull or jerk the reins as this will cause him pain and he is likely to throw up his head and resist. Always yield when he responds. The degree of feel will depend on the lightness of the horse's responsiveness, so begin with a light feel, then ask a little more strongly if necessary. The use of your legs will ensure that the horse's hind legs come under his body and this will keep his outline rounded and correct.

Jog

This is the equivalent of the trot in classical riding. In Western riding, however, the rider usually sits to the jog. The aids are the same as for classical riding: squeeze the sides of your horse with both legs simultaneously and incline your body into the movement, your hands following along your horse's neck. Your spine should be relaxed so that you do not bounce in the saddle, and you should sit as deep as possible, into the movement. The horse must be rounded in outline, showing engagement of the hocks, and even, steady strides.

You should never use the reins to balance yourself, and a good way of testing your balance is to put a finger on the front of the saddle. If you can keep it still, you are sitting correctly to the jog. If you feel insecure, stop, practise at the walk, and then try the jog again.

This rider is sitting well at the jog, although her back appears to be a little stiff.

Lope

This is the equivalent of the canter in classical riding. As with the jog, relaxation of the body, while keeping a secure position, is the key. Maintaining a correct hand position should be easier, since your hands will tend to move less with the rocking movement of the lope than with the more bouncy jogging motion. To lope to the left, keep your horse "between hand and leg", and turn his head slightly to the left (see below), with your weight on your inside seat-bone (but without leaning inwards). Your inside leg, held on the cinch, increases impulsion, while your outside leg, behind the cinch, provides support.

Gallop

The gallop is seldom used in Western riding. It needs an experienced and balanced rider to be performed correctly and should only be used on a good, level surface. The gallop can easily over-excite a horse, which can then get out of hand, so that he runs away with you. To gallop, ease the weight from the horse's loins by leaning forward so that your weight is transferred from the seat to the stirrups and knees. Always keep some contact on the reins.

Turning (Neck-reining)

The Western horse is turned by neck-reining, in which the rein hand is moved in the direction you intend to turn, and the normal leg aids for classical riding are used. For example, to turn right, move the rein hand to the right. Pressure will be exerted on the base of the horse's neck by the left rein which will, in turn, push the horse's head to the right. (Conversely, to turn left, the rein hand must be moved left.) However, the movement of the rein hand should really just be a light wrist movement. If it is too strong it will turn the horse's head against the direction of travel. Your horse must always be looking in the direction in which he is turned.

Rein back

The rein back is an important manoeuvre in Western riding since it tests the horse's ability to go straight back, or to either side.

Neck-reining
The rider's hand has moved very slightly to the right. The left rein is touching the horse's neck and he is turning to the right.

The ordinary rein back (moving backwards in a straight line) is performed in the same way as in classical riding (see page 134). It is executed from a square halt and, after a few backward steps, the horse is urged into forward movement straight away. The rider sits lightly in the saddle but does not lean forward to free the horse's hindquarters, with the legs very slightly back.

To go backwards and to the right, move your rein hand to the right as described in neck-reining, thus making the right rein slightly loose. Guide your horse with your legs by keeping your left leg slightly further back than your right, and by pressing it against his side. At the same time, your hands must ask him to go back with a "give-take" action on the reins. The horse must keep his rounded outline.

Riding side-saddle

A century ago it was considered unladylike if a woman rode astride. Until recently, however, riding side-saddle had waned in popularity: suitable horses, which must be strong-backed and well-schooled, are not easy to produce. Besides this, the side-saddle itself and the riding habits are expensive. Now, many women are rediscovering the art of side-saddle riding, attracted mainly by its elegance and safety.

The saddle

The side-saddle is designed to allow a rider to sit safely with both legs on the same side, yet in a suitable position to ride the horse effectively. It has a flat seat, one stirrup (usually on the left side) and two horns, or padded pommels: the upper pommel, or fixed head, is used to support the higher (right) leg, and the lower pommel, or leaping head, is used for the emergency grip.

Side-saddles vary in design to suit different purposes but it is important that your saddle fits your horse perfectly – otherwise he is certain to get a sore back. It must also fit you – if not, you will sit incorrectly and use the wrong grip, however well you are taught. The length and size of your thigh are the first consideration when determining whether your saddle is the right size. Your left (lower) leg should lie comfortably in the normal position, allowing your seat to remain in the centre of your horse's back without shifting.

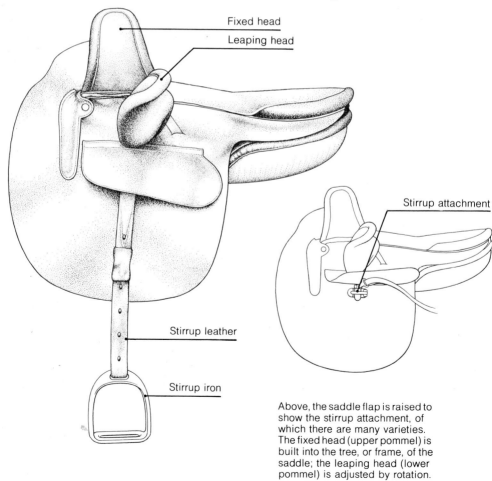

Fixed head

Leaping head

Stirrup attachment

Stirrup leather

Stirrup iron

Above, the saddle flap is raised to show the stirrup attachment, of which there are many varieties. The fixed head (upper pommel) is built into the tree, or frame, of the saddle; the leaping head (lower pommel) is adjusted by rotation.

Side-saddle dress

The side-saddle outfit, or habit, varies in the style and fabrics used, but above all should be practical (for hacking and hunting) yet elegant (for showing, dressage and display riding). Dark colours such as black, brown, navy blue or grey are favoured. It is nice to see a habit which is well-cut and fits neatly; in particular, the skirt, or apron, should be heavy enough at the hem to hang properly without flying about.

Regular breeches and boots are usually worn under the apron, and should be a good fit. An elegant, closely fitting jacket will show off your good posture when riding side-saddle. Some styles have a cutaway front showing a waistcoat underneath, but there are no specific requirements except that the fabric and colour should, ideally, match those of the apron.

A collar and tie are usually worn with a hunting cap or bowler hat. Alternatively, a hunting tie, or stock, can be tied over a shirt (collarless, so that it is not bulky around the neck), and secured with a stock pin. It can be tied in two ways: the crossed version popular for hunting, since it provides extra protection against the elements, and the neater, cravat style favoured in the show ring (see page 128). The correct showing attire is described on page 98.

A side-saddle rider fastening her jacket. Her bowler hat, collar and tie are in keeping with basic side-saddle dress, as are her matching jacket and apron.

Although most of the time they are barely visible, boots should be long and black, but can be brown if a brown or tweed-type habit is worn. Garter straps are usually superfluous, since few breeches have buttons nowadays, but they do "finish" a boot. The single spur is optional for adults; children, however, are not allowed to wear one.

Finally, hair should be swept back in a bun (either your own or a false one): the neater the better. If it is false, make sure that it is properly secured. Children in hunting caps should look neat, either wearing a hair net, or with their hair plaited.

Putting on the apron

The apron is attached by buttons or Velcro on the left hip, and carefully fitted so that it lies smooth and flat. The waist is marked at the centre, and a seam runs from here to the rider's right knee. The apron must have an even hemline when you are in the saddle.

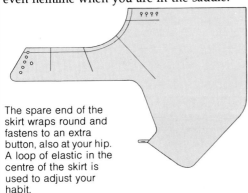

2 Sweep the "spare" end behind your back and bring it round, to fasten it to the extra button at your hip.

The spare end of the skirt wraps round and fastens to an extra button, also at your hip. A loop of elastic in the centre of the skirt is used to adjust your habit.

1 Having fastened one side of the apron at your left hip, hold out the other by the elastic loop, ready to bring it behind your back.

The seat

Your weight must be evenly distributed over the horse's back: although both your legs will be over the left side of the horse, your back must remain straight, with shoulders and hips square to the front (see below, left) so that , seen from behind, the upper part of your body looks the same as if you were riding astride. Concentrate on sitting tall, with stretched spine and neck: it is as well to perfect the correct position at an early stage, since any weight displacement will not only cause you to be badly balanced, but will give you and your horse a sore, aching back and discomfort. A correct leg position is also important: the part of you that is in contact with the saddle – all along the right thigh, from your right seat bone to your knee – will be supporting your weight. To avoid a crooked position, prac-

tise sitting correctly on a saddle stand (see page 43), preferably in front of a mirror, or ask someone to observe you from the ground. Often you may think your back is straight when it is not.

To acquire a good position, first sit astride with your weight evenly on your seat-bones. Next, without changing your weight distribution, swing your right leg over the front of the saddle, resting your thigh on the fixed head. The outer thigh of your upper (right) leg should be in close contact with the saddle, with the lower (left) leg hanging down naturally from your knee, and resting on the front part of the saddle flap. The inside of your right thigh should be pressed securely into the supporting fixed head, and there should be a clear gap of about 5cm (2in) between the back of your knee and the fixed head, to

Right, this rear view shows the rider sitting completely straight, with her weight evenly distributed in the saddle. There is a straight line from the top of her head down to the centre of the saddle, making a perfect right angle with the horse's spine.

Right, the rider is perfectly positioned. She is sitting straight and tall in the saddle, with her shoulders and hips square to the front. She is holding the reins in her lap, and has kept a straight line from the elbow to the horse's bit.

allow some room for manoeuvre, and to avoid friction. Your right knee must never be raised.

The left leg is in a similar position as for riding astride – the stirrup leather should not be so short that the top of your left thigh is pressed hard into the leaping head but not less than 2.5cm (1in) away from it, to allow you to make use of this safety device when necessary (see page 96). Keep your thigh, knee and upper calf turned inwards against the horse, and press down on the stirrup with your left foot.

As when riding astride, a light, sympathetic contact with the horse's mouth should be maintained at all times.

You may position your hands just above your right thigh, over your lap, or on either side of the thigh (see below), with a straight line from your elbow to the horse's bit.

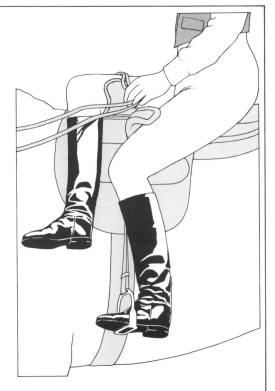

Above, the inside of the rider's right thigh is pressed securely into the supporting fixed head, with the left leg hanging down in a relaxed manner, but placed firmly against the horse.

Faults

Below and right are a number of faults commonly made when riding side-saddle which, if not corrected at an early stage, will affect your balance and, consequently, your horse and your riding.

Right, the rider has leant to the right while trying to compensate for the fact that both her legs are on the left side of the horse (a very common fault). Consequently, her right thigh has moved away from the fixed head and her shoulders are not square to the horse's shoulders or to her own hips.

Left, the rider's hands are too low, and her upper body is stooping down towards them, her legs sliding back.

Left, the rider's elbows are sticking out and her reins are too long. Over-long reins tend to flap and jerk at the bit, causing an unsteady head and very little control.

Saddling and mounting

When putting a side-saddle on your horse for the first time, introduce it gradually. It will feel quite different to him from the usual saddle for riding astride and he may be sensitive to wearing straps touching unaccustomed "soft" areas. It is a heavy weight on his back, and could cause great discomfort if worn for too long, too soon, before his back has adjusted to the feel of it.

Put the saddle on the horse in the usual way (see page 39), and slide it back into position, so that it settles into the lowest part of the horse's back. Using the front two girth tabs of the saddle, attach the girth(s) on the near side, taking care not to pinch the horse's skin with the girth(s) while doing so. The girth(s) should be attached as high as possible, since all adjustments will have to be made on the off side once you have mounted. The balance strap (see below) will prevent the saddle from moving about and giving the horse a sore back.

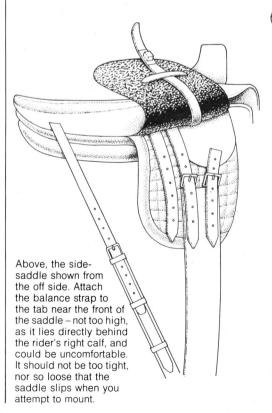

Above, the side-saddle shown from the off side. Attach the balance strap to the tab near the front of the saddle – not too high, as it lies directly behind the rider's right calf, and could be uncomfortable. It should not be too tight, nor so loose that the saddle slips when you attempt to mount.

Mounting

There are several methods of mounting; as you may not always be able to rely on outside help, it is best to be able to get on unaided if required.

The simplest method of mounting, although it requires some practice, is to get an assistant to give you a skilful leg-up, hoisting you straight into the correct side-saddle position.

Another method is to mount astride using the leg-up method on page 41, and then to swing your right leg into position. You may, for a moment, be in a position of

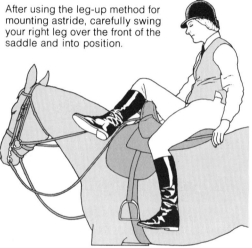

After using the leg-up method for mounting astride, carefully swing your right leg over the front of the saddle and into position.

some insecurity whilst swinging your leg over the front of the saddle; if the horse moves or takes flight you could easily fall or get tangled up in the reins. Keep the reins in your left hand, and your right hand free.

You can also use a leg-up that hoists you high, so that you land facing sideways to the left. You will then have to move your right leg up into position.

Yet another method is to mount unassisted, either from the ground or a mounting block. With your left foot in the stirrup, the apron, if you are wearing one, over your left arm, take the reins in your left hand. Standing clear of the pommels, hold the back of the saddle and spring upwards, turning your left knee so that it is facing the front. Land lightly astride, and bring your right leg over the saddle. Finally, if you are a fairly advanced rider, and are particularly agile, you can use this method to arrive in the correct position in one deft movement.

Once on the horse, you will have to check the girth and balance strap. You will also have to adjust your habit, if you are wearing an apron (see right). If the length of your stirrup leather needs adjustment, be careful not to release the safety catch, or it could drop to the ground.

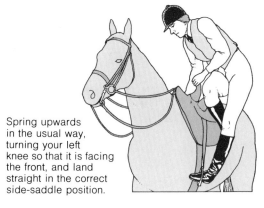

Spring upwards in the usual way, turning your left knee so that it is facing the front, and land straight in the correct side-saddle position.

Dismounting

Take the reins in your right hand, remove your left foot from the stirrup, swing your right leg up and over the pommels and drop lightly to the ground, clear of the pommels. Bend your knees on landing to absorb any jarring. Keep hold of the reins and, thus, control of your horse.

Having removed your left foot from the stirrup, swing your right leg up and over the pommels.

Adjusting the habit

Once on the horse you will have to adjust your apron by wrapping the "spare" end of the skirt around your right calf, and hooking the loop of elastic over your right foot. The apron should then drop down vertically from your left hip and the hemline should be horizontal to the ground. Your right foot should be just covered by the apron, which must also cover your breeches. There should be no unsightly folds.

1 Lay the waist-to-knee seam along the top of the right thigh. Wrap the spare end of the apron round your right calf.

2 Bring the loop of elastic from behind the leg over the right foot to hold the apron in place.

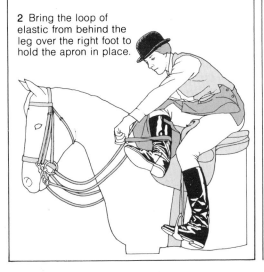

Transitions of pace

Use normal aids (see page 51) when riding side-saddle. You will need to hold a long whip in your right hand to replace the use of your leg on that side. To move off at the walk, apply the whip and your left leg together, using both alternately or simultaneously to increase the horse's impulsion. The whip will also help to stop your horse "falling in", or leaning in, to the right, away from your left leg which is held firmly against him. A supple waist and loins will allow you to follow your horse's movement, and by bracing your back and using a light feel on the reins, you can stop him or check him in a half-halt (see page 121). You will need to apply this aid to some degree before each change of pace or direction. In the case of any sudden movement from your horse, use the emergency grip (see below).

Trot

The suppleness of your body will be tested at the trot – if you cannot absorb the movement you will bump about uncomfortably, giving your horse a sore back. To rise to the trot, your body has to tilt slightly forward into the movement, and very slightly to the right, to remain upright. Your right thigh still bears your weight, and your knees must flex as you rise and fall. If you find yourself hanging on by the reins to keep your balance, hold the fixed head with your left hand; otherwise, hold the reins normally in both hands.

Canter and gallop

Ask for the transition on a bend, to obtain a smooth strike off on the correct lead (see page 55). If cantering right (see below), bend your horse slightly to the right, facing right yourself. Prepare with a half-halt. Your left leg moves slightly behind the girth, while your whip taps him near the girth on his off side. He may respond to a less obvious aid, but if he simply increases his pace at the trot, bring him back with a stronger half-halt and apply the aids again on a corner more strongly if necessary. Eventually a nudge from your right seat-bone should be enough. To canter left, your whip will compensate for the lack of outside leg, until you have learned to communicate your intentions through your seat-bone. Your back should be straight and your waist, although supple, should not bend in any direction or allow you to rock. When galloping you may sit upright, as in the canter, or lean forwards slightly.

Cantering on the right rein
This rider is sitting well, and has her horse well-balanced, but has leaned slightly to the right as she is turning.

Emergency grip
Should your horse make any movement that might unseat you, raise your left thigh into the leaping head, move your right heel back, towards your left knee, and lock this position. If a fall is inevitable, push yourself well clear of the saddle.

Fault
Right, the rider is leaning to her right to compensate for the fact that her horse's left shoulder is "falling outwards". Her hand is too low, pulling back on her horse instead of following the movement.

Jumping side-saddle

Although jumping side-saddle may seem extremely dangerous to those who only ride astride, the expert side-saddle rider insists it is safer than jumping astride, since, if necessary, your emergency grip can be used to pin you to your saddle, leaving your body and hands free to follow the movement of the jump. Your seat should stay close to the saddle and the forward inclination of your body over the jump should be enough to stay with your horse, but not so much that you are bent double. Keep your body and hips straight on, and your right shoulder firmly back. Your legs should be in the normal riding position, with your right knee pressed firmly against the fixed head.

Try to find a good schoolmaster horse to learn on, for you will make some uncomfortable mistakes at first.

As for riding astride, practise first with poles on the ground and cavalletti (see page 68), and then concentrate on perfecting your seat over very small obstacles. If you come forward too soon before take-off you may hit the pommel, as well as hindering the horse with your weight. Should you get left behind, remember to slip your reins to avoid jerking his mouth. Pick them up again quietly after landing. If you are landing with a bump, your position is weak and you are leaving the saddle.

Fault
Above, the rider's lower leg is too far back, tilting her forward over the horse's forehand. She is leaning to her right and has lost her balance and security.

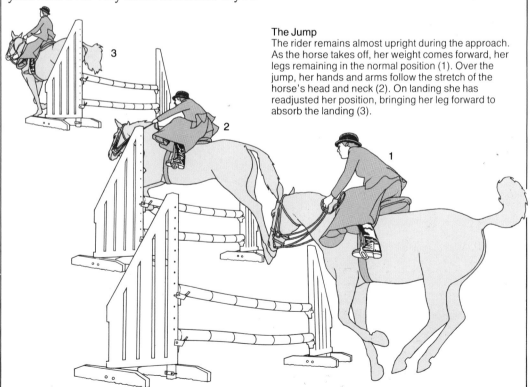

The Jump
The rider remains almost upright during the approach. As the horse takes off, her weight comes forward, her legs remaining in the normal position (1). Over the jump, her hands and arms follow the stretch of the horse's head and neck (2). On landing she has readjusted her position, bringing her leg forward to absorb the landing (3).

Showing side-saddle

Although side-saddle riding is increasing in popularity all over the world, as yet side-saddle competitions are restricted mainly to Britain and North America and, to a lesser extent, Australia, New Zealand, and South Africa.

There are two main types of event: show classes, which are a display of horse and rider where the horse is judged on its various paces, whether as a Show Hunter, Show Hack, or Show Pony; and equitation classes, in which it is the rider's expertise that is tested.

In North America, there are four main divisions: Hunter, Saddle Horse, Western and Period Costume. There are specific rules in these divisions, regarding what you wear and the requirements of your performance in the ring, as well as for the horse's equipment.

What to wear

Dark colours look best for showing side-saddle, with matching jacket and apron. Breeches and boots are worn under the apron: in some equitation classes you may be asked to display your skills without the "cover" of your skirt. A stock, tied cravat-style, and a black silk top hat are worn when showing. A veil, though traditional, is optional; if used, it should fit closely to the face, with the ends tucked neatly out of sight. Gloves must be worn, but a cane – leather-covered or plain – is optional.

Right, a side-saddle rider elegantly dressed in a smart showing habit and top hat.

Trekking and long-distance riding

Trekking is a healthy occupation which you can enjoy provided you are reasonably fit and experienced enough to control your horse at all paces. You should also be used to riding out (see pages 58–65). It provides an opportunity to see the countryside at its best, and is most popular on moorland and downland, in state parks, on ranches, and through forests. It is non-competitive and can take the form of organized trips of groups of riders (such as those arranged by pony clubs all over the world) or informal pleasure rides. It can also include cattle drives and pack trips.

Trekking does not require advanced riding skills – and you are unlikely to have to jump. Nor will you need a highly bred horse – any type will do as long as he is sensible and well mannered. However, he should be experienced, especially if you are a beginner. If possible, try him out beforehand at different paces. When you are satisfied that your horse is manageable, take him amongst other riders and horses, to see how he behaves in company.

The ideal trekking horse is willing, with a calm, steady temperament, but he should not be so lazy that you have to kick him along continually.

A trek may last anything from one hour to several days. For your first venture, one hour or so will be enough – trekking is a far more arduous experience than hacking along roads or bridle tracks. If you are embarking on a long ride, therefore, make

Below, riders enjoying the pleasures of trekking. The variety of terrain offers a challenge to riders at all levels of experience.

sure you are fit enough or it will be miserable for all concerned.

A typical trek is described on pages 101–2. Before setting off, however, make sure you are well-prepared and are wearing the right clothes (see below).

Preparations for a trek

Before going on a trek, you must know exactly where you are going and study the route on a detailed map – even when you are following a guide or instructor accidents can happen, so it is better that you be sure of your way.

Clothes should be workmanlike and comfortable; don't wear loose, flapping garments. It is a good idea to wear bright colours which will stand out if you get lost. Other clothes should be determined by the type of weather you are likely to face. Bear in mind such factors as the time of year, and type of terrain which is to be crossed (whether rivers, thick undergrowth, rocky mountains, or slopes etc.). If it is hot, you could wear a shirt, but on a long ride take protective clothes such as gloves, a sweater, a jacket and a lightweight waterproof. Tie any spare clothes neatly to the saddle.

Jeans, if well fitting, are tough and resistant (and easily cleaned). Some people find them more comfortable than breeches and, if worn outside boots, they will prevent the rain from running down inside them.

In colder weather, leather chaps worn over jeans are ideal – they are protective, warm and strong. Jodhpurs and jodhpur boots are also comfortable, as they are close-fitting and do not rub. A belt may come in useful for carrying a jack knife, compass or watch. It can also be used in an emergency as a replacement for a broken strap. Tall, well-fitting leather boots will protect your legs when you are riding through rough country.

For longer, overnight treks, some extra items will be useful: a jack knife; pliers; a compass; a small flashlight; a plastic sheet; snack food; paper cups; matches (in a waterproof container); a first-aid kit containing insect repellent and sunburn lotion. Amongst your horse's equipment, you will need saddle soap and oil; a saddlery repair kit; a halter and rope; a hoof-pick; a sponge and brush; antiseptic powder, insect repellent and basic first aid.

Check over your horse's tack: it should fit perfectly and be in good condition. Never try out new tack on a long ride – like new shoes, the leather will need working in gradually, and until then could be painful for your horse.

The horse's comfort is vital to your enjoyment. On the ride, his saddle could shift around as you negotiate steep slopes, causing him a sore back from which he may take weeks to recover. He may therefore

Left, riders in an orderly single file, keeping one horse's length apart. An experienced rider has gone ahead to set the pace and to warn the others of possible hazards.

need a breastplate or breast girth to hold the saddle firmly in place (see page 80) if the country is very hilly. There should be no points of stress on your horse's back, so use a numnah or saddle pad under the saddle as protection.

Your horse should be checked over, even if you are hiring him out from a recommended trekking stable. Make sure he has no saddle sores, girth galls or a sore mouth for example. Examine him for signs of strain, and for scratches on his legs or joints, and see that his feet are cool, well shod, and trim. Any risen nails in the hoof or on the shoe should be knocked flat again with a hammer (see page 270).

If you are riding your own horse, make sure you have time to groom him well, bearing in mind that if he is wet it will take longer. He will need to be clean to allow his skin to breathe, otherwise his sweat will clog the pores, causing him some discomfort. If your mount is stabled overnight, he will need a feed at least two hours before your ride, and he should be mucked out and groomed.

Tack him up carefully. The girth (preferably a wide one, for maximum comfort) should be done up tightly to secure the saddle firmly. You are now ready to go out on a trek.

Planning your own trek

There will be several things to organize if you plan your own trek. In a group trek, once you have conditioned your horse properly (see page 261) you should practise together, and choose the most experienced horses and riders as leaders and to bring up the rear. The leader will have the responsibility for the following: setting the pace; following the correct, pre-arranged route; warning the riders of hazards and taking evasive action where necessary; making decisions when the unexpected happens – for example, where to stop in a storm.

All the riders must know how to read an Ordnance Survey map correctly. Practise trekking first in familiar surroundings, then unfamiliar ones, carrying the full supply of equipment, securely packed and tied to your saddle, before attempting a full-scale

venture. Before setting off, you should plan your exact route, knowing what landmarks to look for, how far you will ride at one stretch, and where you intend to make any stops during your journey.

If you will be riding over private property, be sure that you have permission. Also, ask the landowner first if you want to build a camp fire. (It will have to be in a cleared space where dry, dead wood is available – do not break branches from growing trees.) Finally, keep to your schedule or you may run out of daylight. Avoid riding in bad visibility over unknown country where there may be concealed hazards.

A trek

If you are to ride along narrow paths you will be in single file, so arrange the order you will ride in beforehand and try to stick to it. The slowest horses should go at the back to avoid breaking up the group. If your horse kicks, warn other riders before setting off, but preferably keep him at the back so that he is out of the way.

Start out at a walk, to settle the horses and to allow them to warm up gradually. When riding single file, keep one horse's length between yourself and the horse in front, at the walk – slightly more when you are moving faster – to avoid being kicked. Stay alert: a horse shying can cause a nervous chain-reaction. However, you should keep reasonably close all the time, or you will disrupt the ride; if you get left behind, do not rush to make up the ground – you may startle the other horses.

Always follow the leader and do what you are told. If you have to stop or dismount, move aside to let the others pass, and always warn the riders behind you of any hazards such as holes, tin cans, broken glass, barbed wire or boggy ground.

Safety must come first, so never take any unnecessary risks. Should you meet other riders on roads or tracks, pass slowly, keeping to the left. Remember that hikers or pedestrians have the right of way, so do not frighten them by passing too close or too fast. If you wish to pass other riders in your group, warn them on which side you will be passing and do not rush by at a canter or gallop. Only gallop when you are *all* in control, and there is a suitable stretch of ground ahead; you will first have to shorten your stirrups so that you do not bump your horse's back. "Free" his back in the same way when going uphill by raising yourself a little out of the saddle (see page 60).

When climbing, or going down, it is sometimes safer, and easier, for the horse to take a zig-zag path, rather than a straight one. Always go downhill at a walk, and on a long uphill climb stop if he gets tired. If you dismount or remount, do so uphill, on the off side if necessary, having first turned your horse sideways to the hill.

You may also have to dismount when leading your horse across very rough or steep ground; if not, let him have enough rein to lower his head and find the best ground himself. Check his feet for stones or packed mud after crossing bad ground.

If you come to a narrow bridge or gap, it may, again, be safer to get off and lead your horse. Do not try to lead him through water; you will not have enough control should he rush or panic. If he is reluctant to go into it, follow behind a confident horse and rider. If crossing in a strong current is unavoidable, face slightly towards it, and ride definitely but without restricting your horse with a tight rein. If he has to swim, hang on to the saddle or mane, and raise your boots out of the water.

If there are any obstacles to be jumped, the leader should be familiar with them and give you adequate warning, having checked that the landing is safe. The leader should make sure that the entire group is capable of jumping the obstacle before allowing anyone to tackle it, and that an alternative route is available if necessary. Each rider should keep his distance, waiting until the horse ahead has cleared the fence before riding at it. At gateways, the first rider may have to dismount to open the gate, and the last one must shut it.

On the way home, your horse may quicken up in anticipation, but try to get him to relax on a long rein, so that he arrives cool and dry. If he is hot he will have to be sponged down, and then walked until he is dry. However tired you may be yourself, you must always try to help your horse. Don't slouch or ride sloppily – it may give him a sore back; if you do not take care of him, you may find he is no longer fit to ride when you want to go trekking again.

Planning a long-distance ride

Long-distance riding is an increasingly popular form of competitive team or individual riding. An organized long-distance ride varies in distance between a total of 50–100 miles, ridden in a single day, and longer total distances divided into shorter sections over several days.

There is no minimum time, but a maximum time limit is given. The speed you go at will depend on the distance to be covered in the day, averaging between 5 and 15 miles per hour. The terrain will influence your pace, and the judges will check your horse's condition at certain points along the route. The final result of the competition is judged on soundness and condition, as well as time taken to complete the ride. Sometimes less than half the competitors will reach the end.

Your horse must be at least five years old to take part. Before his first endurance test, he should undergo about six months' progressive training, building up to 10 or 15 miles per day, including trotting up hills and long, slow canters to develop his stamina and strength. A seasoned horse will need about two months' preparation, having been fully fit already.

Plan to arrive at the starting point of the ride with several days to spare, to give you and your horse time to adjust to the new environment. Ease up on hard work just before the test and give him every chance to settle down with his usual diet, and the minimum of disturbance. You may need a vet's certificate to show your horse is fit to take part, but in any case it is advisable to have him checked over thoroughly by a vet. His blood should be tested a month before the long ride, to allow time to remedy any deficiencies which may be found.

Right, the leading riders in this trail ride are looking back to ensure that the more inexperienced riders do not get into difficulties or are left behind.

The organizers of a competitive ride will probably arrange accommodation for horse and rider; otherwise you will have to find some yourself. If there are restricted exercise facilities, you may have to lunge him (see also page 197) to keep him on the move, but reduce his oats if he is working less than he has been used to up to this time. Keep your tack well oiled and clean, and check your equipment a final time.

Before the start, water and groom your horse and leave your stable clean and tidy. Allow at least two hours from feeding time to saddling up so that your horse has time to digest his food – his breakfast should be as usual. Saddle him up very carefully, tightening the girth enough to keep the saddle still, without causing the horse any discomfort when he is in action. Once mounted, walk and trot about for a few minutes to warm him up slowly before the start of the ride.

During the ride

Your aim is to complete the day(s) ride within the time allotted and without causing your horse undue stress. There are many tips worth remembering. Take advantage of the best ground, using the most level stretches of good going for cantering. If you keep the canter relaxed, it will take very little out of your horse. Other-wise, trotting will be your usual gait, used over all terrain except the roughest, where you must only walk, or the smoothest, where you may canter. You may prefer to walk down steep hills (see page 60), but bear in mind that you will have to make up this time elsewhere.

Vary your pace to keep your horse happy, and adapt it to suit any changes in the terrain. Mainly use the pace that suits you both the best, remembering to change diagonals regularly when you are trotting for long periods.

After a steep hill, or long, hot stretch, take a short rest. Dismount, slacken the girth for a few moments, wet his mouth with a sponge of cold water and have a drink yourself. Check your horse for any damage. Water your horse a little at a time, when you stop for lunch, and loosen his girth but do not remove the saddle. He will not have time to digest any food so do not let him eat, for his own good. Move on again before you or your horse has a chance to stiffen up or get cold. If he goes lame during the ride, dismount and check his feet for stones, which may be the cause. If you can find no apparent reason or remedy for his lameness, you may have to dismount and lead him.

Plan your ride so that you have time in hand. If you can walk the last half-mile or

Left, Western riders in America about to negotiate a stream. On such trips, mules are often used as pack-horses to carry the camping equipment.

Right, the horse at the front is wearing a breast girth to prevent the saddle from sliding around on his back and causing him discomfort. Breast girths will be particularly useful when riding over steep terrain.

more of each section, your horse will arrive cool, and will not have to be walked around when already weary.

After the ride

After the ride, remember that your horse will be very weary. Take him to his stable, remove the bridle but do not remove the saddle until he has completely dried off, to give his circulation time to return to the area gradually. Loosen the girths little by little, then rub his legs with a stable rubber or with straw, to stimulate his blood flow. When you eventually remove the saddle, massage his back. Wait until his temperature, pulse and respiration have returned to normal before giving him a short drink of water which should be slightly tepid. He may "break out" (sweat up) later, so put a

sweat sheet on him, with a blanket, sheet or rug on top, depending on the time of year, temperature, and whether his ears are hot or cold (a good guide to his body temperature). Give him another short drink, then leave him in peace to eat some hay. Return later and, if he is quite dry, check his legs again, and then groom him, removing all sweat, and making him comfortable for the night. He will need peace and quiet, but should have enough energy to eat a well-earned evening feed and drink as much water as he wants.

Mounted games

Mounted games, in their various forms, have become increasingly popular all over the world. They include a variety of tests invented to test the rider and pony's agility and initiative.

Originally, most mounted games were based on speed races. The British word for such events, "gymkhana", is derived from a combination of "gymnastics" and "gend-Khana", which means "sports ground" in Hindustani. Games on horseback were very popular with the Army in India, before being brought to England by enthusiasts. Mules, donkeys and even camels were used as mounts for this outlet for high spirits and energy. In the USA, mounted games, or "Timed Horse Events", owe their origins to cowboy activities rather than the Indian army and are therefore usually ridden Western style although some of the games are, in fact, the same as or very similar to those in gymkhana events.

Types of event

Popular, well-known events in Britain include: bending (see page 109); the egg and spoon race (the rider gallops to the far end of the ring to fetch the egg, dismounts, then runs beside the pony, whilst carrying the egg in a spoon, back over the starting line); the apple and bucket race (the rider gallops to the bucket, dismounts, and must catch the apple in his teeth, get on the pony, and gallop back again; sometimes the apple is floating in water!); musical sacks (sacks are spaced around on the ground, and all the competitors ride around the outside track. Each time the music stops, they rush to find a sack, jump off their ponies and stand on it. There will not be enough sacks for everyone, since some are removed each time. The winner is the one who lands on the last remaining sack); and the sack race (see page 109). Popular events in the USA are barrel racing (the rider gallops to a barrel, turns around it, gallops to the next, and on to a third in clover leaf pattern, then back to the starting line – see page 77); flag racing (opposite);

pole bending (as above); keyhole racing, and speed and action race (in both of which the horse must gallop, stop and turn with speed and agility), and the rescue race (the rider and pony gallop to the far end, or barrel, and as they turn around it, a second person vaults up behind the rider, and the two gallop for home).

The emphasis is on fun. Many of the games are organized as team events, such as the obstacle race and stepping stones (opposite). The games are always popular as they provide excitement for both riders and spectator. It is all healthy exercise, as well as offering an incentive to improve not only your riding but also your horse or pony's performance.

Most of us have a competitive urge and this is an enjoyable opportunity to use it. If it is your aim to win, you will have to work hard to do better than everyone else. Even if you never win, it will have been fun trying and pitting your skill and progress against that of your friends and rivals.

Ponies are more suitable for these games than horses, being quicker, and small enough to get on and off easily and speedily. Although many adults also compete in mounted games, it is children, with their energy and love of racing, who really excel in them. To enjoy the games neither you nor your pony need be particularly fit, and you need not be an expert rider. When played at the highest standard, however, a very fit pony is required, and a lot of practice is needed.

Equipment

A snaffle bit is generally used on the pony, often with a standing martingale (see page 274). More severe bits are banned from use in formally organized mounted games. Western riders will, of course, use Western tack (see pages 82-3).

For the rider, a well-fitting hard hat and sensible riding boots are the only essentials. Jodhpurs are most comfortable – they do not slip or rub. Try to be tidy, though this is not always possible since some of the games are messy.

Left, obstacle race in which, as the name implies, the riders have to negotiate a series of obstacles during the course.

Below, flag race – a flag is picked up at one end of the arena and dropped in a holder at the far end. The ability of the horse to turn at speed is tested.

The pony

The pony must be fit, and at least four years old. To go fast is a strain on legs, heart and wind, so a mature pony who has worked gradually towards competitive activities is best. A very old pony may have lost his speed, but can often make up for this with experience. Do not push him hard, and, if he loses condition, retire or rest him; a thin, weak, or overweight pony cannot be expected to work hard.

A suitable pony is quick and keen but not excitable. You must be able to control him properly so that he is a safe ride and not a liability to others.

Do not enter too many competitions – preferably only those for which you have prepared your pony at home. Train him to turn, stop and start, but do not always race about. Practise some events at a walk to keep your pony calm and obedient, for if you over-excite him or do too much and sour him, the games will no longer be fun.

Your pony should come first, so never treat him roughly. If he is not doing his best, it is likely to be your fault: he will not perform at his best unless he is happy. Practise leading him, running with him, and, if you can vault on his back, all the better – it is much the quickest.

A skilled pony knows his job. He is very fit and supple, and shows some agile movements of which a dressage horse would be proud: flying changes, canter pirouettes, and even, perhaps, if over-excited at the start of a race, he may perform a levade. However, if he over-anticipates he may start to turn too soon, stop too suddenly, or shoot off before you tell him. You will have to practise sensibly to correct any such faults before they become established. Practices should not exceed half an hour, and this time should be spent mostly on teaching him to stand patiently amid others galloping about, and getting used to strange "spooky" objects, noises and bangs, and carrying and dragging sacks.

When preparing your pony for a competition, you will need to groom him well, and tidy him up if he is not looking his best. Check your tack. Is it clean and safe? He may need an extra feed the evening before, to boost his energy.

Take with you your tack, with spares if possible, a sweat rug, water container, sponge, haynet and feed. He may get hot and sweaty and, if so, will need washing down. You should take a brush to tidy him up. It is also a good idea to take a first aid kit with you as a precaution.

Right, potato race. If the rider drops his potato he has to remount to pick it up – as the rider on the far left has done.

Joining a club

The advantage of joining a club is that you meet people with whom you can compete on level terms. You may have the opportunity to borrow a pony or horse if you do not own one, and to mix with your age group or level of experience, whether you are a novice rider, or a fairly accomplished one. You can all work together to improve your skills: constructive criticism from others will help, and you may discover hidden talents in yourself or your mount.

The Pony Club, a world-wide youth organization, encourages young riders from the very earliest leading-rein stage onwards, to participate in its many activities. Instructional rallies, treks and games, and annual Summer Camps, are organized to further their knowledge and enjoyment of riding. Mounted games are a favourite with most Pony Club members. Through such events, young riders learn that bad temper or violence must be controlled, and that sympathetic yet positive riding is far more successful.

Below, mounted games are great fun. They also test riding skills, and require agility and obedience in the pony.

Right, some games require the rider to pick up an object and gallop back to base with it as quickly as possible.

Hunting

Whatever our views on hunting as a "sport", the fact remains that it is still a popular equestrian activity in many parts of the world – particularly in Britain and Ireland, many areas of the USA, Australia, Canada and Western Europe. Fox hunting is probably the most popular amongst riding enthusiasts – the fox is an adventurous and devious creature, and following the route he takes across country provides an exciting challenge.

Up until the Second World War, most riding in many countries was based on hunting, whether of foxes, stag or boar. The thrill and the fascination of houndwork far outweighed "educated" riding. Whether by skill and guile, raw courage and happy ignorance, or whether with the help of a dose of "jumping powder" (alcohol), people managed to survive a day's hunting. Some would ride only in order to hunt although, nowadays, most of us admit to hunting in order to ride. There is no greater pleasure to the true horseman than an exciting day's hunting: his skill can be tested to the ultimate across difficult country where the obstacles and gradients provide such variety.

Although it is "each man to himself", it is not a contest: Nature alone provides the challenge. The rider will need nerve and common sense but, above all, control of his horse, to perform well. This was not always the case, however. Stories and pictures of hunting men's exploits through the ages can chill the blood, and we marvel, now, how they survived at all, for they invariably sat back, feet forward, reins long with little contact (except to "hang on" over a fence), looking anything but well-balanced. Some great horsemen used this method to maximum effect, but disasters were frequent.

Nowadays, there are few opportunities for heroic exploits, and disasters are, therefore, fewer; our riding has had to adapt accordingly. There are two main styles of riding in the world: one, with a shorter stirrup, and the rider sitting forward, gives a natural, free forward impression, as seen in most parts of Eastern Europe and Asia;

the other is the "educated" Western European style of greater collection and precision, using a "deep" seat. The traditional "hunting seat" was neither of these. The stirrups were long and the leg hung loosely, giving few aids except to "kick on". When a rider wanted to stop, it seemed natural simply to pull on the reins – hard, if necessary. The horse was allowed to travel naturally as he might have done without a rider. With the influence of successful schools and instructors, the forward seat has now replaced the "hunting seat" almost completely.

The hunter

The age and looks of a hunter matter little, but he must be safe, sure-footed, bold and keen. He needs abundant stamina and must have been well-schooled to be a comfortable ride. The hunting man, however, has been known to neglect his own and his horse's education more than most, often regarding the challenge and the dangers of the unknown to be exciting enough, and feeling that too much "science" would spoil the fun. Throughout history, paintings of terrible falls over impossible obstacles show that there have always been sportsmen with more courage than skill. The horses presumably had little choice in the matter. Most horses, in fact, love to hunt: they enjoy the company of others, and are stimulated by the many sights and sounds of hunting. If well-trained and carefully ridden they will not suffer injury. An ordinary horse, given proper exercise and feeding to bring him to fitness and top condition is more likely to finish a hunt in better condition than an ill-trained and less fit thoroughbred racehorse.

Certain types of country will suit some horses better than others. In galloping, jumping country where grass fields are plentiful and fox coverts are small and spaced out, the fox is more likely to go fast and straight. A thoroughbred horse which is a good jumper will therefore be better suited for hunting in these conditions, while a more ponderous horse, such as a cob, will be ideal in steep hill country, or where the ground may be pitted with ditches and other hazards. Being with other horses will give your horse the incentive to exert himself with enthusiasm, and to jump obstacles when hunting which he would never attempt in cold blood. Not all horses will be inspired to great feats of courage, nor all riders. George III, not a renowned sportsman, admitted: "I love hunting, but I fear leaping. A King and the father of a family should not ride bold."

Training and hazards

If your horse has a highly strung temperament, the excitement of sudden galloping and jumping could be too much for him. He could become unmanageable, and a danger to others as well as himself. Valuable racehorses or competition horses with excitable dispositions are seldom risked in the hunting field, where they could come to grief or possibly misbehave amongst a crowd of others.

Unexpected hazards, such as barbed wire or "blind" ditches on the other side of the fence you jump, can be dangerous. Therefore, horses not properly under control are unsuitable for hunting. A placid or lethargic horse, on the other hand, can "come alive" when hunting, revealing talents you never knew he possessed.

Hunting provides ideal training country for a competition horse, with a wide variety of obstacles such as hedges, ditches, rails, streams and, perhaps, banks to negotiate. If it is hilly, the horse will learn to adjust his balance as necessary, in all paces, developing strength and carrying power, and an increased sense of self-preservation.

If you value your horse, hunting is a sport to be undertaken with discretion, according to his temperament, training and fitness, and the kind of hunting conditions that are available to you. If these are unsuitable, stay away.

Although much of the pleasure and excitement of hunting is diminishing due to rapid urbanization, it still provides an opportunity to see the country in the good company of a horse, and with others who enjoy the many attractions of this sport.

Right, this rider is leaning well back, using the traditional hunting seat. He is braced against the stirrups but has not interfered badly with the horse's mouth. This seat, however, should be avoided as it is both tiring and uncomfortable for the horse.

The hunt

Most of the people who hunt have either subscribed to a particular pack for the season, or have come out for a day. The hunt staff consists of the huntsman, who is in charge of the hounds and the actual hunting – he knows exactly where to go to "draw" (cast his hounds to pick up the scent of the quarry); the two whippers-in, who control the hounds, making sure that they do their work correctly; and the Master, who is in overall command of the hunt. He must know the hunting area well, know all the farmers and landowners and, if possible, the followers too. Finally, the Field Master is in charge of the field or followers, and should always be obeyed.

Anyone who can afford to keep a horse and who lives in a hunting area may hunt, as long as he pays the required fees and observes the traditional rules expected of all followers. Ancient rules of dress, manners and language still persist. Although some may now seem outdated, they are all based on practicality.

Hunting dress

The hunt staff usually wear red, or "pink", coats and hunting caps, and carry hunting crops. The huntsman carries the horn to communicate with and encourage his hounds. The subscriber, or hunt follower, may also wear a red coat if he wishes, but with a top hat or skull cap with a black or navy cover. The cut-away version, with swallow tails, looks very smart and can also be in black, again with a top hat or skull cap. Most followers, however, wear a black coat with a hunting cap or bowler. Those who do not possess a dark hunting coat often wear a tweed version, especially during cub-hunting, when clothes are less formal. A "rat-catcher" (tweed jacket) is usually worn, with black or brown boots.

A strong pair of gloves is vital against the cold and wet, and to prevent the reins from slipping in rainy conditions or when the horse is sweating. All the riders wear tall hunting boots to protect their legs in all conditions when on or off the horse. Spurs are not compulsory, but by tradition a blunt pair is usually worn. A warm hunt-ing vest or shirt, with a waistcoat, will help fend off the cold, as will a warm pair of tights worn under the breeches. The hunting stock or tie, correctly tied with tie pin, completes the picture, and gives protection to the neck in case of a fall.

Hunting language

The huntsman's job is to communicate with the hounds, and he needs great concentration to provide a good day's sport for them and for the followers. The huntsman knows the strengths and weaknesses of each hound, and speaks to them in a language in which sounds mean more than actual words. He uses the different notes of the horn to collect the hounds together; to encourage them; to blow "gone away" when the quarry is afoot and has left the covert; when the quarry is caught; when the quarry has "gone to ground"; and when going home.

Hunting manners

Certain rules and traditions are expected to be observed when out hunting, though most manners are, in any case, a matter of common sense and thoughtfulness.

It is considered respectful to the Master to arrive punctually and properly dressed, as neat and clean as possible. You must also remember to say "good morning" to the hunt staff on arrival, and "good night" when you leave to go home – whatever the hour; also, to thank the Master at the end of the day for allowing you to hunt.

If your horse is young or ill-mannered, keep him out of the way. A horse that kicks should wear a red ribbon on his tail as a warning to other riders. Kicking a hound usually results in being sent home, as do the following: riding on seeded or forbidden land; leaving a gate open that should be shut (thus allowing livestock to escape); over-running hounds, or overtaking the Master on a horse out of control and endangering others; and jumping fences when hounds are not running or if the Master is standing quietly.

Right, the huntsman, with a field member, discussing the likely day's sport with a local countryman.

A day's hunting

Your horse must be very fit if he is to stand up to a full day's hunting. Most horses can go hunting, if well-schooled and in good condition. Even the fittest horses are liable to sweat when exerting themselves, and should be clipped (see page 265).

Before hunting

Make sure that your tack is clean and safe, and, equally, that your own clothes are in good condition: you should be well turned out as well as comfortable.

On a hunting morning, start your routine earlier than usual, so that your horse has finished and digested his breakfast well before you leave. He will look smarter if you plait him (see page 264), unless you feel safer having some mane to hang on to. Boots or bandages for your horse's legs are not advisable: they become very muddy, and if your horse slips grit may work under the boot, making him sore. If he needs support bandages, he should not be hunting – his legs will need to be in good shape to withstand the hurly-burly of the chase, which may include fast road work. He may be keener than usual, and a slightly "stronger" bit in his mouth will aid control (see page 275).

If hacking to the meet, allow plenty of time (estimating travelling at about 6.5 km [4 miles] per hour) to arrive cool, and as clean as possible.

While hunting

When you reach the meet, the Hunt Secretary will collect your "cap" money (charged if you have arranged a particular day's hunting, and are not already a subscriber); "field" money may also be charged each time. You should find out what money you will need – it will be more expensive in good hunting country. Like any club, the privileges of membership are not free.

Make yourself known to the hunt staff politely. If your horse will stand quietly, join the rest of the field; if not, walk him about out of the way – the meet can be hazardous, with foot followers milling around, unaware of the dangers from fresh, sometimes excitable horses.

When the huntsman sounds his horn, and moves off, he will probably trot to the first wood, or thicket, known as a "covert", which he will proceed to "draw". If the hounds "find", you will hear them "speaking", and the rest of the pack quickly picks up the scent. The hounds will follow, then the huntsman, rallying them; after him, the Master, and then the mounted followers and finally, if possible, any car and foot followers who may be participating.

Do not sit heavily in the saddle, but adopt a forward style, the weight borne by your thighs, knees and stirrups. You and your horse will not tire if you can remain in balance, without recourse to hanging on to the reins, or falling behind the movement. Your horse may have to stand around for long periods, and so must be well mannered. Walk him about if he is getting cold, but be careful not to disturb the huntsman or the hounds. Following hounds, your horse may be keen, but should not pull too hard; he should be sure-footed and, preferably, a good jumper.

A "good eye for country" is a great asset. It means taking the most economical route from A to B, without jumping unnecessarily or over-tiring your horse, and arriving at your destination as fresh as possible, having done no damage to the countryside behind you. Ride to suit your particular

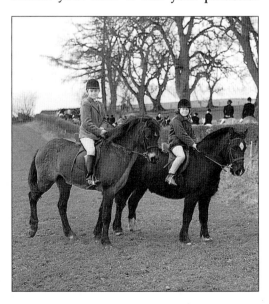

horse, and take care to avoid bad ground, such as ploughed fields. Choose obstacles which will suit your horse best, and remember that the welfare of your horse is your responsibility.

After hunting

At the end of the day, ride home quietly. With so much excitement, even if your horse returns to the stable quite dry, he might break out in a sweat later. Rub him down (or you may prefer to wash him down) to remove any mud. This often helps to cool him off, but rug him up quickly afterwards so that he does not catch cold, and bandage his legs if he has had a long, hard day – it will help his circulation.

Give him his water, slightly warmed, a little at first – he will be very thirsty, and too much cold water may give him colic. He will want his haynet and a hot mash before being left to rest. Return later to check him over, particularly his legs – you may have missed a thorn or scratch – and, if he is still wearing a cooler, or sweat sheet, remove this and put his dry blankets back. Make sure he is warm enough. The next day, he can be led out to unstiffen and relax. He may be very tired, and so should take it easy for a few days; he should be given enough time to recover before undertaking any strenuous exercise.

Introducing your horse to hunting

It is best to give your horse a gentle introduction to hunting, before taking him out for the first time. Cub-hunting, which usually takes place early in the morning, provides an ideal opportunity to do this since there is not a lot of action.

Your horse will soon learn to stand still. Until he does, keep him out of the way or he could be a nuisance. He is likely to get excited by the sounds of the horn, hounds, whip cracking, and the huntsman's voice. Other horses may be galloping about, so avoid hotting up your horse by chasing after them; you want him to attend to *you*, not them. Allowing your horse to develop a "follow my leader" attitude may be dangerous as, when you want to turn away, or jump in a certain place, he may not want to leave the others. A sensible schoolmaster companion will help to teach your horse how to behave, and will give you a lead over an obstacle, if you want.

A quiet introduction to hunting will pay off – there is nothing more tiring, or even frightening, than an inexperienced horse who cannot contain his excitement out hunting. If he is schooled to be a good hunter from the beginning, you will enjoy years of pleasure together.

Young riders ready for a day's hunting. They are on good, strong ponies suitable for carrying them safely and steadily through the day.

Right, the Master leading the field over a ditch and bank. He has approached slowly, to allow his horse time to see what he has to do, before jumping boldly across, on to the bank.

Drag hunting

Although many ardent hunting people believe that it is a waste of good horses to use them for show-jumping, eventing, or even racing, there are, at the same time, fewer opportunities to prove that hunting has more to offer, as suitable countryside becomes scarce and movements are restricted by intensive modern farming. Farmers have supported hunting for centuries, but force of economics often gives them no choice but to ban hunting over their land. In such areas drag hunting may be organized instead. In this type of hunting a trail is laid by a man on foot dragging a sack containing aniseed which produces the required scent. He is followed an hour or so later by a few hounds and the mounted followers. There may be many obstacles on the way, but, because riders will not be able to "take their own line", they may lose the excitement produced by the uncertainty of "natural" hunting.

Those who are against killing the quarry often prefer drag hunting, as do many landowners, since the riders are restricted to a certain line of country where they will do less damage to the land and livestock.

Many riders are content just to gallop and jump, for which drag hunting provides the ideal outlet, for it can be enjoyed anywhere in the world where horses are ridden in open countryside and where there is suitable terrain to lay a drag line that is both safe and fun. Other riders, with an independent spirit, however, love the challenge of the unpredictable, a test of both common sense and riding skill. John Surtees's famous mid-nineteenth-century character, Jorrocks, was adamant:

"Hunting is all that's worth living for – all time is lost wot is not spent in 'unting – it's like the hair we breathe – if we have it not – we die – it's the sport of kings, the image of war without its guilt, and only 25 per cent of its danger."

Right, this drag line has been specially built to provide some fun for the mounted field: the fences are not big, and are wide enough to allow several riders to jump alongside safely. Although the obstacles are predetermined and therefore lack the thrills (and dangers) of the unexpected that occur in natural hunting, they provide much enjoyment in areas such as this, in Switzerland, where there *are* no suitable natural obstacles.

Advanced riding

Improving your riding

In the early stages of learning to ride you should have concentrated on acquiring a balanced seat and on how to use simple aids. Having learned to control your body whatever the horse may do, it is now time to form a closer partnership with him so that you work together in harmony.

The horse

An experienced schoolmaster horse can teach you far more about riding than you could learn from any instructor or book. Since his influence on your progress is so strong, the importance of learning on a well-trained horse cannot be stressed too strongly. The saying "old horses for young riders, old riders for young horses" is invariably proved right, provided you take "old" to mean experienced.

The horse need not have a perfect action or conformation provided he is in sound condition, but he must have a calm temperament, and be willing and obedient. If he has been correctly trained to answer to the aids, you will be able to put into practice all that you have been taught up to this stage of your riding.

The better the conformation of the horse, the easier he will find it to "use" himself efficiently and the more likely he is to be supple, loose and flexible. For instance, if he is built to carry too much of his weight on his forehand, his hocks will trail behind him, spoiling his paces. By comparison, the well-balanced horse will be "light in hand", moving freely from the shoulder, thus giving you a more comfortable ride.

At this stage of your riding the horse must have impulsion. This is not speed, but controlled power. "Freedom" and "control" may sound contradictory but freedom, as applied to the horse's movement, means that he is using himself with maximum facility and minimum effort. To do so, he must be energetic, propelling himself forward strongly, unrestricted by tension in his muscles.

Your sensitive use of the aids will depend on the responsiveness of your mount and the way in which he has been trained. If you are not able to buy your own horse (see page 246), choose a school which can provide you with horses that have been schooled to a high standard, and which are not overworked. Horses used in constant school work soon become stale, however well trained they may be. A horse which is numb to the aids will not provide you with the sensitive "feel" you need, to develop as a rider. However, it may be possible to

Christine Stückelberger of Switzerland schooling under the watchful eye of her Austrian trainer, Georg Wahl. Facilities as good as these are not always available, but an indoor school with a good surface is a great help in improving your riding.

restore the horse's sensitivity and enjoyment in his work by using clear and consistent aids that he will understand and respect, making the constant nagging he has come to expect from a succession of learners no longer necessary.

The rider

The brilliant rider is born, not made, but there are many international stars who readily admit that they are not natural horsemen. Their success is the result of application and effort.

You must have a positive, sympathetic attitude towards your horse. You also need patience and a calm temperament. If you are excitable and nervous, the horse will sense it and become tense and anxious himself. Never lose your temper with your horse: it could damage your relationship with him irreparably.

To ride well enough to harmonize with your horse's movements and to influence his actions, you must develop a two-way communication with him. You will have to learn to feel, through your body, exactly what he is doing with his. This increased sensitivity or "feel" will enable you to get the best results, using the finest of aids, without ever resorting to brute force.

You will, therefore, need to develop your coordination and a sense of rhythm, to know exactly what combination of aids to use: when, and how strongly, to help you to supple your horse and to influence his paces, balance and rhythm. You will learn to feel what each of his legs is doing and the degree of relaxation or contraction in the muscles along his neck, back and quarters. Gradually you will learn what he can or cannot do, and how to make the most of his ability.

Instruction

As well as a suitable horse you will need a good instructor. You will gain more from having individual lessons than from joining a group. You could also take a short concentrated course – three to four days – to include riding instruction and general horse management. Such courses are valuable as they not only provide continuity, but also allow you to learn from other pupils' mistakes.

If you have your own horse, you could ask the instructor to teach you at home, but you must be able to provide a suitable piece of ground for the lessons.

Riding facilities

Avoid riding on wet patchy ground or on very hard rough ground. Either condition will spoil your horse's regular paces and rhythm, and could even lame him. The ground, or "going", must be consistent, with some "give" to prevent jarring his legs.

The horse will concentrate better in a quiet place and the guiding lines of a fence or wall will help you to keep him straight. An indoor school is invaluable since it allows you to ride whatever the weather conditions. If there are mirrors on the wall, they will help you to check your position, particularly when riding alone.

Equipment

At this stage of your riding, your horse should wear a simple snaffle bridle. If he needs something stronger in his mouth, he has not been well-trained and is therefore unsuitable. If possible, buy or borrow a dressage saddle (below) which is designed to help you to sit upright, using a deep seat and long stirrups.

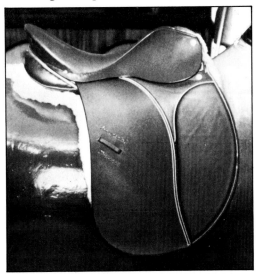

Dressage saddle

Practising your riding

Improving your seat

You will find it easier to follow your horse's every movement when you have learned to ride with balance, not grip, and with increased feeling through a supple, receptive body in which there should be the minimum of movement. Hacking across country will help you to relax and will strengthen your position as will repeating the exercises on the lunge at the trot with or without stirrups (see page 49). You should concentrate on those exercises which help you most to overcome any particular weakness or stiffness. Being lunged removes tension from your body: ten minutes on each rein should normally be enough – if you overdo the exercises you will tire and stiffen up.

When your position is well established and supple, you will be able to use your back muscles effectively. A well-trained horse is taught to respond to the feel of these muscles being braced and relaxed, through the bearing area of your seat. Therefore, your position must be secure – otherwise an involuntary movement will be indistinguishable from an aid. Lungeing without stirrups improves and strengthens your seat, and helps to develop a closer contact with the horse.

You should also practise changing pace and direction on a long rein, to make sure you are riding with seat and leg aids, rather than over-using the reins. You should be able to keep your horse going forward energetically and straight, with regular rhythmic strides. Ride frequently without stirrups to improve and deepen your seat: if you perch on top or on the back of the saddle, you cannot sit deep and still, in harmony with your horse, nor can you apply the aids smoothly. A good seat does not depend solely on a good position, but also on being able to maintain your balance without having to grip.

Improving your hands

You are said to have good hands when they are sympathetic to the horse's movements. They must be able to give and take instinctively as you anticipate his reactions, and used accordingly, whether by restraint, light contact or yielding.

Most riders have one hand more sensitive than the other. For instance, if you are so right-handed that your left hand is seldom able to perform delicate tasks on its own, you will find the muscles of your left arm less developed than those of your right, and your right hand will be more active and stronger than your left hand. If you suffer from this basic handicap (and most people do) you will have to make a conscious effort to overcome it, since the first requirement of a horse is that he should move forward and *straight*, and if you are "one-handed" your horse is likely to be

Even the most advanced riders benefit from riding without stirrups, as is demonstrated here by Reiner Klimke, warming up in the practice arena before a Grand Prix dressage competition at Goodwood.

"one-sided". He should feel equal contact and sensitivity from *both* your hands and legs, otherwise he cannot be expected to move straight.

Remember that your hands must never act alone: they should always be used in conjunction with leg and seat aids, or the horse will resist their action.

More precise aids

Your aim is to make sure that your horse is "on the aids" and "between hand and leg" at all times. In other words, he should be attentive and responsive, ready to perform any movement required of him. Your legs and seat should encourage his hindquarters to move under him, while your hands lightly control his forward movement. He should show a rounded outline, with his hocks coming well underneath

him, and he should accept **light rein contact. His head should be steady with a** relaxed jaw and neck, and he should feel supple as well as light in hand.

At this stage you should be satisfied if your horse accepts your aids and is "on the bit" at the natural "working" paces. At a more advanced stage, particularly in advanced dressage and jumping, the horse will need to achieve greater collection – in other words his hind legs will have to come even further underneath him so that he is carrying most of his own and his rider's weight over them, with the result that his forehand is raised and lightened. However, it would be wrong to ask for too much collection before you have succeeded in getting the horse to move well at the working paces, otherwise he is likely to resist or move crookedly.

The half-halt

This is the most useful and indispensable of all aids, as it prepares the horse mentally and physically for the aid that follows. The half-halt warns the horse, checks or adjusts his balance and "sets him up" for any change of pace, direction, movement or balance. It is also the most effective way of calming a tense or anxious horse.

To make the half-halt, the aids are the same as for the halt, but their intensity varies according to what you require of the horse and how sensitively he will respond. To prepare him to go from trot to canter, for example, a slight tightening of the seat bones, a straightening of the back and a momentary closing of the hands should be enough to ensure a smooth, balanced transition. But if your horse is moving too fast or has become badly unbalanced, with most of his weight on his forehand, a stronger half-halt must be used. You should brace your back, push downwards with your seat bones while tightening the muscles, and apply your legs in the normal position to "collect" the horse under you. This is followed immediately by an increased feel on the reins. The entire action is *momentary*, but it can be repeated more or less strongly until the desired result is achieved. Peformed well, the action of the half-halt is barely visible to the spectator.

To avoid tension and resistance, always

use the half-halt quickly and clearly; never prolong the hand aid, otherwise you will get the opposite effect to the relaxation of mind and muscle you are seeking, shortening or tightening the muscles in the horse's neck and thus blocking communication. If this happens, yield with your hands immediately, and repeat the half-halt firmly but quietly until the horse is more relaxed.

To calm an excitable or tense horse that is pulling, it is useless to tug on the reins. Use the half-halt to slow him down and to obtain longer strides, and to encourage him to stretch his topline (see page 202), lowering his head and seeking contact with your hands in a more relaxed manner.

While you are learning how to make a half-halt, the walk (having the minimum of impulsion) is the most suitable pace to use. It allows both you and your horse more time in which to think out and coordinate your movements. You will have a better chance of controlling him and of feeling what is happening than when travelling faster.

The half-halt is a vital aid in all riding, but may be difficult to learn at first, especially on a less sensitive horse. Practise on as many different horses as possible until you learn to feel when and how, and how much, to apply it. A very well-schooled horse will need less help or warning before changes of pace and direction than one that is less educated.

The walk

A good walk is often the most difficult pace to obtain because it lacks natural impulsion. The horse should move straight, "tracking up" with free regular strides, and with a definite four-beat rhythm. To produce this you need a deep seat, a firm leg position to control the horse's hindquarters and a light but steady contact with his mouth. It is easy to spoil a horse's walk by restraining him with your hands (trying to collect him before his hind legs are truly engaged under him), thus shortening his stride and discouraging his forward movement, while inviting him to move crookedly away from the restriction produced by your hands.

Driving aids

If your horse lacks impulsion and is unresponsive to normal driving aids, increase the pressure of your seat and legs. If this proves ineffective use your schooling whip as well to obtain an energetic walk. Then relax and follow his forward movement the instant he responds. Should your horse slow again, brace your back and tighten your seat muscles: this time it may be enough to send him on. If not, repeat the whole process even more strongly. Eventually he will understand and the slightest tightening of your seat muscles should produce an energetic response. Constant kicking or nagging will have the opposite effect, deadening your horse to your leg.

The working trot

To trot on from the walk, first make sure your horse is moving between hand and leg and then apply the aids in the normal sequence. If using the rising trot, remain

Above, a good walk on a long rein. The rider is maintaining light contact as the horse stretches out with long, even strides. The rider has to maintain impulsion by using seat and leg aids.

Left, the horse showing impulsion and free forward movement at the trot, his hind legs coming well underneath him so that he tracks up (the hind feet overlapping the prints of the forefeet).

sitting for the first few strides – until you feel the horse's diagonal rhythm – before starting to rise. The horse should move with even elastic strides of natural length, as the working trot is neither shortened nor extended. He should propel himself forwards with active hocks, accepting your hands by remaining on the bit, with a supple neck and back. He must not be allowed to "run" with shortened, hurried strides, and with his hocks trailing ineffectively behind him. If his weight is too much on his forehand, he may be relying heavily on your hands to support him. To lengthen his stride, you will need to activate his hindquarters by increased seat and leg pressure, allowing the extra energy created from behind to flow through your hands which should be used to regulate the impulsion obtained.

When you have established a good working trot you have laid the foundations to obtain greater collection or extension of the paces at a more advanced stage (see pages 132–3).

Transitions

All transitions should be smoothly executed which will be possible only if the horse's hindquarters are engaged by the use of firm leg and seat aids, whether increasing or decreasing pace. To go from trot to walk, prepare the horse with a half-halt, then prolong or increase the rein aid, allowing the horse forwards with following hands immediately he changes pace and keeping him balanced and straight with your legs.

In a correct transition to canter the horse must push himself forward from his outside hind leg with his hocks well under him. He must not "jump" or "climb" into the canter as a result of insufficient preparation or impulsion, nor must he "fall" forwards into the canter from a fast, "running" trot. To correct this, use strong half-halts or ask for the transition to canter from the walk. If he makes the transition from the slower pace he is more likely to keep his balance over his hocks, and is, therefore, less likely to fall forward onto his forehand.

Turns and flexions

Turns and flexions are used as school exercises, both to improve your riding and to supple, strengthen and discipline the horse. A well-trained school horse will be experienced in this work. In fact, a highly trained horse whose muscles are properly developed can bend in a regular arc or curve, with his hind feet following exactly in the track of his forefeet, on a circle as small as 6m (25ft) in diameter. However, it is not easy for any horse to bend throughout his length and you must do everything you can to help him.

Turning exercises will help to develop your coordination and his flexibility. The aids to turn a horse are complex and you will need to use "feel" as well as very precise aids to make sure the horse is performing correctly.

To ride a truly round circle with the horse bent evenly throughout his length and with his hind feet following in the tracks of his forefeet, your aids must also be clear and precise. If the horse's quarters or shoulders swing outwards or inwards, the circle will not be perfect.

As you have already learned, each hand and leg plays a separate part when asking the horse to turn. Your *inside* leg creates impulsion, engaging your horse's inside hind leg, encouraging him to bend around it. (This leg forms the central point of his curve). Your *outside* leg is slightly behind the girth to prevent the quarters from swinging outwards; your *outside* hand regulates the impulsion while your *inside* hand controls the amount of bend and also the direction of the turn.

If you use these aids correctly, you will engage the hind legs so that they support the horse on the turn. The more collected he is (that is the more engaged his hindquarters and the lighter his forehand) the more easily the horse will be able to find self-balance.

To check whether you are using the aids correctly, practise walking in a circle of 20m (66ft) in diameter, on a soft surface which has just been raked smooth. You can then study your tracks and see exactly where you are going wrong.

Right, the horse showing an even bend throughout his length while performing a turn at the trot in a novice dressage test.

Below, the correct bend on a circle seen from above. There should be an even curve along the length of the horse's spine.

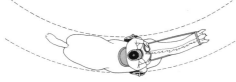

Faults

The common mistakes made when turning, as a result of wrongly applied aids, are shown below. If you find that you are unable to maintain an even bend on a turn, return to practising school figures.

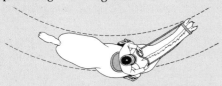

Too much inside hand has been used, causing the offside shoulder to escape.

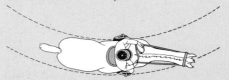

Too much outside hand has been used, causing the nearside shoulder to fall inwards.

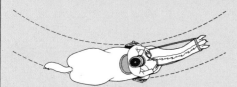

Too little outside leg has been used, causing the quarters to fall outwards.

The common faults are: to use too much *outside* hand so that you pull the horse's head to the outside, thus allowing his shoulder to fall inwards; to use too much *inside* hand to pull the horse around the turn, so that his shoulder falls outwards; to fail to control the movement of the hindquarters with your *outside* leg so that the quarters swing out. Turning a corner too sharply will also result in loss of balance and rhythm.

When changing rein you will have to change the aids. For example, if you are changing rein across the centre of the school, you will have positioned left, turned left and straightened. You must then position right, and turn right. To do so, you will need to change the action of each separate leg and rein aid, which, if you are not careful, could cause the horse to quicken his stride. You can prevent this by using the half-halt before each change of direction, which will also help to improve your horse's balance.

Turning exercises are best performed at the working trot, when impulsion, rhythm and straightness are easiest to maintain. At the walk you will have to work harder on most horses to produce smooth bends whilst moving forward with regular energetic strides. Changes of direction at the canter necessitate a change of leading leg each time. You will have to make the transition at this stage through the trot or the walk.

Straightening the horse

When your horse moves straight his hind feet should follow exactly in the tracks of his forefeet. In fact, it is not natural for a horse to move completely straight because he tends to be one-sided from birth, and this tendency could be exaggerated by your riding if you are particularly left- or right-handed yourself.

If your horse is crooked, you need to know the reasons. It is usually caused by incorrect riding, so check that you are straight. Are you applying the correct aids, for example? Are both your hands being used equally?

To straighten the horse

When your horse is going straight he should move forward with his hind feet following exactly in the tracks of his forefeet. Unless he is very well trained you will have to learn how to prevent crookedness at all paces and in all transitions. You cannot hope to straighten the horse with just your hands, since his legs and body do not necessarily follow his head and neck, so he must be obedient and responsive to independent leg aids. The leg aids to move the horse sideways are the foundation of all future lateral work. One of the best ways of improving your feel for lateral aids is to practise the turn on the forehand, in which the horse pivots around his forelegs (see page 126).

Straightening the horse
The horse, right, is deviating from a straight line with his left shoulder sliding out to the left. His head is bent to the right, and he has dropped contact with the rider's left hand, showing a slack rein. To straighten the horse, the rider is applying her left leg on the girth, to move his forehand to the right, in line with his hindquarters, but she must also take up contact with both reins equally, and ride forward strongly.

The halt

You should no longer be satisfied with simply getting the horse to halt when asked. You should make him stand square, with his weight evenly distributed over all four legs: "a leg at each corner". Now that you are relaxed enough to concentrate on the horse's movements rather than on your own, you should be able to feel if the horse is standing square.

Any crookedness is usually caused by his resistance to one or both of your hands, or by your failure to prepare him sufficiently before halting, so that he is unbalanced and his hindquarters are not sufficiently engaged to support his weight. However, you cannot correct crookedness unless your horse is laterally obedient. To correct a crooked halt you must move his forehand in front of his quarters. The best way of doing this is to ride him forward and halt again. If you shift his quarters over instead, you could throw his balance onto his forehand, making it difficult for him to move on after the halt.

Practise moving from halt to trot to test whether your horse is standing square. With his weight evenly distributed over all four legs, he is able to move forward easily. This exercise will also help to develop your feel for the horse's correct balance when stationary or moving.

If your horse rests a leg at the halt (you will feel it if he does, as his back will slant away to one side under you) nudge him with your leg on the same side or move him forward briskly into a trot. After doing this a few times, he will be more attentive. A tap on the hindquarters with your schooling whip may also be effective, but you must judge how strongly it can be used without him moving forwards or sideways. A slack or sloppy halt reflects a similar attitude in the rider.

Turns on the spot

A turn on the forehand, or on the haunches, through 180°, is a valuable exercise to teach a rider how to use independent lateral aids, and to improve the horse's performance. It is usually executed from the halt or the walk. While learning the aids for this exercise, practise first on a well-schooled horse, and then on a different horse to teach you to adapt your aids according to the horse's response.

It is necessary to obtain flexion to left and to right before you can perform a turn on the spot. If the horse's head is positioned slightly to the outside he will find it easier to yield away from the outside leg. However, all the lateral movements he will be asked to perform after this introduction (see pages 135–42) demand the opposite flexion, towards the direction of the movement, so that the outside legs cross forwards and in front of the inside legs more easily, increasing his suppleness.

Turn on the forehand

The turn on the forehand is useful as an obedience exercise helping to improve the horse's response to the aids, while also serving as an introduction to future lateral work. It should not be taught before straight forward movement, and a steady contact with the bit, are well-established. In the turn on the forehand, the horse must not move forwards or backwards, but must pivot around his inside foreleg, describing an outer concentric circle with his other legs. As this exercise is contradictory to the rules of impulsion and lightening the forehand, it should not be repeated too often, and the pivoting leg should not be completely immobile, but must mark time in the rhythm of the pace.

Turn on the haunches

In the turn on the haunches the horse, at the walk, pivots around his inner hind leg

Flexion to the left
With your left rein, feel the horse's mouth with a taking and yielding action, and ease your right hand forward. Apply leg pressure if necessary to prevent him stepping back.

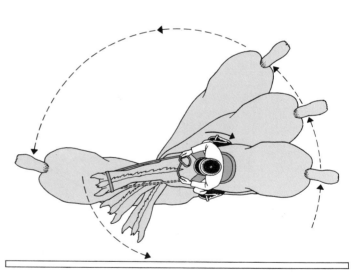

Aids for the turn on the forehand
To turn left, around the inside foreleg, halt the horse alongside a guiding wall or fence. Flex him slightly to the left and then press your leg inwards to nudge the horse in the direction you wish him to turn and to keep him up to the bit. Your right leg should be slightly back behind the girth to control each sideways step and the horse's position. Your seat and hands should be used to keep the horse on the aids and ensure that he does not lose impulsion. You should be able to feel the horse's left hind leg crossing in front of his right hind. Your hands must not cross over the withers, nor should your position move: you should remain upright and square in the saddle.

while his other legs describe a larger concentric circle. It demands not only an accurate and sensitive combination of the aids by the rider but also a high standard of training from the horse. If he has too much weight on his forehand, he will find it very difficult to perform the turn correctly and requires further schooling.

Although the exercise is eventually performed from the halt, it is often easier to start the turn from a walk so that you have the benefit of natural impulsion. The horse's pivoting hind leg can move forward a little, making a small circle, but should never move backwards.

After the first few steps of the turn, the horse reaches the point where his inside hind foot twists awkwardly and he must pick it up and replace it in its natural position. You have to anticipate by feel whether he will put his foot down again in the same spot or whether you must prevent him from wandering. It is this element that makes the turn a difficult exercise for less experienced riders.

If you use your leg aids too strongly, or fail to contain the horse with your hands, he will move forwards instead of sideways, while the reverse of this is a worst fault, as he will then move backwards.

As with the turn on the forehand, do not repeat the exercise too often, and be satisfied, while learning, with a few well executed steps rather than a full 180° turn.

You will find it easier at first to use a wall or fence to guide you. Later you can practise from the halt and, finally, you can try the same exercises in the open, without a guiding fence or wall. You will then have laid a sound foundation for future lateral work at a more advanced level.

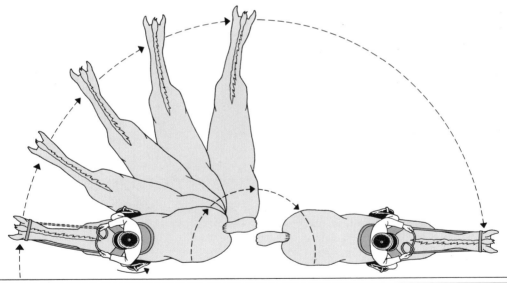

Aids for the turn on the haunches
Halt the horse straight and then apply a warning half-halt, while maintaining light contact with your hands. Flex your horse slightly in the direction you wish him to turn. To pivot right, on the offside hind foot, remain upright in the saddle, with your shoulders square to the horse. Your outside leg will be behind the girth, to control the hindquarters, maintain impulsion, and ask for the turn around the inside leg. Your inside leg should stay against the horse's side to keep the horse up to the bit and in position, and to prevent him from stepping backwards, as well as to limit the sideways movement. Your inside rein leads the forehand into the turn, while keeping light contact, and your outside rein prevents your horse from moving forwards when you apply the leg aids and controls the amount of bend in his neck, as well as preventing his shoulder from falling outwards.

Competing in dressage at novice level

The *Fédération Equestre Internationale* defines dressage as the harmonious development of the physique and ability of the horse to make him calm, supple confident, attentive and keen, thus achieving perfect understanding with his rider.

Dressage competitions are divided into four main categories: Novice (including Preliminary tests for beginners), Intermediate, Medium and Advanced. The rules are set either by the FEI or by a national federation affiliated to it.

When you enter a novice dressage competition, the results of months or, in some cases, years of hard work in the saddle are put to the test for approximately five minutes in a small arena, in front of a judge and maybe a handful of spectators. Having decided you are ready to compete, you must learn the rules, and prepare yourself and your horse to produce a performance that pleases both you and the judge. You will be judged on the freedom and regularity of your horse's paces, the harmony, lightness and ease of his movements, the lightness of his forehand and the engagement of his hindquarters, and his acceptance of the bit without any tenseness or resistance.

Your horse has to give the impression of doing what is required of him of his own accord, remaining absolutely straight in any movement on a straight line, and with the appropriate degree of bend when turning. His walk must be regular, free and unconstrained and his trot free, supple, regular, rhythmic and active; his canter united, light and rhythmic. His quarters must never be inactive or sluggish and he must obey willingly, and without hesitation, responding to the various aids calmly and with precision, both physically and mentally. In all the movements, he must be "on the bit".

However well your horse may have been going for you at home or in the school, he could let you down badly when it comes to "putting it all together" in a competition atmosphere. You are likely to be nervous, and any tension in you will be transmitted

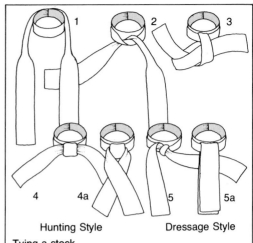

Hunting Style   Dressage Style

Tying a stock
Pass the stock around your neck and feed one end through the loop at the back (1). Tie a knot at the front (2) and then loop one end, passing the other end through it (3). Pull into a smooth knot (4) for hunting style (4a). For dressage style, pull the knot tighter (5), and drape one end of the stock over the other (5a). Secure with a pin horizontally – never vertically.

to your horse. To reduce such tension, avoid competing until you or your instructor feel you are capable of performing at a higher standard than that demanded by the test. Even then you are unlikely to show your true ability at your first attempt: the strange surroundings will make your horse less attentive than usual, and your own excitement and nervousness will not help your performance.

However, competing will allow you to measure your progress, and it will also provide an incentive for you to achieve a higher standard. If you compete and get a very bad mark although you thought you gave a good performance, you have probably not learned, as yet, to feel what your horse is doing and you should seek more experience and expert instruction before competing again.

Preparing for the test
Obviously you are not going to do well in your test unless your horse is well schooled. He must be able to go forward freely and straight, and should be obedient and responsive to your aids, and balanced so that he propels himself from behind and

does not fall forward on his forehand. Your ability to ride a good test will depend as much on practice and experience, and on a suitable horse, as on your natural aptitude.

The day before the competition take care not to upset your horse either by atttemptting any new exercises or by provoking an argument with him. You will want him to be relaxed and willing for the test. Suppling exercises to remove any stiffness are better done the day before the competition, as you want your horse lively as well as obedient. Decide how he will react at the competition and plan your final day of preparation accordingly: perhaps half an hour of schooling, followed by a hack. In some cases it would be better not to school him at all, if he feels stale and "over the top". If he is excitable or tense, however, he may need an hour or more's exercise to settle him sufficiently to produce his best form.

You must be neat and smart for the competition. You will need a hacking or dark jacket, a plain shirt, a stock or tie, a hard hat, gloves, boots, breeches and (if female) a hairnet or elastic band to keep your hair in place. A schooling whip is allowed when riding in, but is not always permitted during the test itself. Your horse will also need to look his best and should be well-groomed, preferably with his mane and tail plaited (see page 264), and his tack well cleaned and in good condition.

On the day

Allow plenty of time on arrival in which to check over your horse, collect your number, tack up and ride in. You must

---

Novice dressage test

A dressage test of novice standard is judged in an arena of 40 × 20m (131 × 60ft). You must learn, and then perform, a specific programme of simple movements at the walk, trot and canter. Each movement will be marked out of a maximum of 10. The merit of each mark is guided by the following scale:

10: excellent   4: insufficient
9: very good   3: fairly bad
8: good   2: bad
7: fairly good   1: very bad
6: satisfactory   0: not performed

A maximum of 30 marks is also awarded for "general impression, obedience and calmness", "paces (freedom and regularity) and impulsion", "position and seat of the rider and correct application of the aids". After the competition you will be given your marked sheet with the judge's comments, which should be instructive as well as critical. The rider gaining the highest number of points is the winner.

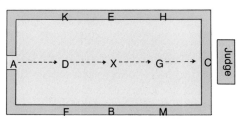

Typical novice test movements

1	A	Enter at working trot
	X	Halt. Salute. Proceed at working trot
2	C	Track left
3	A	Working trot half circle left 20m diameter
	X	Half circle right 20m diameter
4	CM	Working trot
	MXK	Changing rein showing a few lengthened strides
5	K	Working trot
	FXH	Change rein showing a few lengthened strides
6	C	Working canter
	B	Circle right 20m diameter
	BF	Working canter
7	F	Working trot
	A	Medium walk
	KB	Change rein at free walk on a long rein
	BM	Medium walk
8	M	Working trot
	between	
	C & H	Working canter
	E	Circle left 20m diameter
	EK	Working canter
9	K	Working trot
	A	Down centre line
	G	Halt. Salute.
		Leave arena at walk on a long rein at A

The final salute showing a square halt and immobility. However, the horse has raised his head and is no longer on the aids.

decide beforehand how long you may need to warm up. To be safe, allow an extra half-hour for all your preparations.

Both you and your horse will have to supple up and relax, physically and mentally, for the test. Do not squander all your efforts by disorganized timing. If you rush, you will upset your horse. As you want him to perform at his best, give him every opportunity to do so.

On arrival, let the horse look around his surroundings. Then ask him to become attentive to you. If he is disobedient at first, gain his attention by frequent changes of pace and direction. Work progressively towards your goal, and do not allow yourself to be distracted by friends or fellow competitors until you are satisfied with your own performance. When you can perform good, engaged transitions and bends you will both be ready to compete.

As soon as you feel you have reached this stage, stop working him and ride at a relaxed walk. Wait until just before your time is announced, and then run through a couple of the movements to regain his attention. His state of mind must be carefully prepared and maintained. As you gain experience of your horse, you will be better able to gauge his likely behaviour. Finally, it is a good idea to remind your-

self of the sequence of movements and check that your horse's appearance and your own are tidy and polished.

Riding the test

Ride around close to the outside of the arena, as soon as the previous competitor has left the arena. It is a good idea to practise a halt before you start, to make the horse attentive and obedient, and you should let him see the boards and markers at close quarters so that he does not shy at them in the arena. Although you are not yet competing, the judge may notice if your horse is misbehaving, so avoid an argument with him at this late stage, and make any last-minute adjustments out of sight of the judge, if possible.

Begin your test without delay on receiving the signal to start, but do not hurry. If you lose your way during the test (and cannot correct yourself), ride up to the judge who will put you right.

Your entry and halt, the first impressions, should be ridden with straightness and confidence. Your salute should be unhurried and gracious.

If you make a mistake, do not let it upset you, or your horse. Another movement, worth 10 marks, will follow shortly. Try to ride with the same "feel" and aids as you would at home. Accuracy is most important; making your transitions or turns even one stride early or late will result in marks being thrown away needlessly. Prepare each movement in good time, so that your transitions are smooth and exact.

Give the impression that you are enjoying yourself (whatever your true feelings) and that your horse is doing what is required of his own accord. Showmanship, or ringcraft, increases with experience. You will mentally note that there are several areas for improvement, since perfection is rarely attained.

Study your dressage sheet after the competition. The judge's remarks will provoke interest, thought, and self-criticism, with a resolve to do better next time.

Elementary dressage

No horseman or horsewoman has ever finished learning. To achieve the harmony between horse and rider so necessary in advanced equitation you must first have acquired a firm, balanced seat, and an understanding of the aids and their correct use at all paces, providing a sound basis from which your horsemanship can advance. As your seat has improved, you should have learned how to influence the balance, paces and movements of your horse, and how to feel his straightness, suppleness and activity.

You are then able to develop as a "feeling" and "thinking" rider, with an understanding of how the horse reacts in different situations and how you can influence these reactions. You must be aware of what he can or cannot do physically, as well as mentally, and it will help to improve your understanding if you ride as many different horses as possible, learning how to adapt to the different characteristics of each.

You may have been lucky enough to have been well taught by an expert instructor and to have ridden a well-schooled horse or horses, in which case your progress should have been more rapid than those who have struggled to reach the same standard by trial and error. No experience, however, is wasted: even bad experience will provide useful knowledge later if you train a horse yourself.

To perform more advanced movements, your horse must carry the minimum of weight on his forehand. The exercises shown on the following pages help to develop the horse's carrying power of his hindquarters, shifting his centre of gravity and the placement of his weight further back. They can, however, only be performed by a horse that has already achieved some degree of balance, and whose weight is already over his hindquarters. They will also help you to improve and refine your aids and influence. Once you have learned the movements on a well-schooled horse, you will be able to use this knowledge to advantage should you ever train a horse yourself.

Aids for advanced work

A double bridle may be used in advanced work, but should never be a means of forcing the horse to perform an exercise for which he is insufficiently trained. As the double bridle has a more severe action than the snaffle, it must be used with care and sensitivity. It should be fitted properly (see page 275) and the curb chain must not be too tight. There are various ways of holding double reins – the method right exerts the minimum pressure on the curb.

Spurs are used to emphasize leg aids, particularly on horses that lack natural impulsion. They should not be worn until you have established a well-balanced seat, and should be blunt-ended, rather than sharp or rowelled. Only the sides of the spurs should make contact with the horse's body. To see if you have been using them properly examine them after riding – there should be grease on the sides only.

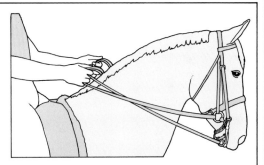

Above, you will be able to exert pressure on the snaffle while keeping the curb rein steady if you run the snaffle rein through between the third and fourth fingers of each hand, and the curb rein between the first and second fingers.

Right, the correct position of the spur when applied to the horse's sides.

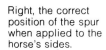

Collection

When a horse is "collected" he appears to be shortened in outline. This is, of course, anatomically impossible but the illusion is created because his hindquarters are lowered on his haunches, as his hocks come well underneath his body, raising his forehand. His muscles contract as his impulsion is contained in short, highly energetic paces. Tightened muscles will be tense and hard, which will hinder your horse's movements, but contracted muscles are supple and elastic, and are able to stretch.

To achieve collection, the horse must be very supple, without any tension. He must accept light contact with the bit, and be responsive to the aids, going forwards and straight. As his energy increases, it must be controlled between "hand and leg".

It may take several years for the horse to establish enough self-balance to be truly collected, particularly if he is built heavily on his forehand. Collection should not be forced but without it in some degree, progress cannot be made, as it forms the basis of all precision riding.

Maximum collection is achieved when the horse carries most of his weight and that of his rider over his hind legs, which come right underneath his body. Without it, the advanced movements of dressage, such as piaffe and passage, would not be possible.

The half-halt is the most valuable aid towards collection and when you have mastered its execution you will find that a slight bracing of the back is all that is needed on a well-trained horse to gain his attention with a collected effect.

To achieve collection

Use the half-halt, followed by stronger driving aids with seat and legs into a more restraining hand which, at the same time, is elastic enough to allow and encourage the forward straight movement of the horse. Be careful not to ask for too much collection before the horse is balanced, or evasions will result (see page 211). Your horse must not tense against these collecting aids. If he does, he will either move away crookedly or will resist in some way.

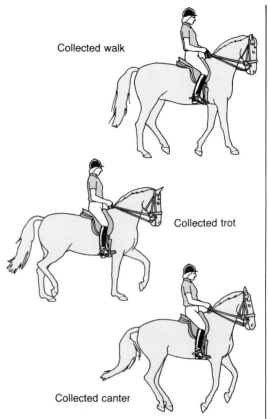

Collected walk

Collected trot

Collected canter

Irina Karacheva of the USSR on Said demonstrating good collection in the piaffe. This high-school movement demands great impulsion, controlled between the rider's hands and legs. The horse's steps are short but elevated, showing equal flexibility in all four legs. He is in perfect equilibrium.

Extension

Collection acts as the spring from which the energy generated in the hindquarters, and contained in strong elevated steps, is released. When allowed to do so, the horse will spring forward in extended steps, covering the maximum amount of ground in a single stride. His impulsion should be used to the full whilst a regular rhythm is kept. He must be on the bit, not leaning on it, coming above it or rushing, although his nose can be slightly ahead of the vertical. His head and neck will stretch lower than in collected, medium and working paces.

A horse extending correctly brings his hind legs as far as possible underneath his body and shows regular steps. Extension should never be achieved at the expense of regular strides, rhythm and balance. The exaggerated extension of the forelegs, as seen in the Spanish walk, is an artificial movement rather than a true extension, as the hind legs are not the propelling force.

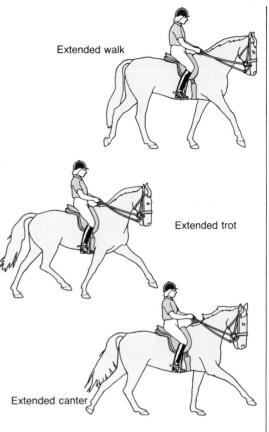

Extended walk

Extended trot

Extended canter

To achieve extension

To teach a horse to extend you must first work towards greater collection, building up his impulsion and power with progressive exercises.

Increase the impulsion with strong driving aids but contain the energy in your hands, using elastic rein aids. Make sure your horse is straight and if he resists in his mouth, neck or back, ride him on a small circle to collect him. Then straighten him and release this energy gradually, keeping the horse moving ahead of you. At first, do not extend around a turn or your horse will lose balance and rhythm. If you over-push he may lose balance and rhythm, and even break into a faster gait.

Elena Petouschkova of the USSR on Pepel showing admirable extension at the trot. The horse is using the release of muscular energy generated by collection to great effect. He shows perfect balance and is moving straight with a lightness and freedom rarely seen.

The rein back

The rein back is the walk backwards. Instead of picking up each leg separately as in the forward walk pace, the horse raises and sets down his legs alternately in diagonal pairs. The rein back should have a regular two-time beat, and the horse must move back straight, taking a definite number of well-defined steps. He must remain on the bit throughout, neither rushing backwards nor hollowing his back. If he is accepting your leg aids and rein contact, he will slightly lower himself on his haunches, appearing to round his back. When the movement is performed in perfect balance, he will be ready and able to move forward again immediately when asked to do so.

The rein back is a difficult movement for the horse as you have always previously stressed the importance of forward movement. It should be practised with patience as it may take some time to perform it well. Never yield to the temptation to pull up and rein back sharply if your horse is disobedient or becomes badly unbalanced. Such an action could severely damage his joints and muscles. You should never try to force the horse backwards by pulling on the reins. If you do, he will resist, either in his mouth, neck, back or through his length.

Your first attempts should be made with a fence or wall as a guide. When you can perform the rein back smoothly and accurately, practise it in the open to see if you can keep the horse straight.

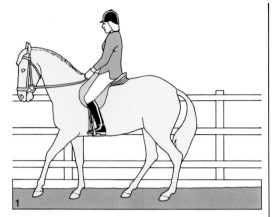

Fault
The horse has not been well prepared for the rein back. The rider is using too much hand, and the horse has resisted, raising his head and hollowing his back. The tension has caused him to take uneven steps.

How to rein back
Halt your horse alongside a wall or fence, on level ground. Make sure he is standing square and then brace your back to gain his full attention. Apply both legs equally just behind the girth, and use an elastic rein action to prevent him from moving forward. Place your weight slightly forward of the vertical to help send him backwards (1, 2, 3).

Lateral movements on two tracks

When you can ride turns and circles with your horse bent evenly throughout the length of his body, and when you can keep him straight without relying on your hands, you are ready to learn lateral work on two tracks. This is the term used to describe any movement during which the horse's hind feet do not follow in the tracks of his forefeet, but step sideways, with one pair of legs crossing in front of the other pair. All lateral movements on two tracks can be performed at the walk, trot or canter, but it is usually easier to learn them at the walk, until your coordination and feel are well established. You will then find them easier at the trot, which has more rhythm and impulsion.

The various exercises on two tracks are: leg yielding, shoulder-in, travers, renvers, and the half-pass, and they are described on the following pages. Each exercise supples the horse and teaches him to be obedient to the lateral aids. The degree of flexion can vary in each movement, but you should not demand too much until the horse is supple enough to cope with it. Nor should he ever be asked to stretch sideways beyond his natural reach at the particular pace you are using.

Always practise the lateral movements for short periods only, and ride forwards strongly after each exercise to confirm the importance of going forwards and straight. The movements should be performed equally to left and right when training a horse, in order to prevent one-sidedness from developing.

By using selected lateral exercises, you can also help cure one-sidedness where it already exists by encouraging the horse to bend on his "stiff" side: in the opposite direction to that which he finds easiest.

Neck flexion

The exercise below tests your ability to keep your horse straight while flexing his neck to one side or the other. Unless you can do this, you are not ready to attempt the lateral movements on the following pages, as your inability to perform the exercise almost certainly stems from too much rein influence rather than effective leg and seat aids. The exercise is also useful as it will reveal any stiffness along your horse's ribs or back. You should practise it first at the walk, although it will be valuable later when performed at the trot and canter, as a preliminary to the other lateral movements at those paces.

How to flex the neck
Half-halt, then ask for left flexion by feeling on the inside rein, allowing his head and neck to bend round by yielding the outside rein, while controlling your horse's straightness and impulsion with your legs. Ride straight for a few paces before asking for right flexion, reversing the instructions above.

Right, horse and rider demonstrating, correct neck flexion at the halt: 1 flexion left; 2 straight; 3 flexion right

Leg yielding

This is more an obedience and suppling exercise than one for improving balance, as the horse's hind legs need not move very far underneath him. It helps to develop the rider's feel for moving the horse sideways and forwards, as the outer pair of legs cross in front of the inner pair. When learning leg yielding do not ask for too great an angle at first.

Leg yielding should be practised parallel to a wall or fence, first at the walk and then at the trot. It should be executed to the left and right equally. There should be slight flexion away from the direction of the movement, and the steps should not be hurried. Practise the preliminary exercise shown below before trying the diagonal

Leg yielding
The rider is practising leg yielding to the right at the trot. She is asking for a considerable amount of bend away from the direction in which she and the horse are travelling.

leg-yielding exercise far below. If the horse resists at any point, ride away in a circle and put him between hand and leg before starting again.

Preliminary exercise (right direction)
Position your horse at the halt, facing a wall or fence. Ask him to walk directly sideways away from your outside leg, keeping him as straight as possible. Control each step and stop when necessary to check your aids and position.

Aids for leg yielding (left direction)
For leg yielding at the walk, turn down the centre of the arena, parallel to the wall. Half-halt to prepare your horse. With slight flexion to the right to lead him in that direction feel on the left rein, opening it out a little if necessary while applying your right leg behind the girth so that he moves away from it, crossing in a forwards and sideways movement. Your left leg is used to prevent his body deviating from the correct straight line.

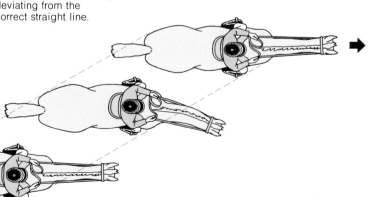

Shoulder-in

The shoulder-in is a useful exercise to develop your coordination, feel and timing and for learning how to straighten and position your horse while maintaining impulsion. For the horse it is an obedience lesson as well as a test of suppleness and physical development. In the shoulder-in the horse should move obliquely forward, his inner hind leg stepping under his centre of gravity in the track of his outside foreleg, while maintaining the bend away from the direction in which he is moving: the angle should not exceed 30°.

You will find it easier to ride a correct shoulder-in if you first ride a 10m (33ft) diameter circle in the corner of the arena to ensure you have the correct flexion. Do not overpush your horse: his strides must be even and of medium length. Feel for his inside hind leg coming right underneath you, taking your weight and thus relieving his forehand. Do not cross your hands over or bring either of them across his neck. If you lose impulsion when moving sideways leave the exercise and ride forwards strongly before recommencing the movement. Finally, when you finish the movement, continue in the arc of your original circle rather than turning your horse back on to the track.

Shoulder-in
Rider and horse are demonstrating the movement at the correct angle (about 30° to the side of the arena). The horse is bent evenly to the right, around the rider's right leg, while his hind legs remain on the track.

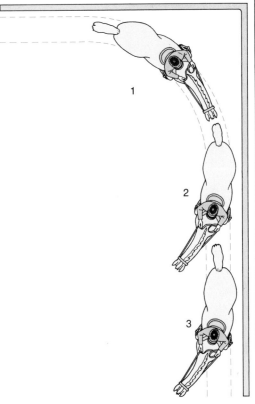

Fault
The horse is positioned at too great an angle to the track, making it difficult for him to move freely and to maintain his impulsion and length of stride at the trot. The horse is not sufficiently bent around the rider's inside leg.

Aids for shoulder-in
Prepare to apply the aids for a shoulder-in with a half-halt (1). As your horse arrives at the point where his forehand is one stride off the track (2) you must direct his impulsion sideways and forwards along the side of the wall without losing the even bend you established on the turn (3). To perform the shoulder-in, press with your inside leg near the girth, keeping your outside leg just behind the girth to support your horse and to prevent him from rejoining the track. Your outside rein controls the impulsion, the angle of the horse from the track and the amount of flexion in his neck. The inside rein helps maintain the correct bend which is held with your legs.

Travers and renvers

In these lateral exercises, the horse moves forwards and sideways along the track. In travers, his forehand remains on the track,

Travers

Renvers

and his hindquarters are carried in from it at an angle of approximately 30°, whereas in renvers, as the name implies, the movement is reversed so that the hind legs remain on the track and the forehand is brought off it, again at an angle of about 30°. In both movements, the horse is flexed through the length of his body in the direction in which he is travelling.

When performing travers, it is best to start the movement after a turn so that you obtain the required flexion before you travel along the side of the arena. Renvers is slightly more difficult because you will have to straighten the horse after coming around the corner of the arena, and then position him in left flexion.

In both movements, try to keep an even bend throughout the horse's length. Too much angle may result in loss of impulsion

and rhythm and may cause the horse to strike himself. If you lose the bend, circle right (or left, as appropriate) and start the exercise again. As in all lateral work on two tracks, you must remain upright and square in the saddle.

Once you are able to give the aids correctly at the walk, perform the exercises at the trot, as it has the benefit of the simple diagonal rhythm and more impulsion.

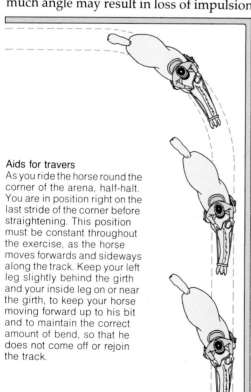

Aids for travers
As you ride the horse round the corner of the arena, half-halt. You are in position right on the last stride of the corner before straightening. This position must be constant throughout the exercise, as the horse moves forwards and sideways along the track. Keep your left leg slightly behind the girth and your inside leg on or near the girth, to keep your horse moving forward up to his bit and to maintain the correct amount of bend, so that he does not come off or rejoin the track.

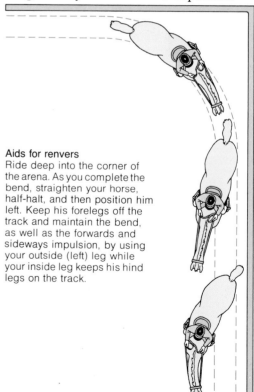

Aids for renvers
Ride deep into the corner of the arena. As you complete the bend, straighten your horse, half-halt, and then position him left. Keep his forelegs off the track and maintain the bend, as well as the forwards and sideways impulsion, by using your outside (left) leg while your inside leg keeps his hind legs on the track.

Half-pass

The half-pass is similar to travers and renvers, except that it is performed free of the track (which makes it more difficult), and there is only slight lateral flexion. It must be performed with the forehand slightly in advance of the hindquarters. The horse moves diagonally forwards and sideways on two tracks, flexed towards the direction in which he is travelling.

The half-pass is a valuable exercise for improving the rider's coordination and sensitivity when applying the aids, as well as being an excellent way to supple the horse, since it increases the flexibility in his shoulders, hindquarters and joints. He has to bring his hocks well under his body which increases his impulsion and leads towards greater collection.

You should practise at the walk until you are certain of the correct aids.

You will find it easier to perform the movement correctly if you first walk a small circle of approximately 10m (33ft) in diameter, in a corner of the arena. (Bear in mind that the horse is more likely to prefer to face towards "home".) On the circle,

Half-pass (to the left)
The horse and rider, right, are performing a half-pass to the left. The horse's right foreleg is crossing in front of his left foreleg, and he has the right amount of lateral flexion, as he moves diagonally forwards and sideways on two tracks.

check that your horse is correctly bent around your inside leg, as you will need to maintain this same bend when executing the half-pass.

The half-pass can then be performed at the trot and, at a more advanced level, at the canter. At the trot the extra impulsion and easier rhythm will help you, but to make a good half-pass you will need to plan and apply your aids earlier and use them with greater precision.

On completing the half-pass, straighten the horse by riding strongly forwards along

Faults
Common faults in the half-pass are: to allow the hindquarters to lead the forehand, with too much bend (far right, half-pass to the left); for the rider to lean to one side instead of sitting straight and square (right, half-pass to the left) and for the rider to take her inside hand across the horse's neck (below, half-pass to the right).

the track. If both the near-fore and near-hind leg join the track at the same time or if the hind leg arrives before the foreleg, you may have been travelling more sideways than forwards, with a probable loss of impulsion and regularity of stride. Riders often neglect to use their inside leg with the result that the hindquarters are pushed too far over and the horse either loses the inside bend or leads with the hindquarters. If this happens, ride forwards strongly and start the exercise again.

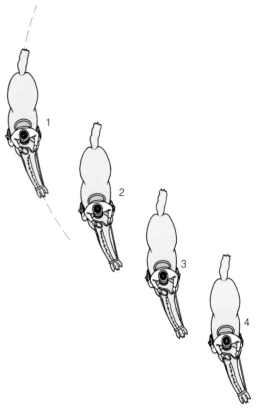

Aids for the half-pass to the left
Half-halt just before (1). Your position at (1) must be maintained throughout the movement back to the track on the long side of the arena. Both you and your horse should look left, and your weight should be on the inside seat-bone, although you must remain square. Your hands can move slightly to the left, your inside hand guiding the horse's direction and keeping left flexion, while your outside hand limits the amount of flexion and regulates the impulsion and forward movement. Apply your outside leg just behind the girth to move your horse to the left, but remember that the inside leg maintains the left bend and keeps the horse going forwards (2, 3 and 4).

Half-pass – counter change
This is a half-pass in zigzag form in which the horse, on changing direction, has to change the flexion evenly throughout his whole length. How easily and quickly he can do this will depend on his suppleness and correct training. Remember that the forehand must lead the hindquarters slightly, in both directions. At a more advanced stage the counter half-pass can be performed at the canter.

Aids for the counter half-pass
To make the half-pass first to the left and then to the right, half-halt immediately before H and position left. Half-pass left and then, immediately before X, half-halt and straighten the horse for one or two strides before positioning right, and making the half-pass right to K.

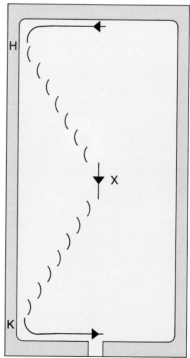

Lateral work on a circle

Lateral exercises on a circle are useful for helping to develop the balance and suppleness of the horse and for improving your sensitive coordination of the aids. You can increase and decrease the size of the circle by applying the lateral aids.

Ride a circle of approximately 20m (66ft) diameter, then gradually decrease the size of the circle using the half-pass, and without changing the bend you have already established. Do not let the quarters lead the forehand, and never allow the sideways movement to be more pronounced than the forward impulsion. Your outside leg should press the horse inwards while your inside leg controls the impulsion and maintains the bend. You should feel the horse's outside hind leg crossing under you, increasing the carrying power of his hocks.

When your circle is reduced to approximately 10m (33ft) in diameter, you can then increase it again using the lateral aids, feeling the horse's inside hind leg moving across under you this time, controlling the bend with your outside hand.

Variations of this exercise can be performed to straighten out any deviations in the horse. Travers on a left-handed circle, for instance, will help to prevent the horse from carrying his quarters to the right. If he tends to carry his quarters to the left, perform the travers on a right-handed circle. Shoulder-in on a circle can be used to move the horse's hindquarters to the outside if he tends to carry them inwards on either rein. Any deviations, once diagnosed, can be cured with such corrective exercises, provided they are performed accurately.

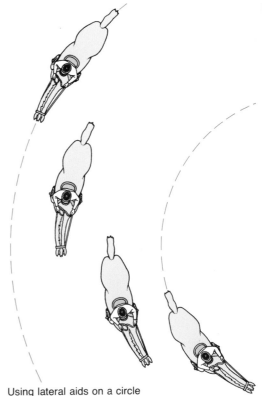

Using lateral aids on a circle
A useful exercise to improve the rider's effective application of lateral aids, while increasing the horse's suppleness and obedience, and obtaining greater engagement of the hind legs. The rider is using the same aids as for the half-pass but is applying them on a circle, which becomes gradually smaller in size, finally reaching a true 10m (33ft) circle.

After completion of any exercise demanding a considerable degree of collection, ride your horse forwards strongly to relieve him of any tension, and to remind him that "forwards and straight" is still your chief priority.

Advanced transitions

You are familiar with the simple transitions of pace – walk to trot, trot to canter, for example – but you will now have to learn to increase and decrease pace from walk to canter, and canter to walk. You will also need to be able to increase or decrease the length of stride within a specific gait. The half-halt is used before a change of pace or stride alteration. How strongly or how lightly you apply the aids at a particular moment will depend partly on your sensitivity and partly on that of your horse. When going from a canter to the walk or halt, for example, a more pronounced half-halt will be necessary to prepare the horse as the hocks must be engaged well under him so that he is sufficiently balanced to achieve a fluent transition. To lengthen or shorten the stride within a specific gait, an almost imperceptible half-halt may be all that is needed.

Counter-canter

The horse is in counter-canter (also known as false canter) if he leads with his outside legs on a circle or bend instead of the natural inside lead. This exercise is useful for developing your sense of balance and feel, as well as for straightening out any deviations in the horse and suppling him. It will show up any stiffness, in particular on the turns.

The horse should move on a single track in regular rhythm. If he is not sufficiently balanced to maintain a slow canter on the normal inside lead on a bend, he will become more unbalanced if you attempt the counter-canter and will try to change back on to the more comfortable legs, or may become disunited (see page 216). If he does, trot or walk briefly before applying the aids to canter again on the required leg. When you have mastered the counter canter you can make serpentine loops, and complete circles at counter-canter.

Aids to counter-canter
To strike off directly into the counter-canter, use the normal canter aids but in reverse: flex your horse towards the intended leading leg, with your inside leg behind the girth to prevent the quarters from coming in, and your outside leg on the girth to create opposite bend and to control impulsion. The outside rein asks for the outside bend and together with the inside rein controls the horse's direction while regulating the amount of bend. Your weight presses down over the leading leg, but you must sit upright and square.

Elementary dressage test

At this standard the test will be longer and demand a higher standard of training. The horse must show a more rounded outline than at novice level, as evidence of his progression towards collection. Through improved muscular development, suppleness and impulsion, he should be able to perform the required movements without any difficulty.

You will be expected to show clearly defined differences in the variations of pace, whether working, medium or extended, as required. Your control of the horse's impulsion and his balance will be tested by changes of bend and exact transitions, as from walk to canter or a simple change of canter lead through the trot or walk, and also by precise figures: 10m circles, and serpentine loops for example. Some strides at counter-canter and some lateral work may be included in tests at this level, and these will display the degree of suppleness and collection achieved, as well as further proof of the horse's obedience to your correctly applied aids, as you move together harmoniously.

The elementary test can be performed in either a snaffle or simple double bridle.

Movements of an elementary test

1.	A	Enter at working trot
	X	Halt. Salute. Proceed at working trot
2.	C	Track left
	E	Turn left
	B	Track right
3.	K	Circle right 10m diameter
4.	EX	Half circle right 10m diameter
	XB	Half circle left 10m diameter
5.	M	Circle left 10m diameter
6.	HEK	Medium trot
	KAF	Working trot
7.	FXH	Change rein at medium trot
	H	Working trot
8.	C	Halt (6 secs)
		Proceed at medium walk
9.	MXK	Change rein at free walk on a long rein
	K	Medium walk
10.	Before	
	A	Working canter
	FBM	Two loops, each 2m diameter in from track
11.	C	Circle left 15m diameter
12.	HXF	Change rein with change of leg through trot at X
13.	A	Circle right 15m diameter
14.	KEH	Two loops each 2m in from track
15.	B	Turn right
	X	Simple change of leg
	E	Track left
16.	K	Working trot
	A	Down centre line
	X	Medium walk
	G	Halt. Salute
		Leave arena at walk on a long rein at A.

Advanced dressage

At this level, the rider should be able to perform the most advanced transitions, as when producing maximum activity from immobility – an extended canter from a halt (and vice versa). A typical advanced test might include transitions of: halt – canter – canter – halt – rein back for six strides – canter. If such transitions can be performed without any resistance or deviation, both horse and rider have reached a very high standard of training.

The movements performed at the advanced and Grand Prix level of dressage include the volte (a circle of only 6m in diameter), the pirouette (the turn on the haunches through 360⁰), the half-pass and the flying change of leg. At this standard, lateral movements can be ridden at the

The flying change

In the flying change the horse changes leading legs simultaneously during the moment of suspension which follows the third beat of the canter. He must spring from one pair of leading legs to the other in one fluent movement. Correctly performed, the flying change is the smoothest way of changing direction at the canter (or at the gallop) but it is an advanced movement in that the rider must give exact aids, with split-second timing, fractionally before the moment of suspension. If the rider fails to prepare the horse, or asks for the change too early or too late, the horse may change the lead in front or behind only, resulting in a disunited canter, or he may change the lead on both legs, but not simultaneously.

To perform the flying change, the horse must have reached the stage of collection which enables him to use his hind legs actively. If he has not, the canter may become disunited, or he may rush or jump into the change. Resistance and crookedness are other possible results.

Flying change

At first, the flying change should be made on a bend, as you turn from one direction to the other. Repeat frequently until your aids are precise, and then ask the horse to make the change from the counter-canter, before progressing to making flying changes on a straight line.

In advanced tests, the horse is asked to make flying changes every three, two and at every stride.

Aids for the flying change
Start by asking for the transition on a bend, as you plan to turn from one direction to the other. Prepare by collecting your horse with a half-halt (1). Reverse the lateral canter aids, so that you have the "new" inside leg on the girth and the "new" outside leg now slightly behind the girth. At the same time your hands also reverse roles to change the flexion. As you nudge with your outside leg, the flying change should be made (2), but be careful that you do not move the quarters sideways when applying the leg aids. The horse should then move forward correctly on the new lead (3).

143

canter, and must show the same rhythm as when on a single track. They require great balance and suppleness. The volte is often ridden before the canter half-pass to obtain the desired degree of collection and flexion. The half-pass is often made across half the length of the arena, which demands considerable skill and precision. A test at this level may also include a counter change of hand in the centre of the arena at X, using a flying change, and on completion of the movement the horse must either remain in counter-canter or make a flying change of lead onto the inside leg without any change of rhythm.

Although advanced movements are exciting to perform, the main priorities when riding – "forwards and straight" – must never be lost. These are demonstrated best at the simple working paces, particularly the trot. Lateral work is used to help develop the perfect trot by increasing

The pirouette

The pirouette is a full circle of 360°, with a radius equal to the length of the horse. The forehand moves around the pivoting hindquarters, as in the turn on the haunches, and the lightness of the forehand is essential if the horse is to perform the turn correctly. Pirouettes may be executed at the collected walk or canter. The necessary degree of collection may take years to achieve, but even then, the rider must apply the correct aids with precision.

The aids for a pirouette at the walk are the same as for the turn on the haunches (see page 127) but away from a guiding fence. In a correct pirouette, the pivoting inside hind foot marks time on the same spot, or just in front of it, in the rhythm of the pace. The horse is bent slightly towards the direction in which he is turning, and should remain on the bit, showing no resistance to the rider or to the movement. He maintains impulsion throughout the turn.

At the canter, when there will be greater impulsion, the aids for the pirouette may need to be applied more strongly, since collection is vital to the success of the movement, and the horse will have to decrease pace rapidly – from 12–15 mph to a standstill. When learning the movement, the rider usually begins with the demi-pirouette on a small radius – 2–3m (6–10ft) – before reducing the area covered by the turn. Eventually a full pirouette at the canter should require only six to eight strides

A good pirouette shows suppleness, lightness, regularity and some elevation (at the canter only).

The canter pirouette performed by Christine Stückelberger on Merry Boy (right) and by Dr. Reiner Klimke on Ahlerich (far right). Maximum engagement of the hocks is needed for this demanding movement.

the horse's suppleness and strength as the ultimate high school dressage movements, the piaffe and passage, are based on a powerful trot. They are the culmination of balance and impulsion produced by improving and developing the horse's natural paces and physique.

The piaffe and passage demonstrate the result of long, careful training. Normally the piaffe is taught before the passage. It is similar to a trot on the spot, with very col-lected, elevated steps, the quarters lowered over bending hocks and the forehand raised. The horse must show his desire to go forwards, while the rider, who creates the urge, restrains him, so as to produce a perfectly balanced, dancing movement. Force should never be used to produce the movement, but a long whip helps to main-tain the horse's energy and rhythm. A good piaffe shows lively impulsion, as the horse springs rhythmically from one diagonal

to the other, without signs of physical or mental tension. He is always ready to spring forward into an extended trot.

The passage is a very collected, elevated trot with a long moment of suspension, as if the horse were floating effortlessly above the ground in slow motion. His hind legs push him forward in high springy steps, showing maximum impulsion and balance. The horse must be straight during this demanding movement. The excellence is governed by the strength and ability of the horse, and the skill of the rider in producing and regulating the required impulsion to achieve regular, even strides, taken by both fore- and hind legs, and in controlling the horse's muscles and joints. At its best, this is a beautiful movement.

The ultimate test of dressage training is for horse and rider to perform a smooth transition from passage to piaffe with uninterrupted rhythm.

Left, Robert Dover of the USA on Federleight demonstrating the skill and harmony between horse and rider necessary for advanced dressage movements.

Right, Christine Stückelberger of Switzerland on Granat, performing a half-pass to the right, using the great power and reach of this horse as he takes long, elastic strides in perfect balance.

Below, Jennie Loriston-Clarke and Dutch Courage, of Britain, performing the piaffe – only the horse's tail shows slight signs of resistance.

Advanced jumping

At the preliminary jumping stage (see pages 66–75) you will have learned how to jump simple obstacles, probably no higher than 1m (3ft 6in), separated by easy distances and usually with a ground-line to help your horse judge his point of take-off. As your standard of riding improves, however, you may wish to take your horse out hunting or cross country, where you may have to face bigger fences, sometimes at awkward angles. You may also wish to compete in horse trials, or show jumping competitions.

The jumps you will face when competing at an advanced level may not vary much in appearance from those you have experienced in small competitions, but they will be more difficult because of their greater dimensions and their position, both in relation to one another (as in the case of doubles and trebles) and to the terrain on which they are situated.

When out hunting you may encounter a variety of large fences such as vertical gates, water-filled ditches, and hedges, often on steep gradients. On cross-country courses your ability and courage will be tested by every possible type of obstacle,

both natural and artificial; they will be fixed and solid, and are often made of strong rails to form uprights of up to 1.2m (3ft 11in) and spreads of up to 3.5m (12ft). These rails may also be placed over water troughs, straw bales and brush fences. Many of the jumps will be built on slopes, and may take the form of ramps and platforms; banks which cannot be cleared in one leap; drop fences (in which the landing level is much lower than the take-off); steps up and down; and water, which you can jump into as well as over. In horse trials, where speed becomes an additional factor, there will be even more emphasis on accurate riding, as when approaching a jump from an angle.

Speed can be still more important to the results in top show jumping competitions, which are the ultimate test of the horse and rider's jumping ability. Uprights may be as high as 1.8m (6ft) – and spreads as wide as 2m (6ft 7in). Courses will include combinations – at least one double and probably a treble. These will be made more difficult as the distance between each element of the combination will not always be ideal, often requiring some adjustment in the horse's stride so that he meets the obstacle correctly. It is also important to be able to use the flying change to make sharp turns.

In your early jumping lessons you will have concentrated mainly on keeping a good jumping position without interfering with your horse. As he had more experience in jumping than you at this stage, you will have relied on him to a large extent to negotiate the obstacles. As your standard of riding improves and you progress to the larger and more difficult jumps set by course-builders in show jumping competitions, you will no longer be able to leave decisions such as where to take off, and how many strides to take between jumps, to him. From now on you will have to know how to help and influence him to make his task as easy as possible.

Natural ability in horse and rider will be an advantage but it must be supplemented by constant practice as well as further training from an expert to develop your skill and

Jumping saddle
The jumping saddle should be forward cut to allow you to ride in the correct jumping position, with your thighs lying flat across the saddle and your knees against the saddle-flaps in close contact with your horse.

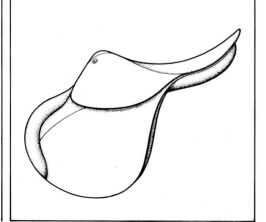

your horse's ability. If your horse has good conformation, this will also be an asset (see page 243). You will find it easier to use a special jumping saddle (see opposite).

As the jumps become bigger and more difficult, the margin of error narrows and it is essential, therefore, to take off at the correct point. The arc, or parabola, that a horse makes when he jumps (see page 67) will vary slightly in shape according to the type of obstacle. He will, for example, form a wider, flatter arc over a spread such as a water jump, and a higher, rounded arc when he clears an upright (see below).

Jumping an upright
The arc of the jump will be high and rounded (a) when taking off within the optimum take-off zone (d). If the horse takes off from too far away (b) or too close (c), it will probably result in a knockdown.

Jumping a spread
The arc of the jump will be wider (a). Lines b and c again show the results of taking off too far and too near.

However, unless the arc starts and ends in the right place, the horse will have to adapt his flight to clear the jump. This will not always be possible over a big obstacle, resulting in his knocking it down, or, possibly, refusing. It is the rider's responsibility to prevent this from happening by making a good approach, taking off within the optimum zone for each particular jump. This zone will vary according to the height and type of jump: as a general rule, the higher the fence, the narrower it will be, since there is less room for error.

You can improve your judgment of the approach by working with grids, varying the distance between each element. A "placing" pole in front of a jump will ensure that your take-off spot is correct.

The diagram below shows an example of using a placing pole before an upright. The height of the jump (a) is 1m (3ft 6in) and the distance between the pole and the jump (b) is 3m (10ft).

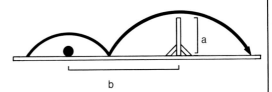

However, accuracy of take-off spot will be useless unless it is supplemented by correct balance, impulsion and speed: if a horse is unbalanced, he cannot "use" himself effectively when jumping. Without enough impulsion he will have to take off closer to the jump and make a big effort to clear it, and if travelling too fast he must take off from further away and make a long, flat parabola, risking a knockdown or even a fall. All these factors may, in turn, be closely connected with the length of the horse's stride (longer strides for greater speed, shorter ones for less speed), which may need adjustment to ensure that he arrives at the correct take-off point.

Adjusting the horse's stride
To shorten the stride, use a half-halt (see page 121), followed by positive rein actions to engage the horse's hocks, while restricting the extension of the shoulders and forelegs. To lengthen the stride, stronger leg action is used, but the rider should not lean forward in anticipation of greater speed or he will overload the forehand. All adjustments to stride should be made early in the approach, not just before take-off.

If it is necessary to adjust the horse's stride in an awkward distance, it is better to do so immediately after recovering from landing over the previous jump. For instance, if the distance between two jumps is a tricky four and a half strides, you must lose the extra half-stride as soon as possible to arrive at take-off for the next jump on a normal stride. Two examples of

Advanced jumping

Three examples of jumps requiring advanced jumping skills from horse and rider. Opposite, this high upright is being jumped successfully by the American rider Franke Sloothaak on Mon Plaisir; it has necessitated an accurate approach and take-off. Left, a gate, blocking a muddy track, which is typical of the kind of obstacle met when out hunting. Horse and rider are jumping at a slight angle, and the rider is carefully studying the landing side to avoid the worst ground. Below, this difficult cross-country obstacle, with an awkward approach down a steep slope, is testing British rider Diana Henderson's ability to control the balance, speed and impulsion of her horse, Kingmaker.

correct and incorrect adjustment of stride in such a situation are given below.

The first diagram (1) shows an incorrect adjustment. The dotted line shows how, after four normal strides, the horse must

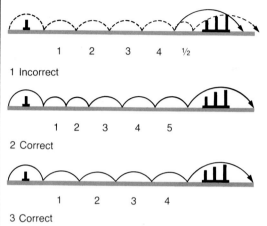

1 Incorrect

2 Correct

3 Correct

"put in a short one" before take-off. This will cause him to jump awkwardly, probably faulting at the fence, or he may even refuse. It is too late to interfere with the stride at the last moment. The unbroken line shows how horse and rider, realizing there is not enough room to take another stride, stand off too far and may not have the scope to reach the far side without hitting the jump.

The next diagram (2) shows how, after landing, the rider has shortened the next two strides to make the extra half-stride into a full extra stride without affecting the correct take-off. On a horse which lengthens stride more easily than he shortens it, yet does not lose balance when extended, the alternative method is to ask for four regular strides of longer length, as shown in the third diagram (3).

You can practise adjusting your horse's stride in an enclosed arena. Using a medium-length canter stride, practise lengthening then shortening your horse's strides, keeping his hocks well underneath him so that he remains well balanced and can change from long to short strides smoothly. When you can regulate his stride easily and accurately, count the number of strides he takes on a certain stretch, and

plan to take one more or one less the next time by making smooth adjustments using half-halts which should be almost invisible to the onlooker.

The rider's skill lies in having a fine control of the horse's balance, impulsion and speed, and in coordinating them well, so that one is not emphasized at the expense of another. For example, if you lengthen your horse's stride and increase his speed by using more leg action than rein restraint you will lose both balance and impulsion. If you shorten your horse's stride by using too much hand and too little leg action, you may have him balanced, but it may be at the expense of impulsion and speed.

Sometimes, when you cannot adjust your horse's stride, or when it is too late to do so in the approach to a fence, you may have to allow yourself more room by jumping it to one side instead of in the middle, making the change as early as you can.

Riding turns at speed

When riding a show jumping course, you will need to make frequent changes of direction, and the horse has to change his canter lead to remain well balanced. To change legs through the trot will break his rhythm, but to remain in canter, which is obviously better, necessitates a smooth flying change. Practise trotting the route of a jumping course without the jumps. When the horse will do this same exercise at a balanced canter, with short, springy strides, he is ready to make flying changes of leg on each turn. As you change direction, ask for the change of lead (see page 143). If the horse does not respond, you will have to change legs through the trot, since a false canter (on the "wrong" leg) is uncomfortable for both horse and rider.

Show jumping

Of all equestrian sports or pastimes, show jumping competitions are the most popular. They test the rider's ability to present his well-trained horse at each jump correctly and accurately so as to clear it. They are easier to organize than cross-country events, since less space and fewer officials are required. The judge, course-builder and a time-keeper are necessary, and at least two active helpers must be available to rebuild fences and replace poles when competitors dislodge them; a steward in the collecting ring is needed to send riders in to jump in the right order.

Riders find show jumping competitions exciting and often fascinating; also, since each rider is in the arena for little more than one minute, hundreds get the opportunity to compete in one day.

Meanwhile, the spectators can sit beside the ring in reasonable comfort and, at the bigger shows, may recognize well-known local horses and riders, or even some nationally known stars. The rules are easy to follow and the competitions themselves can be very exciting, with competitors riding against the clock to win, often displaying remarkable skill.

Although most show jumping competitions are held in outdoor arenas, indoor competitions are becoming increasingly popular, partly because they are so practical: they can be held despite bad weather or unsuitable ground conditions outside.

Types of competition

There are two main categories of show jumping competition: those that are affiliated to the rules of the official national show jumping association (in this country, the British Show Jumping Association) and non-affiliated competitions, which are run independently, often by local riding clubs, and are usually judged under the same rules. Classes at these shows range from the elementary "minimus" competitions to "open jumping", for the more proficient.

Most horses and riders start in the non-affiliated competitions. These may be acceptable for beginners but the standard of organization is sometimes low. For example, the course-builder and other officials may not be recognized by the national show jumping associations concerned, but instead may be inexperienced volunteers. As a result, the courses and jumps may be badly designed, and possibly unsafe. If in doubt, consult an experienced competitor before taking part. Advice as to what constitutes well-organized competitions is given on page 162.

Once the horse and rider have gained some experience in non-affiliated competitions they can then progress to affiliated competitions. To jump in these, both horse and rider must make sure they register with their national show jumping association. This categorizes horses so that an inexperienced learner or novice competes against horses of a similar standard, and does not have to jump fences designed for the more seasoned campaigners. No horse may compete until it is four years old, and only registered horses are officially graded. The grading will depend on the total prize money won in "affiliated" classes. In Great Britain the grades are A (the most advanced), B (intermediate) and C (novice). Junior classes in affiliated competitions are graded JA and JC on the same basis. Once the horse has won more than the limit stipulated for his grade, he will then be upgraded to the next level. The rules which govern the size of jumps and how a particular class will be judged are available annually from the British Show Jumping Association. At non-affiliated shows, the emphasis for the competitors is on having fun and gaining experience, and not on financial gain. Top-class show jumping, at the other extreme, has become a business for some, and at times does not even resemble "sport", with a danger of the best horses being over-exploited.

Judging

Most competitions are judged under standard rules (Table A) or speed rules (Table S). All jumping classes have a pre-arranged time allowed to complete the course. This begins from the moment horse and rider cross the starting line to the time they pass the finishing post or flag. If the time

These pictures show horses and riders at four different stages of competition: junior, novice, intermediate and advanced. Left, a pony and rider competing in a junior class at an indoor show. They are jumping this parallel confidently in good style, and look all set to progress to a higher level. Below, Michael Whittaker on Monsanta stretching out over a large spread. The big fences encountered at top-class level require very accurate jumping, and success at this level requires many years of training and experience. Right, a horse and rider jumping in an intermediate level competition. The horse has tucked up his legs neatly to clear the spread. He may not develop into a top-class jumper, but his technique here is good. Below right, in this novice class the rider is helping his young horse as he stretches to clear this small spread, but they have taken off too soon. With further training, a more controlled approach will allow the horse to jump fences more accurately and easily.

allowed is exceeded, they will be penalized with time faults and if twice the time allowed is taken, they are eliminated. When a horse refuses and displaces a fence, the clock is stopped to allow the jump to be rebuilt before the rider re-presents his horse at the jump. The winner is the one with the fewest penalties or faults.

If more than one competitor has a clear first round there will be a "jump-off" over a slightly raised and shortened course. The first jump-off may or may not be "against the clock" (i.e., the fastest wins). If, as under Table A rules, it is not, in the event of equality of faults after the second round there will be a further, timed jump-off. To jump both fast and accurately demands great skill. It is not necessarily the horse which looks the fastest which wins but, rather, the well-trained, balanced, accurately ridden horse, which can take the shortest route, turn quickly and respond to the finest of aids exactly.

In some jumping classes, speed is the deciding factor in the first round.

Faults
The horse is penalized for disobedience when he refuses to jump by stopping in front of the fence; runs out by veering off to the side of the jump(s); resists by, for example, napping (turning away, rearing or going backwards) or refusing to even approach the fence; or if the rider has to make a circle, thus crossing his tracks. He is penalized for a knockdown if, as a result of touching the fence, any part of it is lowered in height. The numbers of faults incurred for each mistake are shown below.

Penalties table

Mistake	No. of faults
1st disobedience	3
2nd disobedience of the whole round	6
3rd disobedience of the whole round	elimination
Knockdown	4
Fall of horse/rider	8
Exceeding time allowed, for each commenced second	¼
Exceeding time limit	elimination

Jumping at a show
Before competing, make sure your horse is fit, and able to cope with what is required of him. As in dressage contests, you should begin by competing at a grade slightly below the standard of training you have reached at home. When you are jumping clear rounds at this level, you can progress to more advanced competitions.

Before going to a show, check that you have all the equipment you will need (see page 174) and a haynet for the return journey. Work out your schedule to allow enough time on arrival to check in with the officials, collect your number, and study the layout of the showground; meanwhile, your horse can stand quietly after his journey.

Remove any travelling gear from your horse, and tack up. Next, prepare yourself, making sure you are correctly and tidily dressed, with boots, spurs (optional), hard hat, jacket, number (if worn), gloves and whip, if used. Walk the course (see below), then warm up your horse with a series of exercises at the trot and canter. When you feel he is ready, you can take him into the practice jumping area and then into the arena itself. Make use of any spare time by watching others jump, and noting which jumps present particular difficulties.

Walking the course
You must walk the course before the class is due to commence, in order to study both the jumps and the route you will take between them. Make sure you know the rules under which a particular class is to be run. A plan of the course is often available in the collecting ring, or near by. Study this first for the layout, and note which fences will be jumped in the jump-off, and whether or not this will be against the clock, so that you can plan ahead should you jump a clear first round. The importance of speed in the timed jump-off makes it essential to work out the shortest route possible around the course (see opposite).

When walking, plan each approach, noting the state of the ground, and decide how you will tackle any problems on the course. Walk any combination jumps with

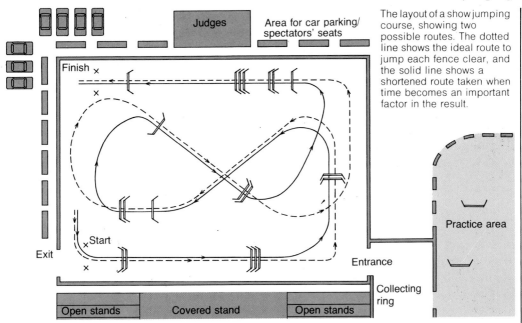

The layout of a show jumping course, showing two possible routes. The dotted line shows the ideal route to jump each fence clear, and the solid line shows a shortened route taken when time becomes an important factor in the result.

care, measuring the distance between each element to judge the number and length of strides required. If the jump follows a turn you should allow at least four strides of straight approach in the first round, particularly before spread fences, which should be jumped straight and with stronger impulsion. Plan exactly where to turn to allow a perfect approach to each jump. (This may be more of a consideration in indoor arenas, where the jumps are often set more closely together.) Upright jumps will require greater collection and accuracy, especially when following soon after a spread or combination.

The practice jumping area

Use this to help supple your horse in preparation for his first round. Approach a low jump (approx. 0.8m [2ft 6in] high) at the trot, to encourage your horse to jump off his hocks. Then canter slowly at a slightly larger jump – say, an upright with an inviting ground-line pole. Then, at your normal pace, jump the upright at the approximate height it is built in the arena, and a spread of similar dimensions. Vary your practice to keep your horse interested. Finish up over a lowered practice fence to boost his confidence before entering the ring.

Jumping the course

You may be sent in before the previous competitor has finished jumping, in which case walk quietly along the side of the arena so as not to distract him. It is polite to salute the judges just before starting your round.

After the bell rings to indicate you should start, you have a minute to prepare yourself. Do not rush, as you may tense up or change rhythm. If you have decided to approach the first jump on the right rein, pick up a right lead at the canter and settle into your rhythm.

Half-halts to balance the horse and control his impulsion may be necessary after every jump. These may have to be stronger after a big spread or water jump to re-collect him, transferring the horse's weight back towards his hindquarters if he has become too low or heavy on the forehand.

If your horse refuses, knocking down or moving the jump as he does so, the bell will ring. While it is being rebuilt, get into position ready to approach again as soon as the bell goes. The clock is stopped from the time the first bell rings until it sounds again. After three refusals, the bell will signal your elimination. On completing your round, your horse should remain on the aids until you have left the arena.

ADVANCED RIDING

Three examples of excellent style by international riders: Irish champion Eddie Macken on Boomerang, right; Johan Heins of Holland on Romeo Z, below; and John Whitaker of Britain on Milton, opposite. In each case the rider's sympathetic hands and perfect balance are giving the horse every assistance possible.

Jumping faults

Show jumping faults are categorized as knockdowns and refusals. They are mostly caused by the rider, and are usually the result of bad presentation. Jumping technique can be improved by practising on a good school horse. However, your horse's physical condition is also important when jumping. He may refuse if he is overworked or weak, or if bad riding causes him pain. His discomfort may be caused by a severe bit used in insensitive hands.

A horse may fault through lack of training, but even a well-schooled show jumper will make mistakes if presented badly at a jump. For example, approaching on an uncollected, unbalanced stride may make the horse hollow his back instead of rounding it, resulting in a "flat" jump, so that he is less likely to clear the obstacle. Alternatively, the rider may have made a good, collected approach, but in the last stride before take-off, slacken the reins. This sudden loss of contact with the horse's mouth will destroy his balance – if the rider also comes forward, the horse will find it even more difficult to raise his forehand over the jump, and may knock it down with his forelegs. Knockdowns with the hind legs usually result from approaching too fast, so that accuracy is lost, or from the rider's weight being too far back, behind the horse's centre of gravity, forcing his hind legs to drop on to the fence.

Bad presentation causes most refusals too. If the approach is too fast, with the horse's hocks not sufficiently engaged, you are more likely to misjudge the take-off point, whereas if the approach is too slow the horse will not have enough impulsion and energy to jump. A horse may also refuse when meeting a fence "wrong" (too near or too far off), although if the jump is not big and he is balanced and has impulsion, he should still jump. A crooked approach invites a run-out. This often happens in a jump-off if a rider angles a jump too sharply. It can also happen in a combination if the initial approach was not straight. Slackening the reins, and thus dropping the horse's head just in front of the fence, can unbalance a horse enough to stop him jumping, and overfacing your horse with jumps which are too big or too difficult for him may also provoke a refusal. Inexpert course-building with wrong distances between combination jumps can cause a horse to refuse if he finds himself too far from, or too close to, the final element. This, can be avoided by a more skilful approach (see pages 148–9).

The rider must give his horse confidence since a negative attitude can transmit itself to the horse. You must intend to jump and, once committed, should ride strongly towards the obstacle. A wavering or timid approach may result in a loss of impulsion and rhythm, so that you have little hope of jumping the fence without a refusal, knockdown or run-out. This can be cured at home by asking your horse to follow a keen, reliable horse over several easy obstacles, until he is going straight and evenly of his own accord.

Lack of balance can cause every kind of fault, and may also make your horse slip on wet ground, or become unnecessarily jarred on very hard ground. Although some horses have bad natural balance, this can usually be improved with the help of good weight distribution from the rider.

Finally, one-sidedness in a horse may not actually make him refuse, but could be bad enough to cause run-outs if you cannot get at the fence because your horse is "hanging" away to one side. The problem may seem to be in his mouth, but it is more likely that the horse is one-sided through his body, or has one hock working better than the other. Like humans, horses are born left- or right-handed, and must be schooled to work efficiently on both reins. Supple him with groundwork, and practise jumping on a circle and at angles, until you are completely satisfied that you have ironed out this problem.

If your horse appears to lose confidence during a show jumping round, you can gain nothing by continuing. The best thing you can do is retire, study the problem, and work on regaining his form at home. Never use force, especially as it may well be your rough and insensitive riding that is causing him to refuse.

Three examples of horses and riders faulting. Left, this horse has stopped suddenly because his rider has made a crooked approach after a sharp turn. The horse is lacking the necessary impulsion to clear the obstacle and has refused. Below, in an attempt to jump fast, horse and rider have become too unbalanced in the approach to this gate, and have pushed it on to the ground. Far below, David Broome is seen here making an uncharacteristic mistake. He and Philco have lost their accuracy, making a long, flat jump; Philco has knocked out the top of the wall with his forelegs.

Courses and jumps

When taking part in show jumping competitions it is important to choose contests that are well organized. Whatever your level of riding, try to find shows run by knowledgeable organizers, providing a spacious, level ring and well-built courses from which you can gain some experience.

The length of a show jumping course will vary between 450m (492yd) and 2,000m (2,185yd). The arena should be large enough to contain 10 to 12 jumps, including at least one combination. The start and finish must be clearly marked, and the jumps should be numbered at one side, against the wing. They may also be flagged; a red flag on the right, white on the left. The ground should not be rough or uneven, nor boggy or hard. A small collecting ring at the entrance to the main ring will be used for competitors to await their turn, and there should be a steward to control the order of jumping.

All well-organized shows should have a practice area near the main arena where competitors can warm up and use the practice jumps before competing. The jumps should include one upright (single pair of wings, two to three poles), and one spread (two pairs of wings, three poles).

Show jumps should have a strong and solid appearance, to encourage bold, confident jumping, and thus to avoid constant rebuilding. All show jumps must knock down easily, but without bringing the wings with them, which means the cups holding the poles must not be too deep. Round poles should be held in round cups, not more than half the diameter of the pole; planks should rest on flatter cups, so that they can slide off when hit. Similarly, an octagonal pole must only be used on an angled cup which allows it to fall.

The wider the aspect of the jump, the more attractive it is to the horse. If the only poles available are short, the widest possible wings must be used. Remember that big, brightly painted, colourful jumps may please spectators, but can startle the horse if they look unnatural.

Course-builders will provide a variety of jumps which are interesting for the riders, and also less repetitive for the horses, as well as making the competition visually more exciting for spectators. The first two jumps on a course should be natural-looking and easy to encourage the horse. The first should be sloping, with a good ground-line, the second could be a small upright. Spreads and uprights should alternate round the course to provide variety and interest.

To encourage a flowing style with no breaks in stride, a minimum of 18m (59ft) should be allowed between each fence (the distance will be shorter in indoor arenas, see page 157), so that you can rebalance your horse before the next jump. In combination jumps the distance will be measured from the back of the first element, or part, of the jump, to the front of the second. Equally, the turns on a show jumping course should follow a smooth route, with enough space to straighten and balance the horse in front of a fence (particularly before a combination, big spread, or water jump). An experienced course-builder who understands jumping can build a variety of good courses and get a fair result without resorting to tricks. He will position each obstacle at a suitable distance in relation to the next, so that a minimum adjustment to the canter stride of the horse should be necessary (see page 149): "wrong" distances between jumps will upset the horse's rhythm and balance, and may make him lose confidence.

A typical selection of jumps for a show jumping course is given on page 164: Although these will consist basically of uprights and spreads, they can vary in appearance. The water jump, for instance, can be used with a small hedge, or similar object, placed in front of it as a take-off guide (known as "open" water), or may have poles over it. If there are poles, the jump is judged as a knockdown obstacle; if it is without poles, the horse must land clear of the far tape, to avoid a penalty. He must jump between the red and white flags placed on each corner, but will not be penalized if he knocks over the small brush fence on take-off. The water jump should not be longer than it is wide, and the brush fence should not be narrower than the water. You should not ask your young novice horse to jump water in a competition unless he has practised over water before, at home.

A hedge can be a useful "filler" in a fence to make it look substantial and inviting to jump. Whether artificial, or a permanent, planted one, it should not be higher than any pole placed beyond it. The pole should be clearly visible to the horse, so that he can judge the height and width of the obstacle. A brightly painted, or white, pole is more obvious than a rustic, brown or green pole.

Combinations can be either doubles or trebles. A double consists of two jumps spaced at one or two strides apart. The gap between should not exceed 12m (39ft) – and this is only suitable between very big, wide jumps. A treble is a jump with three elements, again with each one spaced either one or two strides apart. The distances between will vary according to the height, and whether the jumps are uprights, spreads, or a combination of both.

On a showground where competitions are held frequently, special permanent jumps may be built to make the arena interesting and attractive to riders and spectators. However, under wet conditions the ground around the take-off and landing areas can become very cut up, taking a long time to recover, and therefore permanent fences should not be used too often, particularly if the course must be used again soon afterwards.

The water jump must be sited so that it can be avoided easily when not in use. Smaller water jumps, or water-filled ditches, can be used under or in front of poles, as variations.

Ditches add variety to a show jumping course as long as they are dug deep enough to be well defined, but not so deep that a horse could become stuck in them. Slopes are also popular, but banks are controversial. Many riders consider it unfair to ask a horse to jump on to, then off, a bank, when they have been schooled always to clear every obstacle without touching it. Others argue that a horse jumps a bank naturally, and will not be confused if well presented

Platform

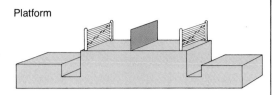

Ramp

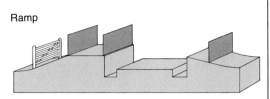

Sunken road

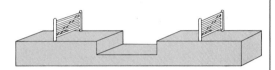

The platform, ramp and sunken road are three examples of permanent jumps which can be adapted to varying degrees of difficulty according to where the obstacles are placed. In the diagrams above the obstacles have been suitably positioned to test the horse's agility, neatness and obedience; alternative positions are indicated by the rectangular shapes. All three jumps will demand skill and accuracy on the part of the rider and, in some cases, considerable courage from the horse. The platform can be jumped from either side; the ramp and sunken road are jumped from left to right.

at an attractive-looking bank which is obviously too big to be cleared in one leap (known as an Irish bank).

There are many permanent combination-type fences which can be built such as pens and boxes, but there must always be an exit, in case the horse refuses and cannot extricate himself. Alternatively, the top rails must knock down. Examples of permanent obstacles seen in some advanced courses include ramps, platforms, or other variations using raised or sunken ground levels (see above).

A typical selection of fences at top-class show jumping competitions. Left, John Brown of Scotland on Our Gaytime, negotiating a water jump. It is attractively presented, bordered by flowers and plants to make it look as natural as possible; the small brush on the take-off side makes a good ground-line for the horse. Right, Nick Skelton of Britain jumping a parallel on Apollo. A parallel is an upright and spread combined and requires an accurate approach.

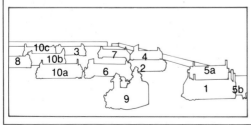

Layout of a show jumping course
1 Oxer of rustic poles over wall base; **2** Gate; **3** Parallel rustic poles; **4** Spread of poles; **5** Double: **a** upright poles over brush; **b** parallel poles over brush; **6** Spread of poles with staircase effect; **7** Upright planks; **8** Wall with upright poles; **9** Curved wall; **10** Treble: **a** wall; **b** spread of poles over brush; **c** parallel poles over brush

Eventing

"Eventing" is a term used to describe the exacting sport of one- two- or three-day events (also known as "horse trials") in which horse and rider must show their ability in three separate disciplines: dressage, cross country and show jumping.

In Britain, all official (affiliated) horse trials are governed by the British Horse Society, but they are organized and run by individual enthusiasts. Since these competitions are expensive to lay on, financial help or sponsorship may have to be found. Horses have to be registered to compete in official horse trials, and must be at least five years old. They start off in Novice events (Grade I), progressing through Intermediate (Grade II) to Advanced level (Grade III). All riders must also be registered members of their national ruling organization. In one-day events, all three phases are completed on the same day – an arduous test when competing at advanced standard.

In the three-day event the first day is confined to dressage, and preparations for the full-scale Speed and Endurance test on the second day. This will consist of four phases: A: roads and tracks, in which competitors must average approximately 1km in four minutes over a distance which will vary in length between 3 and 8km, depending on the grade of competition or on where the steeplechase is sited; B: steeplechase, a course of racing-type fences which varies from 1 to 3km in length; C: roads and

tracks, again of varying distances, but usually longer than A; and D: the cross country, probably between 4.5 and 7.5km long and consisting of 20 or more varied obstacles, depending on the grade or standard. The show jumping course on the final day is seldom difficult, but serves to show that, after the endurance test, the horse is still fit and supple, willing and obedient.

The two-day event includes a short steeplechase section and some roads and tracks, but the one-day event does not include any extra endurance tests in the cross country phase.

Success in eventing depends on a thorough training of horse and rider. For most competitors, the main attraction is the thrill of cross country riding. The course is designed to test the horse's obedience, agility and boldness as well as the rider's ability, judgment and courage when jumping fixed obstacles at speed.

It is a good idea to attend as many horse trials as possible, as a spectator or, preferably, a helper, so that you gain as much all-round experience and knowledge about eventing as possible. Take every opportunity to gain experience of riding across country over all types of fences and terrain – hunting or drag hunting provide ideal practice. You will also need guidance in dressage and show jumping from an experienced instructor or competitor. Take part in as many combined training competi-

The cross country course at the Wylye Three-Day Event, renowned for its huge variety of fences for every standard of eventer. This competitor is preparing to jump a combination of rails and steps down, and has her horse poised, perfectly balanced and fully "on the aids".

tions as you can find, to help improve your skill and techniques in these two disciplines, before entering a one-day event.

Before embarking on a full-scale three-day event, however, it would be advisable to compete in at least one two-day event. This will help you to adjust to the format of this more arduous form of eventing, in which you must learn to judge pace over longer distances, and understand the meaning of true fitness – the key to three-day eventing.

The novice event rider would do best to start off with a horse which has learned to take care both of himself and his rider by taking the initiative in awkward situations. He should have gained experience, whether competitive or in the hunting field, and should be a reliable all-rounder.

Horses of all shapes, sizes, types and breeds can be successful in Novice events, where special ability is less important than

The plan of Badminton Horse Trials – a successful layout that has been used at this famous three-day event for over two decades.

Combined training

In combined training, competitors are judged on their dual performance in dressage and show jumping. Penalty points from both phases are added together to obtain a result. This is a useful form of competition as it promotes the closer relationship of dressage and jumping training, which is so often neglected, and it is also a useful stepping stone to eventing.

There are classes for every standard from preliminary to advanced. All horses schooled to elementary dressage level should be capable of jumping a small course of show jumps approximately 1m (3ft 3in) high, and those trained to medium level should find no difficulty over jumps of up to 1.3m (4ft). Equally, correctly trained show jumpers should be able to perform an obedient dressage test, demonstrating their suppleness, good balance, impulsion, and smooth transitions of pace. The rider's ability to regulate his horse's stride– so important in the jumping arena – will also be tested, at elementary level and above.

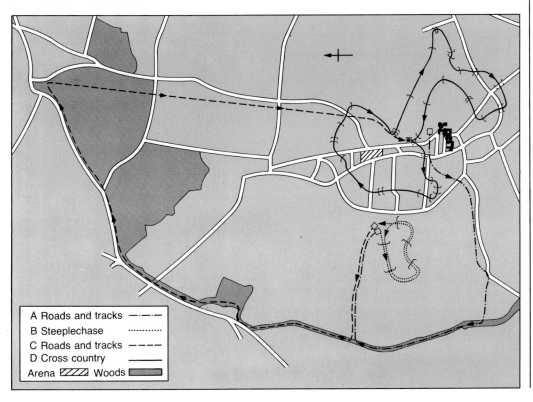

A Roads and tracks —·—·—
B Steeplechase ···········
C Roads and tracks — — — —
D Cross country ——————
Arena ▨▨▨ Woods ▉▉▉

Left, the Australian rider Andrew Hoy performing the dressage test at Badminton on Davey. He is completing the half-pass at the trot.

Below, Otto Ammerman of West Germany on the stallion Volturno in the show jumping phase at the World Championships in Lexington, USA, in 1978. Although looking down has caused his weight to tilt forwards, the rider is in no way interfering with his horse.

Right, Mark Todd of New Zealand and Charisma at the 1988 Olympics, on their way to a second individual Olympic gold medal. The rider is keeping his weight well back as they take this long drop into the water.

The challenge of the cross country course is probably eventing's greatest attraction for competitors, and spectators too. Water obstacles (left) in particular can provide dramatic moments, adding to the excitement of this sport, while uphill and downhill gradients before or after a jump (right) test the skill and balance of both horse and rider.

a good preparation and training in the dressage and show jumping tests, and the cross country is well within the scope of most horses. At three-day event level, however, the horse should be a strong, well-trained athlete, and as fit as a steeplechaser. Good conformation is an asset, since this gruelling sport will reveal any weakness in the horse, although if he has extra talent this may compensate for any possible handicaps.

Typical week of an event horse

Monday (1–1½ hours) After a rest day the horse is fresh, so start with trotting and cantering on both reins until he settles. Practise school exercises: transitions, bends and lateral movements for obedience, suppleness and balance. Hack, including trotting up hills and a short canter.
Tuesday (1–1½ hours) Schooling exercises as Monday; grid work, short hack.
Wednesday (1–1½ hours) Warm up with exercises on the flat to prepare for show jumping practice. Hack and long slow canter for equal distances on either leg.
Thursday (1 hour) Practise simple exercises and dressage movements. Hack.
Friday (1 hour) Schooling to brush up on weakest points. Short, sharp gallop ("pipe-opener").
Saturday The event.
Sunday Day off: walk out, or turn out in field.

Preparing your horse

Your horse's preparation will include months of systematic training and conditioning to bring him to his peak (see also pages 260–61).

Horses which have been fit before a winter break need about 12 weeks to prepare for their first one-day event. If the horse has not had a break, but has been working or hunting during the winter, he may need a short rest before starting on more intensive preparation.

Ideally, your horse should be fully fit with a week to spare before the beginning of the event, so that he can be allowed a comparatively easy run up to the competition without over-exerting himself.

A typical week of an event horse before his first one-day event of the season is shown left.

A week before his first three-day event, your horse will need at least one "school" over steeplechase fences. These are usually made of brushwood or birch, and are 1–1.1m (3ft 3in–3ft 9in) high.

At your first attempt, ride at a strong canter pace, similar to your cross country speed. The slope of the fences invites a long, flattish jump, not demanding great accuracy, so checking or slowing down is unnecessary unless the horse is badly balanced. Your only adjustment should be a slight alteration of balance in the last two or

Judging

All horse trials are judged on a system of penalties awarded in each phase: the competitor with the least number of penalties wins. Elimination from one phase will incur elimination from the whole competition. All horses in intermediate or advanced classes must carry a minimum weight of 165lb (75kg) on the cross country phase.

In Novice one-day events, the optimum time for completing the cross country is based on a speed of 525m per minute. For more advanced one-day events this speed is calculated at 600m per minute. In three-day events, the cross country phase is between 4,500 and 7,410m to be carried out at a speed of between 520 and 579m per minute.

| Cross Country penalties table | No. of |
Fault	penalties
1st refusal, run-out, circle of horse at obstacle	20
2nd refusal, run-out, circle of horse at same obstacle	40
3rd refusal, run-out, circle of horse at same obstacle	Elimination
Leaving the penalty zone jumping the obstacle (where penalty zones are used)	20
Fall of horse/rider at obstacle	60
Error of course not rectified	Elimination
Omission of obstacle or boundary flag	Elimination
Retaking an obstacle already jumped	Elimination
Jumping obstacle in wrong order	Elimination
For every commenced period of 3 seconds in excess of the optimum time (one-day events)	1
Exceeding the time limit	Elimination

| Show Jumping penalties table | No. of |
Fault	penalties
1st disobedience	10
Knocking down an obstacle	5
Touching boundary mark of water or feet in ditch	5
2nd disobedience in whole test	20
3rd disobedience in whole test	Elimination
Fall of horse/rider	30
Error of course not rectified	Elimination
Omission of obstacle or boundary flag	Elimination
Jumping obstacle in wrong order	Elimination
For every commenced period of 4 seconds in excess of the time allowed	1
Two-day events and three-day events: for every second in excess of time allowed	¼
Exceeding the time limit (twice time allowed)	Elimination

three strides, in order to help the horse relieve his forehand.

As an event rider you must learn how to slip your reins properly, as jockeys do, so that if you are leaning back to avoid being shot forward on landing at a drop, for instance, you will not cause interference by pulling on your horse's mouth.

Speed should gradually be increased once you have become accustomed to flying the fences, and a watch can be used to gauge your speed in metres per minutes (the required speed in an international three-day event is 690m per minute).

As you gain speed with increased confidence, shorten your stirrups to allow you to fold up neatly and move with your horse, absorbing his movement, yet clear of his back. The rider only sits down in his saddle to drive his horse strongly, or to increase his stride or speed before a fence. The faster you are galloping, the greater impact you will feel should he hit the top of a fence, or stumble on landing, and the shorter stirrups, with your feet braced forward, will help you stay in position. If you aim for a smooth, even gallop stride, your horse will jump well and enjoy himself.

Above, Nils Haagensen of Denmark on Monaco in the cross country phase at Badminton, skilfully negotiating The Slide. He is sitting centrally to give his horse every possible assistance.

Below, the British rider Lucinda Prior-Palmer (Lucinda Green) and Mairangi Bay, on the steeplechase phase of the Badminton Horse Trials. Horse and rider are in perfect balance.

Right, the American rider Bruce Davidson on J.J. Babu, making this log fence at Downlands One-Day Event look particularly easy.

One-day event

You cannot just turn up at a one-day event as you can at some shows – entries must be sent in well in advance. When you have registered yourself and your horse, you will receive the rule book and details of all events. As event courses vary in difficulty and type, find out, before making your entries, if the local competitions you have probably selected are suitable for you and your horse. If the competition is far away – more than two hours' travel, for instance – you will have to make arrangements to stable your horse overnight. Remember that you will need time to walk the cross country and show jumping courses carefully (there is often not enough time between the phases to do this), and extra time will also be needed to prepare yourself and your horse before the dressage. Some riders take their horses to the grounds of the event on the day before the competition to let them look around and settle, so that they can prepare for the dressage in competition surroundings. Decide what is best for your horse, as his performance the next day will depend on his well-being, obedience and calmness.

Make sure you have everything you need. This will include grooming and plaiting equipment, a first-aid kit, and all the normal tack which you would use for the different phases of the competition, including spare girths, stirrup leathers and reins, and an extra set of boots or bandages. If stabling the horse overnight, you will need his normal feed plus spare rations, mucking out tools, tack cleaning kit, and spare rugs. Apart from the formal riding coat and hat used for the dressage and show jumping, you will need a sweater and crash helmet for the cross country phase. On the day, take someone with you who

Right, a rider and her horse waiting at the start of the cross country phase.

Left, a competitor weighing out in the Advanced class of a one-day event.

Below, a horse being washed down after the cross country. Removing the sweat will help him dry off easily.

can help with your horse and walk the course with you. On arrival, check your horse after his journey, then collect your number and a programme. This will contain a map of the cross country course, which you should now walk if you have not already done so.

Next, tack up your horse and prepare yourself for the dressage test, making sure that everything is clean, neat and straight, and that your boots are well polished. Oil your horse's feet, unless the ground is muddy or wet. If he is turned out looking his best, it will enhance his performance in the arena. The demands of the dressage test at novice level are simple: the walk, trot and canter on both reins, a halt, and perhaps some lengthened strides at the trot. Remain calm and relaxed throughout your test, whatever happens. Never blame your horse for what goes wrong; if you are angry with him, he will become upset and nervous, which could easily affect his performance in the show jumping phase which follows.

If there is a long wait, put your horse back in the horsebox, untack him and make him comfortable. You can offer him a short drink if there are at least two hours before he works again, but no hay. Never feed hay during a competition day, however long your horse must wait. A short feed of "hard food" – not bran or chaff – can be given if there is a gap of four hours or more, but most riders prefer not to risk possible indigestion or discomfort.

Walking a cross country course

Walking the course is as important as the way you ride it. Your final score will depend on quick, economical jumping and careful preparation of your route between fences, and not just on how fast you gallop. Choose a route which will best suit your particular horse. The quickest way is usually the most direct, but sometimes it will be necessary to sacrifice a little time by taking a more cautious (and less risky) route: for instance, you or your horse may lack the necessary experience, as yet, to take on a Double Bounce (see page 182) or a difficult corner fence, and you may decide to jump the alternative offered, although it takes longer. Take into account the ground conditions, hazards such as "blind" or ill-defined ditches, or anything else which might cause a stumble or even risk injury or a fall.

Make sure you know exactly where the turning points are, if any (these will be marked with flags – red on the right, white on the left): missing a compulsory flag incurs elimination.

Try to see each fence as your horse will, remembering that an obstacle which seems formidable to you may be less so to him, whilst a bad approach to the simplest fence could make it impossible for him to jump it.

Watch out for false ground-lines which could make a fence deceptive to your horse. Shadows, too, can cause optical illusions, so try to walk the course at the same time of day that you will be riding it, especially in a three-day event, to see the effects of the light on a particular fence.

Study and assess each jump to decide where the problems lie, paying special attention to combinations (see page 182), which need particularly accurate riding. These are either numbered as separate fences or as part of the same obstacle. Make sure you are clear about the appropriate ruling. If a combination is marked as 9a, 9b, 9c, it is judged as one obstacle, and the third refusal at any part of it will eliminate you. If you refuse at any one element, you are allowed to retake the entire complex if this gives you a better chance to clear it, or you can retake it from the element you have refused. However, separately numbered elements – 9, 10, 11 – are judged separately, although positioned together, and you are permitted two refusals at each of these jumps without being eliminated. If you retake 9, having refused at 10, you will be eliminated for retaking a jump already jumped, as it is numbered as a separate jump.

Certain obstacles invite refusals (see page 183). For instance, water can be a "stopper", and must be ridden strongly, yet carefully. Wade through it yourself to test it for depth and a level base, before you plan your route. Remember that most surfaces will deteriorate eventually if all the horses are landing in about the same spot. If you are riding late in the order, you may be wise to jump slightly to one side, to avoid a dangerous patch.

Use any spare time to watch fellow competitors in the show jumping ring, or on the cross country course, and see how different horses and riders cope with various problem fences.

Start getting your horse ready at least half an hour before you are due to show jump, as you will need about 20 minutes to warm up. Tack him up, and put on the boots or bandages he normally wears, then dress yourself tidily.

You will need a helper at the practice jump. Use your usual warming-up procedure – you will know by now what works best for your horse. When satisfied that he is jumping carefully and well, walk him about until it is your turn. Do not sit around, or he will get cold and stiff or "switch off". Keep calm when in the show jumping ring, and remember the main principles of balance and impulsion.

After this phase, return to the horsebox or trailer. There is usually at least an hour in which to prepare for the cross country.

In an Advanced class of a one-day event you may want to "weigh out" before the cross country phase. This means weighing yourself, plus saddle and weight cloth (if carried) on the scales provided, to make a minimum total of 75kg (165lb). Your hat will be included, but not your whip or bridle. Before saddling up, distribute the lead evenly in the weight cloth, so that it is not bulky or uncomfortable.

Secure the safety strap on your crash helmet, and the tapes on your number-cloth, and check your horse's tack before getting on. Adjust the stirrups to their most comfortable yet effective length for jumping at speed, and check the girths and surcingle again for tightness, after walking around for a minute. Then find a suitable place to give your horse a "pipe-opener".

Arrive at the start area at least five minutes early. It will probably be a standing start, but the starter will warn you of the procedure and will give you a countdown. As he says "Go!", the time-keepers press the timing button for you to start the cross country phase (see page 180).

Left, the British partnership of Diana Clapham and Martha, folding up well over a solid tree trunk.

The three-day event

Three-day event competitors usually arrive at least two days before the event is due to commence, to allow their horses to settle down in new, exciting surroundings. This time can be used for brushing up your dressage and to do some practice jumping or cantering. There will be a preliminary briefing, when any special instructions or information will be issued. This will be followed by a conducted tour of the roads and tracks and the steeplechase course, in which you must study the route, noting the best ground and the most direct path to take. There are many factors to consider, which will influence your decisions. For example, your horse will probably need to walk during the first kilometre of Phase C (roads and tracks), to recover after the arduous steeplechase, and this lost time must be made up later on in this phase. You must decide which is the most suitable ground to canter, and where to trot.

On the steeplechase course, take the shortest possible route, as every second will count. A twisty, or irregular-shaped track may include some sharp bends, and hugging the rail or ropes too closely may cause you to slow up, losing rhythm, time and possibly balance.

You will also be shown the layout of the "box" – an enclosed collecting area where you will spend the 10-minute compulsory halt before Phase D of the Speed and Endurance test.

This will be followed by your first inspection of the cross country course. This can be walked several times, in groups or alone (see page 175). During the preliminary walk round, you will get your first impression of the course. On the second, you can take an adviser with you, and should study each fence in detail from all angles, to decide which route is the best – that is, the safest, quickest and most suitable for your particular horse. Finally, you should walk the course alone, following the exact route you intend to take, and memorizing it.

At the first veterinary examination, before the dressage starts, the horses will be tested to ensure that they are fit enough to take part in the competition.

On the first day of the actual event, which is the dressage phase, you and your horse should be well turned out. Before the test itself, competitors will ride in as usual, remembering that very fit and keen three-day event horses may need a longer preparation to produce a calm, obedient performance. It may help to allow your horse to stand quietly and watch, gradually taking in the atmosphere, so that he is mentally as well as physically prepared to perform at his best. When the "ordeal" is over, you should return your horse to the stable, cool and relaxed, to rest in preparation for the Speed and Endurance test.

Meanwhile, you will probably return to the cross country course for another look. You must also collect together the equipment you will need in the box the next day. This must include buckets, sponges, and a sweat-scraper for washing down; spare reins, stirrup leathers and girths; a spare set of shoes, and studs (if used); waterproof sheets or rugs, and veterinary equipment. Competitors must also work out their timing schedule for the roads and tracks in advance. (Each kilometre will take, on average, just under four minutes. You should plan to allow two minutes to spare at the start of the steeplechase, for adjusting girths and stirrups.)

The second day of the event is the Speed and Endurance test. The day begins with the usual stable routine of feeding and mucking out – your horse must be fed at least two-and-a-half hours before it is due to start and his water removed at least an hour before.

Have your horse led up to the start of Phase A, the first road and tracks. This will conserve his energy while you "weigh out" on the official scales provided at the start. After this, saddle up your horse, 10–15 minutes before he starts Phase A. On the roads and tracks, use a relaxed trot, or slow canter. If there is a suitable stretch of good ground, this is useful for a short, sharp sprint (gallop) as a "pipe-opener" which will clear his wind before the next phase.

Arrive at the steeplechase and relax the horse, if possible, by walking about calmly and quietly. You will have to check the

Above, the preliminary veterinary inspection at a three-day event.

Right, a competitor at Badminton 1982, clearing the Whitbread drays – an ingenious obstacle whose daunting appearance is, fortunately, more alarming to the riders than the horses.

Below, a competitor on Phase C, the second roads and tracks section of the Speed and Endurance test.

girths and adjust the stirrup leathers for riding the course at near-racing pace. The steeplechase course must be ridden within the horse's capacity, according to his ability, fitness and energy, although you will have aimed to complete it without time penalties. Pull up carefully at the end, since a rough or sudden stop may cause your horse to go lame.

On the second road and tracks (Phase C), you should walk at first to allow your horse to regain normal breathing, and until he is willing and ready to trot on. This phase

The Speed and Endurance test

On the cross country course, try to stick closely to your carefully planned route, as any unprepared change of approach could prove disastrous. Your decisive attitude is essential to inspire your horse with much-needed confidence.

Although you will be moving fast when riding the course, you must not allow your horse to become too low on his forehand, or you will risk hitting these fixed obstacles. Too much weight on his forelegs restricts the free movement of the horse's shoulders and his hocks are likely to be out behind him, which will make jumping more difficult for him. Balance is all-important. To help your horse to jump easily, therefore, you will often need to sit up a little more on the approach, to allow him to adjust his balance in order to overcome any awkward situation or obstacle he may encounter on the course.

You will have to adapt your riding to varying weather conditions, which could affect a course drastically: a deluge of rain on the day, for instance, will make the ground heavy, with poached or boggy take-offs and landings.

Start off strongly. Although the first fence is usually comparatively easy, with a straight approach of at least 46m (50yds), your horse may not yet be fully concentrating or settled into his rhythm, so insist on his full attention. Check his balance, then take it in your stride. By the time you reach the second fence, you should have picked up the stride and rhythm that you will be using over most of the course ahead. After jumping the last fence on a course, resist the temptation to gallop wildly to the finish. It is even more important than usual to hold him together when he is tiring, so pull up gradually at the end.

If your horse tires towards the end of the course, keep an even rhythm and give him extra support between hand and leg. You may have to take easier, alternative routes at some of the last fences, so bear this in mind when walking the course.

When a horse which normally jumps well starts to falter at, or hit the fences hard, he is probably tired or could be in pain,

should be completed with the horse as cool and relaxed as possible, preferably at a walk. On arrival at the box, the horses will be inspected for soundness by a veterinary panel. When passed as fit to continue, the next 10 minutes are used to refresh the horse as effectively as possible. While one person holds him, the saddle is removed and the horse sponged over quickly with clean water. He is then walked around to dry off and relax, but must not get cold – he should wear a sweat rug, at least. During the 10-minute halt, riders may seek helpful information as to how the course is being ridden. Then, with three minutes to go, it is time to remount.

Once on your horse again, you must adjust your girths and stirrup leathers.

As horses often get excited before the start, most riders do not enter the starting box until the last possible moment, to avoid a false start or unnecessarily agitating their horses. In extreme cases, the horses are sometimes held.

After the cross country phase, the horse should be washed down, and led away to his stable for rest and sustenance.

On the final day of the event, a veterinary inspection is held to examine the horses' condition before he takes part in the show jumping phase. The jumps will not be particularly demanding, but are designed to test whether the horse has retained his suppleness and is obedient after his Speed and Endurance test.

There may be a parade before the jumping, followed by prize-giving.

and you should pull up. It is a disgrace, as well as a distressing sight, for any rider to allow his horse to become exhausted. If his breathing is laboured, and he loses his rhythmic action and starts to sway, do not jump another fence: it could prove fatal.

The cross country course

You will encounter a wide variety of fences on a good course (see below), each one demanding a different approach.

Straightforward obstacles such as the Log Pile (fence 2), although inviting-looking, may have a wide spread and must therefore be approached strongly.

You will also need impulsion, but less speed, when jumping up, as, for instance, out of a road (fence 12), but you must be prepared to come well forward on take-off to stay with your horse.

By now, your horse should be used to jumping ditches without hesitation. However, this should never be taken for granted, as a hole in the ground can often take him by surprise: prepare with collecting aids early in the approach, and be ready to ride on strongly in the final strides, in case he peers at the ditch for too long. Often, there is a fence built over the ditch, making it a Trakehner (fence 13). When

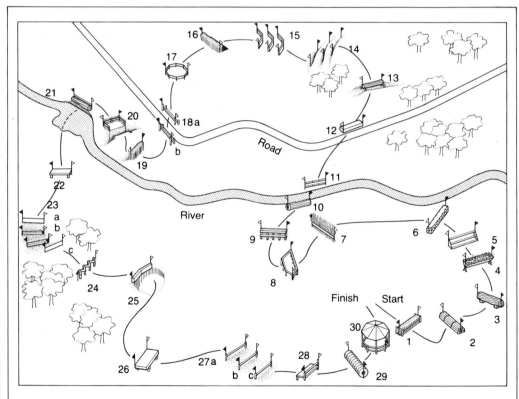

Layout of advanced cross country course for a three-day event

1 Rails and Gorse Heath	11 Rails out of River	21 Trout Hatchery
2 Log Pile	12 Bank out of Road	22 Table
3 Tree Trunk	13 Trakehner	23 Double Coffin (a, b, c)
4 Hayrack	14 Step Down	24 Zig Zag Rails
5 Sloping Rails	15 Double Bounce	25 Quarry
6 Stone Wall	16 Hedge and Ditch	26 Wagon
7 Bullfinch	17 Cage (circle)	27 Downhill Rails (a, b, c)
8 Corner or Bounce Rails	18 Rails: a into road; b out of road	28 Chair Fence
9 Hedge and Oxer	19 Hedge and Drop	29 Tyres
10 River Crossing	20 Normandy Bank	30 Arrow head

Above left, this horse is showing incredible scope as he takes off a long way in front of this log pile spread fence, making a huge, spectacular leap that will carry him safely clear of the obstacle.

Above, a horse and rider perfectly balanced to spring up out of a road on to a stone-faced bank.

Left, the take-off and landing on this Trakehner are uneven, and have caused the horse to jump into the bank, stumbling before recovering his balance.

Riding the steeplechase course

Riding a steeplechase course requires a special technique, and you must practise before competing in your first three-day event (see page 174). The rider's aim is to cross the fences fluently and fast, with economy of effort, but at the same time avoiding time penalties.

Captain Mark Phillips of Britain taking a steeplechase fence in the 1988 Olympics.

When learning to jump at great speed, the rider may become left behind, with only his hands on the reins to save his balance. Do not, therefore, shorten your stirrups too much before you can maintain your balance without hanging on to the reins.

If you tug at a hard puller, he will fight back, which will throw you about in the saddle, and exhaust you both. Brief, sharp checks will be more effective, offering a light rein between each check, to encourage him to settle. A lazy horse, on the other hand, may drop his bit, and will need encouragement. Keep your horse balanced, particularly when approaching each fence, so that he can easily take off far away ("standing off"), or put in a short stride if necessary, and avoid asking for very long jumps, especially when he is tiring.

At the end, pull up gradually, rather than suddenly or in jerks, which could possibly lame your horse.

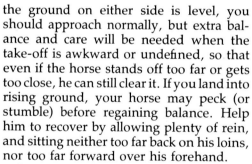

Above, Steps Down, requiring an extra secure position from the rider.

Top right, the Double Bounce – a complex combination which

necessitates an accurate approach.

Right, a hedge and drop test a horse as he cannot see the landing from the take-off side.

the ground on either side is level, you should approach normally, but extra balance and care will be needed when the take-off is awkward or undefined, so that even if the horse stands off too far or gets too close, he can still clear it. If you land into rising ground, your horse may peck (or stumble) before regaining balance. Help him to recover by allowing plenty of rein, and sitting neither too far back on his loins, nor too far forward over his forehand.

Steps up or down (fence 14) require different degrees of impulsion. When jumping down, the horse must see where he has to put his feet. A trot approach is often best, since he will gain impetus with each step, particularly if your weight is too far forward, unintentionally pushing him on too fast so that he may lose his footing. You should lean back slightly to avoid this, and allow him all the rein he needs, while retaining enough control and impulsion to keep him going straight, and smoothly.

When jumping combination fences, the most direct route is then the most difficult

and you must decide whether this, or an alternative way, will suit your horse best. Whichever approach you choose will require accurate riding. At a Double Bounce (fence 15), the most direct route is straight through the middle, jumping each element without a stride between them. Unless your horse is a bold, athletic jumper, this way could prove too difficult for him, both mentally and physically. He must be perfectly balanced and obedient, so that you can achieve an accurate take-off at the first and most vital element. Alternative routes can be taken by approaching from the left or right, but these could prove more difficult as well as more time-consuming as awkward turns are involved.

A big fence with a drop on the landing side (fence 19) must be attacked strongly, to

Left, a hesitant approach at this bank has caused the horse to change his mind at the last moment, as he was lacking sufficient impulsion or confidence to clear it.

Above, the Trout Hatchery at Burghley, a notoriously difficult obstacle which demands courage, balance and a correct approach.

give your horse every chance to land far out, which lessens the shock of a steep descent, as he can keep on going. Remember to sit well back, and grip tight, with your feet braced against the stirrups to take the impact, but allow him sufficient rein to recover his equilibrium.

Refusals must be avoided at all costs: it is often safer to jump than stop! (fence 20). A ramp or bank in front of a drop (such as a Normandy Bank) requires two changes of balance. The bank could cause your horse to falter in his stride; to prevent any loss of energy you must help him by riding into it with increasing, but controlled impulsion, aiming to land well out of the far side, otherwise the horse will meet the ground heavily, with unhappy results for both horse and rider.

Another type of obstacle that often causes refusals is a water jump (fence 21) in its various forms. You may either have to clear the water in one leap, jump over a fence in the water, or jump directly into the water. The latter requires courage, good balance and trust in the rider, for the horse does not know its depth.

Always approach water positively, since any hesitation will be transmitted to the horse, but never so fast that you risk toppling over in the water, since the weight of water stops a horse dramatically. You must therefore brace yourself against this, grip tightly and lean back, allowing him to use his neck and head freely, as always. Once in, keep going, as he will need extra energy if he has to jump out again or climb a steep bank. Lean well forward, or you will be 'left behind and impede him. Some horses are too bold when jumping into water, and it is then wise to approach it at a strong, balanced trot in case they over-jump; others are nervous of it, and must be ridden with sympathy but determination.

The Double Coffin fence demands a bold, athletic and obedient horse. The rider must ride accurately particularly in the initial approach, and maintain a well-balanced position throughout, to help his horse.

The first two pictures show the horse bouncing over two ditches without a stride between them; the third shows the horse jumping the final element of this combination fence, after one stride on the bank.

Below, a Pagoda. Unusual obstacles such as this, test the courage of the horse, which must have complete trust in the rider, who in turn must ride accurately.

Jumps where the landing side cannot be seen can frighten the horse. Coffin-type fences (fence 23) ask a horse to be bold, athletic and clever. It is the rider's responsibility to approach using the right combination of speed and impulsion, on a perfectly balanced shortened stride, to give the horse every chance to negotiate it smoothly. Your own balance is equally important, not only to stay on, but to help your horse to adapt to the changes of gradient. The central or direct route is often the best. The first element is crucial, but once over this, he should have little trouble with the following parts; you must always approach such combinations positively, to avoid a refusal, and be prepared for your horse to hit the first element, as he may suddenly use it as a "brake" when he sees the unexpected hazards ahead of him.

The nature of cross country fences will vary according to the contours of the land, and the skill of the course-builder, and also ground conditions can be drastically affected by the weather. This means that your horse must learn to expect and accept anything you face him at, but you must never abuse his trust by overfacing him or making an impossible approach. Even the simplest upright rail demands accurate riding, so you should never lose concentration. Occasionally a horse is asked to jump "unnatural" fences, such as the House at Lexington (World Championships, 1978) (fence 30), or a painted wagon or boat, and you must give him the confidence he needs. There is no place for hesitation in good and successful cross country riding.

Training the horse

The early stages

Training a horse for riding begins when an unbroken horse is prepared to be backed and ridden. Once he is broken in, he can be schooled to respond to the rider's aids so that he can be enjoyed as an all-round riding horse. However, some horses may then go on to specialized further education (for dressage, show jumping, for example). The average horse and rider do not usually reach this later stage, either because the horse lacks special ability or because his preparatory education was either inadequate or non-existent. (Most spoiled horses, however, can be retrained using the methods outlined later in this section.)

Aims

While learning to ride, you will have gained experience from handling a wide variety of horses, adapting your approach according to their individual characteristics, and becoming increasingly sensitive in your understanding and application of the aids. Unless you are an experienced horseman, with a thorough knowledge of horses and how they work, do not embark alone on training a young horse. However experienced you are, a good assistant is essential when starting to train any horse. He or she should have a quiet, reliable temperament and must be physically fit.

Make sure both you and your assistant are clear as to your aims in training, and how you expect to achieve them: conflicting or vague instructions will confuse the horse. Specific training programmes and schedules will vary depending on the type and character of your horse, his intended future under saddle, and your skill as a trainer. Remember that your principal aim when training the young horse is that he should enjoy being ridden and be pleasant to ride. He should not only be willing to comply with your wishes but should also be physically capable of doing so with ease.

A positive approach is vital from the start, for you need to gain the horse's confidence and respect – to provide a firm basis for training. Lessons in obedience can begin during the first weeks of a foal's life,

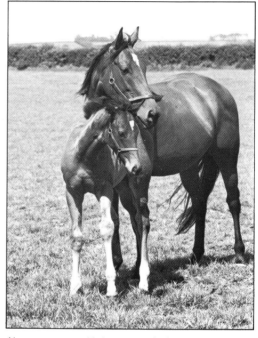

Above, a mare with her young foal.

and should be progressive – teaching him first to obey your voice and hand, and the whip, and eventually the aids, which become increasingly refined.

Understanding the horse

To train a horse successfully you must have a basic knowledge of a horse's conformation and anatomy. This will help you to understand the individual characteristics of each horse so that you can avoid making unsuitable demands. Quite often, a physically mature and self-confident three-year old is able to work harder than a poorly developed nine-year old.

Muscles cannot be built in a matter of days, but with systematic work they will develop greater strength. It is therefore important to understand the anatomy of the horse so that you can help him to perform easily and efficiently. Although people speak of "fat being turned into muscle", these are two different substances and such a conversion is impossible. But it is possible to reduce fat with gradual conditioning work, and to increase muscle with skilful and patient training.

Physical ability alone is not enough. The horse must *want* to use his ability and produce it happily, otherwise it will be squandered. If any horse is overtaxed, he will become disobedient. To persuade the horse to work for you and with you at all times, it is important to understand his mentality as well as his anatomy.

The horse has limited intelligence and powers of concentration but he is usually a willing and generous animal who wants to please. It is up to you to encourage these qualities by putting the lessons across simply and obviously. To do this requires common sense, experience and sensitivity on the part of the trainer. For instance, each lesson should be planned in advance, with specific goals to suit the individual horse and his stage of training. The trainer cannot always keep rigidly to his plan and there may be setbacks. But it is up to the trainer to judge accurately how much training to do, and for how long, without tiring or boring the horse. The trainer must retain the horse's full attention by varying the exercises, keeping them short and giving praise whenever appropriate. The lessons should be fun, otherwise the horse will become idle or even uncooperative. Never use force except as a last resort, and only then to win a battle. A good trainer, however, always remains in control; if the trust and confidence of the horse is lost, it may never be regained completely.

The difference between "yes" and "no" must always be made clear to the young horse, and both praise and punishment should be given immediately. Punishments such as jerking the rein, or using the whip or voice harshly usually do more harm than good. The horse will not necessarily have understood what he did wrong (if he had, he would probably not have misbehaved), and he will become nervous and jumpy as a result.

A horse cannot be bribed with titbits to perform well in the same way that a dog can, because his reasoning powers are not developed in this way. The best reward is through his sensitive response to feel and hearing – by a pat, a kind word or, best of all, release from restraint (giving him a loose rein, or dismounting, for instance).

Training a riding horse is always a two-way communication. Once you have established a good working relationship, you can set about producing a well-trained and well-developed horse.

Left, training a young horse on the lunge. All young horses are trained from the ground before being backed and ridden, and lungeing the horse is one of the most important preparatory phases in his development.

Preparation in hand

The newborn foal

It is never too soon to give a young horse his first lesson. Foals, unless born in the wild, can and should be handled from birth to accustom them to human contact. This is achieved easily if the foal is born in a stable or barn, but it may be some days before you can approach a foal born outside. Some owners like to use a special foal halter soon after the foal is born, so that he can be held, and led to and from his pasture if necessary, instead of running loose. It also allows the foal to be handled more easily, and is useful if he has to be treated by a vet. The halter must be soft, and must fit the head closely so that it cannot catch on anything. If the foal is stabled at night, the halter should be removed, for safety. As he grows rapidly, the halter must be checked frequently to make sure it still fits.

Handling the young foal

Foals can be surprisingly strong. Therefore, to hold a foal, you should put one arm under his neck, near the chest, and the other arm behind his hindquarters. A second person can then quietly slip the halter on him, while talking to him soothingly. When handling the foal, always keep your voice and movements quiet and gentle, to give him confidence.

Gradually accustom the foal to being touched all over, starting with his neck, back and quarters; it may take several days before he accepts this human contact. When he does, teach him to pick up each foot, as this training is essential for later hoof and foot care. Although he may be difficult, never become angry or impatient, and always reward him with kindness when he responds to the smallest demand.

Some foals are groomed. Although this is excellent handling, it is not necessary unless the foal is being shown, and it is inadvisable if the foal lives out, because you will remove the grease from his coat and he may get cold.

If possible, avoid tying up a young foal. If he struggles, he may injure himself, and will certainly be frightened. If you must tie him up, make sure he is attached by a string which is fine enough to break easily should he pull back. Tie up the mare rather than the foal if they are feeding together in a stable or shed.

Once halter-broken, the foal should be taught to stand still when held, and to move over when asked.

Leading a foal

As the foal gets older, stronger and more independent, he must be taught to "lead" – that is, to be led on a rein or rope without pulling away, forward or back. Loop the rope through the halter rather than tying or clipping it on, so that it can be released quickly. At first, lead the foal beside the mare in an enclosed area with all possible exists closed, so that if he gets loose he can be caught again easily.

Progress to leading the foal behind the mare, then in front, and then slightly apart from her. Then teach him to stand still; first beside the mare, then behind, then in front and, eventually, on his own.

Although discipline is not vital before the foal is weaned, these early lessons are never wasted, if sensibly taught. Be careful not to overdo the training because he will only understand simple commands.

When leading the foal, stand level with his shoulder. You may carry a whip in your outside hand to encourage him to go forward if he refuses to move, but it is better at first for your assistant to walk behind the foal, urging him forward if he stops.

Never twist the foal's lead-rope or rein around your hand. If he is startled and tries to break away, your hand could be crushed or burned. It is better to let go than to try to "anchor" the foal in this way. If you can possibly prevent the foal getting loose, however, do so. A loose foal can cause havoc, and if he escapes, he may try again.

To hold a foal securely, take the rein in your right hand close to the halter, just behind his chin, holding the end and folds of the slack rein in your left hand.

Showing the foal

Some foals are taken to shows, so that mare and foal can be judged for good conformation, condition and type. This can be a good

Above, this foal has learned to graze alongside his mother and will soon be ready for weaning.

Left, when handling young foals, take time to gain their confidence.

Above, leading a mare and foal – the halter (as here) or a slip rein can be used on the foal.

Weaning

The foal is separated from the mare at about six months, so that he can be weaned. Initially the foal may be frantic, and for this reason it is better to wean two or three foals together so they can take comfort in each other's company. They should be shut together in a barn or stable where they cannot injure themselves or escape. After a few days they will relax, become more interested in "adult" food, and be ready to be turned out into a field.

After weaning, the foal's education continues with lessons on leading, stopping, starting, walking straight, and turning. You must lead him from both sides to prevent one-sided habits developing.

Never use a bridle, however wilful the foal may be. The bit will damage his soft young mouth and the pain may possibly cause a permanent aversion to it – acceptance of the bit when the young horse is ridden is of paramount importance. Accustom the foal to being tied up. Stay with him at first to watch his reaction, and always use some form of quick-release knot. To begin with, keep him tied up while you pick out his feet and handle him. If he is happy,

education for the future, as the foal will become accustomed to the excitement of many different sights, sounds and smells.

Before showing a foal, make sure that you can control him. Practise at home, and get him used to cars, tractors, and people, for example. Practise, too, leading the foal into a trailer or horsebox, with the mare, until he enters with confidence. On the day of the show, it is better for both mare and foal to travel in the box loose, as it would be unwise to tie the foal up at this stage.

Be careful not to travel him or show him too much: over-education at this stage can lead to training problems later. Be careful also not to spoil a youngster by feeding him titbits. He may learn to bite, and this, along with any other bad habits, must be stopped at once.

leave him tied up, preferably giving him a haynet. But do not leave him for too long as he may become bored and restless. Once he will stand quietly in the stable, tie him up outside, in a safe place, where he cannot come to any harm if he pulls loose. Also accustom him to cross-ties (see page 262).

Make each lesson short and enjoyable, frequent repetition is the best method of instructing the foal. Always be firm but never rough, and reward him often with your voice and hands.

As the foal grows into a yearling, his legs will become stronger and he can learn to trot up in hand, and to stand properly.

Trotting up

To teach the foal to trot up, pull on the head collar a little to suggest a faster pace, but do not try to drag him along or jerk the rope, as it could have the opposite effect of making him unwilling to move on. Instead, teach him to respond to your voice. Ask your assistant to follow behind the foal and,

when you want to trot, say "Trot", click your tongue and, with your outside hand, flick the whip or rope behind you, at his flank or rear end. At the same time, your assistant may have to urge the foal forward from behind, waving a schooling whip or tapping him with it if necessary. He will understand eventually, and will learn to respond to your voice alone. Run straight, your shoulder level with the foal's.

Standing square

Good deportment is important for young horses, and you should teach yours to stand up straight – a leg at each corner. At first you can pick up and arrange his legs, rewarding him when he is "square". Some horses naturally stand more tidily than others; weak, gangly and immature youngsters, however, should not be expected to cope with this exercise until older.

Below, a two-year old (left of picture) and a yearling – some yearlings are mature enough for their first lessons on the lunge.

The yearling

A reasonably mature (well-developed) yearling can be lunged a little, although only for a few minutes on each rein. As the joints are not yet fully formed at this stage (he has little muscle), there is an obvious risk of injury. An experienced trainer will know how much to ask of a yearling or whether to delay the first lessons on the lunge until the horse is two or three years old. If you are uncertain as to your yearling's development, seek advice.

Thoroughbreds destined to race on the flat are broken in during their second winter – while still yearlings. Many of them are lunged, long-reined, backed and ridden and have started cantering before their second birthday. Most horses cannot be broken as yearlings, however, because they are insufficiently developed. A racehorse can be reared with a view to racing at two years, but even then he may be too "backward" to be trained for racing until he is a year older. The process should be carefully planned. If it is not, only the toughest or the lucky will survive this hard training without permanent damage.

All yearlings, however, should learn to obey your hand and voice and to tie up quietly. Before going on to lunge him, you should complete your horse's training "in hand" so that he obeys voice commands, and light hand signals on the lead rein. By now he should walk and trot beside you without pulling against the rope; he should also stop when you say "whoa" or "halt" (remember to use one or other of these, not both) and should walk on and trot on when you tell him. He should stand still until asked to move on. If you press your outside hand on his flank as you say "walk on", he will not be surprised when you use your leg aids later on to give a similar signal.

Training facilities

Once the horse is ready for training, you will need the appropriate equipment, described overleaf, and a suitable area where he can first be led, then lunged, and finally long-reined. The area should be on good level ground, preferably enclosed by a high fence to block out distractions such as noise or the sight of other horses.

Although it is possible to train a horse directly from the field he lives in, your task will be made easier if you have the use of a stable, as it will be easier to control him within its confines.

An indoor arena is ideal provided it has a good floor surface. However, some excellent outdoor all-weather surfaces have been developed, functioning most successfully on well-drained land, such as chalk or sand. Clay-type soils provide an unsuitable base, and will involve you in expense if you try to improve the drainage and surface by laying stones or gravel as a base under the all-weather surface.

Without a good indoor or outdoor enclosed arena, you must make the best of what you have. If you have access to a field, use one corner. This will provide you with two "sides" for guidance; four open sides invite trouble and make it difficult for you to ride straight lines and accurate circles.

If possible, mark out your own arena, using boards on two sides at least. Alternatively, you can use a white, marked line, or a mown line. Since you want your horse to go straight, so that he develops on each side equally, a guiding line is of great assistance in his training.

Plastic cones or wooden boxes can be used as markers. Bright pegs stuck in the ground can also be used but these are less safe, as the horse may trip over them.

A well-worn track helps to guide a young horse but he should not become too reliant on it because, at an early stage, he must learn to go wherever you want, without deviating. An over-used path can become deep and muddy, spoiling your horse's paces and confidence, or it may bake hard like a rough road. If you must use a "fixed" outdoor arena, try to keep just inside or outside the track.

Lungeing equipment

Make sure the equipment you use is in good condition, and that it is soft and supple: your horse's comfort is important for good results. The various items of equipment that you will need are:

Boots These (like bandages) are used to protect the horse's joints and tendons from knocks (see page 278).

Bandages These can be used in the same way as boots, and may cover the fetlocks; they must be applied correctly, as shown on page 278.

Knee caps Your horse should wear knee caps if he has to go on the road or over rough, stony ground, as there is a risk that he may stumble onto his knees, if frightened.

Lungeing cavesson This is a vital piece of equipment as it is used to control the horse while he is being lunged. It can be adjusted to fit the horse perfectly, and is well-padded so that it does not rub. It must not be too heavy as the extra weight will affect the horse's balance. However, the lungeing cavesson should be very strong.

Lunge-rein This should be made of strong webbing ideally and should be about 10m (35ft) long. A snap-hook fastening is easy to clip on, but a buckle is also safe to use. A swivel joint is useful as it prevents the rein from twisting. If you use a rope instead of a lunge-rein, it could hurt your hands if the horse pulls away suddenly. Always wear a strong pair of gloves to prevent rein burns.

Lungeing whip This should be as light and as long as possible. A short whip is useless because, if you have to reduce the size of the lungeing circle to reach the horse, you will strain his legs.

Side-reins These are used to improve your general control of the horse and his bearing. They are usually made of plain

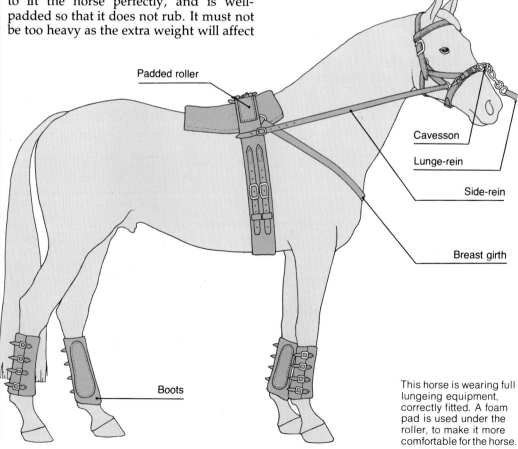

Padded roller

Cavesson

Lunge-rein

Side-rein

Breast girth

Boots

This horse is wearing full lungeing equipment, correctly fitted. A foam pad is used under the roller, to make it more comfortable for the horse.

leather and should be light, with plenty of holes to allow for adjustment. A clip-hook on one end with an adjusting buckle at the other is normal. Elasticated side-reins tend to have too much "take" in them, cancelling out any "give" they may allow.

Padded roller with breast girth attachment This is used before the saddle is introduced. A foam pad can be placed under it, in the saddle area.

Bridle and bits A simple snaffle is suitable for early training. Key-ring bits are used by some trainers when the horse is first introduced to a bit, as the horse plays with the keys, producing saliva. A "wet" mouth encourages a horse to accept his bit, whereas a "dry" mouth can become sore, leading to resistance. A very thick mouthpiece will be uncomfortable as the horse will have difficulty closing his mouth, while a thin bit is sharp on the bars of the mouth, causing discomfort, and also leading to evasion. An eggbutt snaffle bit, which does not pull through the horse's mouth or rub at the corners, is normally used. It should fit perfectly and must never be too wide, otherwise the action of the bit will be painfully severe. A straight bar bit has the advantage of discouraging the horse from putting his tongue over it – a habit that is hard to cure. However, because it has no "play" or "give", the horse tends to lean on the bit.

Saddle This must fit perfectly, with or without a numnah. Make sure that from the first time you "back" your horse the saddle puts you into the correct place over the horse's centre of gravity.

Schooling whip This should be approximately 90cm (35in) long.

Neckstrap This is useful, as is a martingale, in some cases.

Lungeing the young horse

Lungeing enables you to train and exercise a horse from the ground. Indispensable throughout the riding horse's life, its first and most vital role is to provide the foundations of his education. It is possible to train a horse on the lunge to a very high standard, as shown by the Spanish Riding School and other experts.

To lunge a horse, you stand still and send the horse around you in a circle, on the end of the lunge-rein. It is a skilled art, even in the elementary stages. You should, therefore, assist an experienced trainer before trying to lunge a horse yourself. If you are not an expert, but have experienced help, keep the lungeing to its simplest aims: to teach the horse obedience to voice and whip, to move forward freely and willingly, and to stop on command, and to accustom him to wearing a saddle and bridle and to the feel of the bit.

Under expert guidance, lungeing also teaches a horse to balance himself on a circle while gradually improving his paces, rhythm and impulsion. By lungeing a horse, you will soon notice his weaknesses, many of which can be lessened or even eradicated before he has to cope with a rider. For instance, an idle horse can be driven forward more effectively from the ground than by a rider whose aids the horse does not initially understand, and whose weight will discourage him from the proper, active, forward motion.

How to lunge

The first time that you lunge a young horse all you need for equipment is a simple cavesson, a lunge-rein and a whip. See that the cavesson fits closely so that it will stay in place even if the horse pulls away violently. Remember also to protect your horse's legs when lungeing him, with bandages and boots (see page 278).

Attach the lunge-rein to the ring on the noseband and start working from the near side, as the horse is more accustomed to being led from this side. Later on you should vary the side that you start with, and lunge him on both reins to keep an even balance. Bear in mind, however, that an immature horse must not be lunged for more than ten minutes in either direction or he may strain his limbs, heart or lungs from over-exertion.

Before picking up the lungeing whip, arrange the spare end of the rein in folded loops so that you can release it easily in sections when necessary.

If your horse is already obedient, you may not need your assistant to walk with him, but most horses are reassured by a guide during this first lesson, and will learn more quickly as a result. Your assistant should walk on the outside of the horse, gradually releasing his or her hold on the cavesson until merely walking beside him. When the horse has completed a few circuits, he is ready to continue alone; the assistant can then stand back ready to help again, if necessary. The assistant should never speak to or distract the horse. All instructions to the horse come from you, as trainer, alone. It is vital to concentrate fully while you are lungeing the horse. Young horses can move very quickly, often in the wrong direction, and a skilled person should be able to anticipate such moves and prevent them with a quick command, or a flick of the whip. Some horses will become excited on the lunge or try to take advantage of the relative freedom. If this happens, keep calm, speak to the horse firmly and, if he does not slow down, reduce the size of the circle, giving short, sharp pulls on the rein to bring him back under control.

A very lively horse, so eager that he may escape from you, must always be lunged in an enclosed area, preferably on deep sand. This will slow him down and eventually tire him, without doing any damage.

Positioning

When lungeing, position yourself behind the point of the horse's shoulder so that he is always moving ahead of you. In this way you are in a good position to control the horse; your lungeing hand controls the head, and the lungeing whip, in the other hand, controls the hindquarters. Start with a 15m (48ft) circle, which is small enough to keep the horse under control but not so

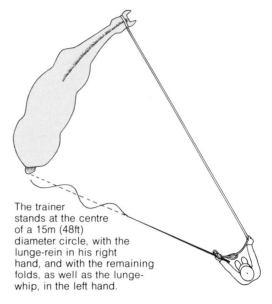

The trainer stands at the centre of a 15m (48ft) diameter circle, with the lunge-rein in his right hand, and with the remaining folds, as well as the lunge-whip, in the left hand.

tight as to strain his legs. Provided that the horse is under control, the larger the circle the better. Watch him carefully all the time.

Circling

On a left circle, hold the lunge-rein in your left hand with your right shoulder nearest to the horse, and the whip and the folded remainder of the rein in your right hand. To circle right, reverse this position. To start the horse off, you or your assistant should take him to the outside of a small circle, where he should be made to stand until you lead up your position in the centre. Tell the horse to move on and, if necessary, click at him or flick the whip behind him. He should move off calmly, without rushing, so adapt your aids accordingly.

Gradually increase the size of the circle once the horse is moving by releasing a section of the folded lunge-rein as he takes up the slack.

At first you will be satisfied if your horse is obedient to the commands of "walk, trot, walk, halt". He should stand still when halted and not turn in towards you looking for a reward. As yet the horse will not be ready to balance himself at a canter on this small circle. Use a low soothing tone to slow the horse down, and a sharper pitch to make him go faster. The horse will learn from the alteration in sound of your voice.

With the first stage completed, your horse is ready to be introduced to a bit, roller and side-reins.

Introducing the bridle

By now your horse is used to wearing a head collar, and probably a lungeing caves-son. The bridle is different only because the steel or rubber bit goes in the horse's mouth. As the bit will be an important means of communication between horse and rider, the horse must never have cause to resist, evade or dislike it in any way. With care, such problems can be avoided.

The bridle itself will not surprise the horse, if you have handled him well around his ears and neck. Neither reins nor nose-band are necessary at this stage, especially if a lungeing cavesson is to be used over the bridle. Before fitting the bridle, remove the bit from it.

Put the headpiece over the horse's ears, and then pull his forelock gently over the browband to ensure a snug fit. Do up the throat lash. Next, attach the bit to the cheek piece on the far side. As an extra precaution, make sure the bit is warm, not ice-cold; it can be dipped in sugar or treacle to make it more pleasant for the horse and to help produce saliva.

With one hand, ease open your horse's mouth by feeling the gums inside the top corners of the mouth above his teeth. With your other hand, gently but quickly ease the bit into his mouth and attach it to the cheek piece on the near side before he can reject it or before it knocks against the lower teeth. If he is properly prepared, the horse will accept the bit.

Make sure the bit fits correctly and is the right size. It should rest on the bars of the mouth, not jangling against the teeth, and should just wrinkle the corners of his mouth when in position.

Leave the bridle on for a few minutes for him to become used to the feel of it. Repeat the process either on the same day or on the next, leaving the bridle on for a longer period or while you lunge the horse.

When lungeing at this early stage, do not attach the reins or side-reins to the bit, but continue to improve the horse's balance,

suppleness, paces and obedience with the lunge-rein attached to the cavesson.

Gradually your horse's "bearing" will improve, and then side-reins can be attached to the cavesson in order to encourage this improvement. The side-reins should *not* be attached to the bit until the horse has learned to accept its action and has acquired some self-balance. The sensitivity of the horse's mouth must be maintained if he is to be a responsive ride: any sudden jerks on the mouth will be painful and one thoughtless movement could cause a major setback by destroying the confidence you have carefully built up during his training so far.

If the side-reins are attached to the bit before the horse is sufficiently balanced to carry his head in the correct, still position, he will be forced to do so unnaturally. Problems such as evasions, being behind or above the bit, resisting it, or setting the jaw are then likely.

The more time you give your young horse to get used to the feel of the bit in his mouth, without reins attached, the easier your task will be when you come to take up contact through the reins, particularly if he has already started to adjust his balance and muscles as the result of correct training on the lunge.

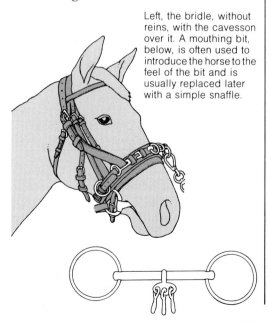

Left, the bridle, without reins, with the cavesson over it. A mouthing bit, below, is often used to introduce the horse to the feel of the bit and is usually replaced later with a simple snaffle.

Introducing the roller

Provided the roller is introduced gradually it should not create a problem on a well-handled horse. It is best to introduce it to the horse after working him, so that he is less fresh and more relaxed. Start by leaving stable rubbers draped over the horse's back while you are grooming him in the stable. Then progress to using something heavier such as a stirrup leather, or sack. In turn, make the sack heavier by filling it with small objects. Meanwhile leave the roller over the stable door or the manger so that the horse can sniff and touch it, to remove any suspicions he may have. When you finally drape the roller over his back, he will hardly notice it. Put a soft pad under the roller for comfort, and leave the girth end hanging down while you continue to groom him. Next, standing by his nearside shoulder and reassuring him, quietly reach under him to take hold of the roller and bring it slowly under his stomach. If your horse is worried, hold the roller close to his stomach until he is used to the feel of it. Some horses are naturally apprehensive of this completely new sensation, so make sure yours has accepted the roller before fastening it loosely.

Leave him to stand in his roller, in the stable, once you are able to fasten it more securely. It must not be tight, but neither should it slip round or back. To prevent the latter, a breast-girth attachment is a wise precaution.

When the horse first moves with the roller on, the sensation may alarm him and he could take fright. If it is introduced gradually in the stable, however, and the horse is walked around a few times, all should be well. Let your horse enjoy his feed while wearing the roller; he will soon learn to accept it. Once he has done so, he can be lunged with it on, but always make sure it is properly secured.

Introducing the saddle

Find a small, light saddle for this lesson. Soft, supple girths will be the most comfortable and a numnah will also help. (Remember that your horse should also be wearing protective boots.)

Again let the horse sniff and touch the saddle in his stable in order to allay any distrust. Although your horse is by now well-used to wearing and working in a roller, this larger object could surprise him, as it will cover most of his back.

Remove the stirrups and leathers and introduce the saddle in the same gradual way that you introduced the roller. When the horse moves, the saddle may feel uncomfortable to him. Be ready for this, and allow the horse as much time as he needs in the stable before venturing out with it on his back.

Next lead and lunge your horse with just the saddle, without the stirrups and leathers. When replaced, these must be secured so that the irons do not slide down, banging against his sides. After a few days, however, they should be left hanging down. The sequence for lungeing the horse is as follows:

1 With the cavesson, bit, roller, and breast girth;
2 With the cavesson bit and saddle, but without stirrups;
3 With the cavesson, bit and saddle, and with the stirrups tied up;
4 With the cavesson, bit and saddle, and with the stirrups down, but tied together under his belly.
5 With the cavesson, bit and saddle, but with stirrups flapping.

If your horse bucks against his saddle, replace the roller with a large pad over his back. Usually, however, a firm word and some perseverance will be enough to cure the problem. Your assistant must be ready to help, particularly if your horse breaks away, and you should remember to keep all gates shut.

When you attach side-reins to the saddle, fasten the end to the girth strap, above the buckle guard.

Using side-reins attached to the bit

Before attaching loose side-reins to the bit, fit the normal bridle reins so that the horse can feel their weight on the bit. At first, do not apply any tension on the rein; then lead your horse along, one hand on the rein attached to the bit, the other on the lunge-

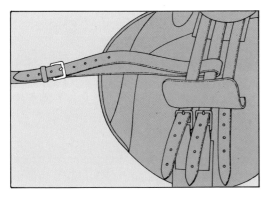

The side-reins attached securely to the girth straps, with an adjustable buckle. They should be loose enough to allow reasonable head movement.

On the lunge

Next, attach both ends of the side-reins to the D-rings on the roller or to the girth flaps on the saddle (see left). Wait until your horse has settled on the lunge in the usual way, and has let off steam. Then halt him in order to fasten the reins, at their longest length, to the bit; contact is made only when the horse stretches his neck down long and low.

Encourage your horse to stretch downwards in this way, seeking contact with his bit. This will not happen all at once. Concentrate on free forward movement, plenty of impulsion and a good rhythm. If progress is slow, shorten the reins so that contact is inevitable, and lunge him in this way for a few circuits, on either rein. Then let the reins out again; your horse should instinctively reach forward to find the contact. In this way you will achieve your aim of stretching the muscles along the neck,

rein attached to the cavesson. In this way, if your horse is startled, you can use the cavesson to stop him. If you can imagine a piece of thin metal in your mouth, your reactions and the use of your hands will be more sensitive.

Common faults of lungeing

1 Lungeing a horse alone if you are inexperienced – it is a skilled art.
2 Lungeing on a deep heavy surface, which could strain your horse's legs, muscles and back.
3 Lungeing on rough, hard surface which will jar the horse's legs.
4 Using too small a circle, which may strain the horse and cause incorrect bending.
5 Using too large a circle which may cause you to lose contact or control.
6 Lungeing a horse that is too young, or too weak, or too immature, causing tendon or muscle strain, pulled ligaments or bone damage.
7 Lungeing a horse too fast or too slow – the horse will lose his balance and rhythm in the former case, and will not use himself properly in the latter.
8 Using your voice so frequently and unnecessarily that the horse becomes confused and fails to listen to other instructions.
9 Scolding the horse too much and never praising him, which discourages him.
10 Jerking the reins, even when only attached to the cavesson, as it will cause loss of confidence and fear of contact – if the horse

fails to stop when commanded, reduce the circle drastically or face the horse into a wall.
11 Misusing the whip which should only be used to encourage forward movement or to support your voice, never to punish him.
12 Lungeing on one rein more than the other, causing one-sidedness.
13 Losing your concentration so that the horse loses his with the result that he becomes lazy or uncontrolled, and his respect for you is diminished.
14 Using side-reins attached to the bit before the horse has learned to carry himself in balance.
15 Adjusting the reins too tightly causing resistance, overbending, hollowing of the lower neck and back, leaning on the bit or tongue over the bit.
16 Tightening the inside rein, so that his head and neck is bent to the inside and his shoulder is thrown out, with the result that the rest of his body is unable to follow such an exaggerated curve and the quarters are also thrown out of line.
17 Tightening the inside rein, causing the wrong bend and development of his muscles – the bend should be through the whole length of the horse from poll to tail.

back and hind-quarters, thus encouraging a rounded, soft outline which will remove tensions in the muscles and spinal cord.

If you shorten the side-reins to obtain this result, be careful that you do not allow the horse to retract or "shorten" his neck, becoming behind the bit or overbent. If this happens, lengthen the side-reins and drive him forward again.

Some trainers, when lungeing, make the inside rein shorter than the outside one, to encourage correct bend. The danger of this practice is that the horse is only bent at the neck and not, as he should be, in a continuous curve. It can also restrict the movement of his inside shoulder, and he may resist the greater contact on the inside of his mouth by "setting his jaw" or by some other evasion.

Side-reins of equal length are normally used when training the young horse. There is a case for a shorter inside rein when lungeing an older, trained horse on a tighter circle, where more collection is asked of him.

Introducing rein contact

Before the young horse is ridden, he must be prepared for hand contact through the bit. Long-reining, in the hands of an expert, is often the best method (see opposite), but it is an art rarely acquired by most people. The following is an alternative to it.

Procedure

Put the bridle on your horse in the stable. Take both reins in your hands, equally, and feel backwards and upwards with soft, vibrating movements (above right) as if you were on the horse's back and holding the reins. Continue the movement until your horse answers by mouthing the bit, submitting to the slight pressure by relaxing his jaw. If he resists, be patient, and increase the vibrations slightly until he gets the message. If he backs or throws his head, you are using your hands too strongly. Then reward him by relaxing the contact. You can then progress to feeling one rein more than the other, until your horse yields either side of his mouth when asked, bending his neck very slightly at the poll.

Rein contact
Above, getting the horse used to the feel of the reins by vibrating them upwards and backwards with a "give and take" action.

Right, introducing a turning aid by using a vibrating action on one rein while the other is left slack.

Repeat these exercises in the yard, leading your horse in the bridle at the walk, asking him to soften his jaw at the lightest of pressure, then practising to the left and right. You can teach him to halt by using your usual vocal command, whether "whoa" or "halt", while feeling with a vibrating motion on both reins equally, yielding the pressure the instant he stops. Your horse's reward when he responds is a "giving" rein, which must be obvious as well as immediate. A long, rough or even a steady pull will cause him to resist or "lean" against the bit. Avoid it by vibrating the reins and using either hand separately.

Turning, too, can be taught in this way. Walk beside your horse, a rein in either hand making equal contact. To turn the horse towards you, feel with the hand on the nearest rein, and give with the other rein. As his neck bends a little, release the tension on the nearest rein and walk with him through the turn.

Long-reining

Driving a horse in long reins is a delicate art. Like lungeing, it is best not to do it at all, rather than do it badly. Done well, however, there is no more effective way of curing a horse's problems. It is possible for an expert to bring a horse up to Grand Prix standard on long reins – most of the work with Lippizaners at the Spanish Riding School in Vienna is done in this way.

The main difference between lungeing and long-reining is that two reins are used for long-reining. They are attached to either side of the horse's head, first to the cavesson and later to the bit, when the contact is similar to that of the reins when the horse is ridden.

The principal aims of long-reining are to introduce hand aids, to make the horse more supple by practising turns and bends, and to improve his impulsion from behind. On long reins the horse can be driven straight ahead or can be turned: the outside rein passes along his far side through the ring on the roller, or the stirrup iron on the saddle, then below the tail but above the point of his hock, and back along to the trainer's hands.

The main advantages of long-reining are to obtain forward movement or impulsion, to supple the horse on turns and to straighten him. Skilful handling is vital.

There are various disadvantages to long-reining, however. The most obvious is that the horse's mouth can be ruined by insensitive hands, especially if you lose control of an untrained youngster. Just the weight of the long reins on the horse's mouth can cause evasions or resistance. When turning right, for instance, there will be pressure on his left side as the left rein drags against his body, inevitably pulling on the outside of his mouth, however much the trainer may "give" with the left hand.

In addition to these drawbacks, there is also the danger when long-reining that the hands become too important as aids, so that you will confuse the horse when you later reverse the whole process as he is ridden and taught to respond to seat, leg and weight aids. Finally, unless the trainer is very fit and agile he will tire more quickly than the horse!

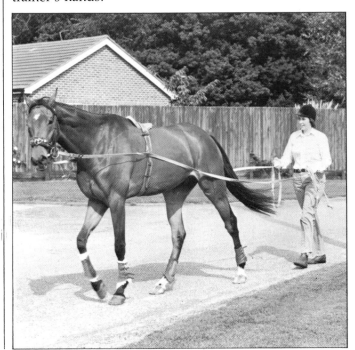

Left, the correct position for long-reining a young horse – just close enough to maintain control.

Below, when using a saddle, run the long reins through the irons, and secure the irons to the girth to stop them flapping.

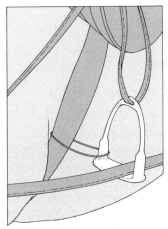

Backing the horse

This is a simple procedure if your young horse has been thoroughly prepared, but it is essential to have an assistant. You will know that the horse is ready to be backed when he has completely accepted the stages already described, including being lunged in riding tack.

Only attempt to back a young horse when he is completely relaxed. After working him on the lunge, return to the stable yard but do not remove the tack. If he is calm, you can proceed.

Bring the horse alongside a bale of straw, and ask your assistant to hold the horse's head. Stand on the bale and rub your hands over his back or groom him, talking gently all the time. When he is used to your height beside him, and is relaxed, move to the other side and repeat the process. Then gradually lean your weight on the saddle until you are across his back. Stay there until the horse is relaxed, and then do the same again on the other side.

The next step is to put your foot in the stirrup, as if to mount, and to gradually put some weight on it. The girth should not be very tight, so ask your assistant to hold down the other stirrup with equal pressure. Then remove the bale and repeat the process from the ground, until you can lift yourself up on the stirrup. Do not mount in the stable, because, if your horse becomes frightened and panics, you could both be badly hurt.

Lead the horse to the schooling area and repeat the preliminary moves, including the initial work on the lunge. Then, if he is quite relaxed you can mount fully, being careful not to kick him on the rump as you swing your leg over the saddle.

Do not sit on the back of the saddle; lean forward a little over the horse's centre of gravity, near the withers. Your assistant should lead him forward immediately for a few steps – the horse is better able to adjust to your weight in the saddle when he is moving, although he may get upset when he feels the shift in his balance. Stop after a few strides and stand still for a minute or two, making much of him before dismounting. Each time you get on, in future, repeat the preparatory stages first, to ensure that the horse remains relaxed throughout.

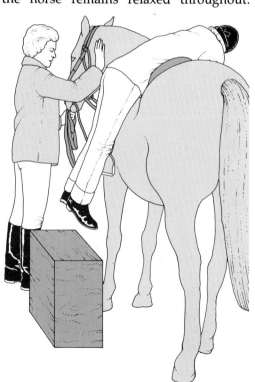

Above, introducing the horse to the feel of the rider's weight by leaning against his side. A block or bale of straw should be used to stand on.

Right, the horse taking the full weight of the rider on his back. Again, a block helps to avoid any extra pressure or movement.

Continue with the preliminary lungeing until you can trust your horse to be well-behaved when fresh out of the stable. A horse that lives out in the field, however, should not need such lengthy preparation.

As your horse gains confidence you can gradually increase the number of steps he takes while you are in the saddle. Your assistant should continue to lead the horse but you can take up the reins with a light contact. You may need to use the neckstrap if you lose either your balance or your nerve, but never use the reins.

Sit still on the horse, your legs hanging loosely against his sides, in the correct position. Resist the temptation to kick him or he might react from fright. Instead use your voice, repeating the commands already familiar to him on the lunge. At first, you should be content just to sit on him while he becomes accustomed to your weight and readjusts his balance.

Introducing leg aids
Gradually introduce leg aids, quietly squeezing his sides to move forward, just after you give the command "walk on".

Do the same for "halt". With the assistant still at his head, ask the horse to "trot on"; only the rider should speak, supporting the voice with a light leg aid. Use the rising trot only – the sitting trot would cause tension in the horse's back muscles. You may need to hold the neckstrap on one hand, as the pace may be jerky and he must not be pulled in the mouth.

The assistant can leave you alone once you have enough control. If you find it difficult to steer a large circle, you could go on the lunge with your assistant in the middle, taking up the controls. Then remove the lunge rein and stay on the same circle, with your assistant still in command, while you introduce light but obvious aids for direction and simple walk-trot-walk-halt-walk transitions. Eventually your assistant can stand aside while you continue to use both voice and aids until the horse responds. When you can use simple aids, without the voice, the first stage of training is complete.

Below, getting the horse used to the feel of the rider's weight in the stirrup.

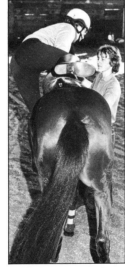

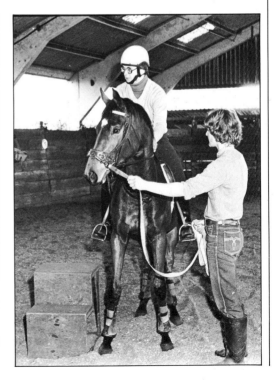

Above, when mounting, your leg and foot must not touch the horse's back.

Right, backing the horse. The assistant should hold the lunge-rein.

Off the lunge

Introduction to simple aids

To control your horse off the lunge, you must teach him to obey the simple aids at the walk and ordinary trot. Bear in mind that the horse will need time to adjust his balance to the feeling of your weight on his back. He should, therefore, be prepared gradually to accept contact with your hands, without resistance. To achieve this, the muscles along his "topline" must first of all be made to stretch and contract by encouraging him to extend his neck downwards and forwards. This can be achieved by the exercise below, at the halt, with the horse standing squarely. Your success depends on the sensitivity of your reactions: you must free the reins at precisely the right moment.

When your horse has learned to extend outwards and downwards to a loose rein, repeat the exercise but maintain a light contact as he stretches, your hands following along his neck as they would when you are jumping, for example.

Then repeat the exercise at the walk. Your horse should accept contact with your hands without tension or resistance. Stretched and relaxed in this way, his muscles are ready to begin to work efficiently. But your hands must still remain passive: pressure on the reins, or jerking them, would destroy his carefully built-up confidence in the feel of your hands. Do not give your horse any reason to resist or falter. At a later stage in his training, the horse's topline will need to be stretched further, see page 206.

Acceptance of the bit

Your ultimate aim when taking up contact with your horse's mouth is that he yields to your hands without resistance, and that he holds the bit confidently, neither evading it nor leaning on it.

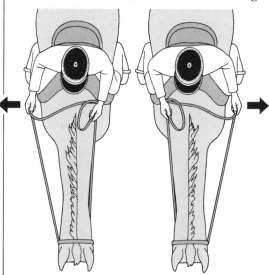

Stretching the topline
To teach a young horse to stretch his topline, open your hands wide to the left and right (above) with a gentle rhythmic sideways movement until his mouth yields. Then give him the reins: he should respond by stretching downwards and forwards with his head and neck (right).

It is vitally important for your horse to accept the bit because it is your direct means of communicating your intentions to him. To teach your horse to take the bit, ride him forwards energetically at the walk, and then increase the impulsion with stronger leg aids. (If necessary, give extra encouragement by tapping your schooling whip behind your leg.) As he moves forward strongly, take up gentle contact with his mouth, encouraging him to extend his neck downwards. At no point should he lose impulsion, so do not restrict his stride with stronger contact. Be sure to stay relaxed, allowing your shoulders, elbows and wrists to follow his natural movements. Do not try to force your horse's head up when he wants to carry it lower: it would upset his natural equilibrium, resulting in resistance, hollowness and the development of the wrong muscles. Your young horse will probably be on his forehand during the first year of training. But as his balance improves and his hindlegs are brought further under his body, his forehand will raise itself naturally, lightening the load over his forelegs. (Remember that this is a gradual process.)

Circling
It is easier to get a horse to yield to the feel of one hand rather than to both of them simultaneously. As a result, training in these early stages is done by working mainly on a circle; going in a straight line puts the young horse's muscles under too much pressure.

Ride your horse on a circle approximately 25m (82ft) in diameter, using a long rein. When he is walking on freely, take up light contact with both hands. If he tries to stop or deviate, ease your hands, and ride forward strongly again before repeating the contact. The contact between your hands and his mouth should be similar to holding a fine thread – not so tight that it could break, nor so slack that it is looped.

Simple turns
Plan ahead when turning so that the turn is smooth, without loss of impulsion, rhythm or balance. Your horse cannot yet be

Schooling area
School your young horse in a defined area. It need not be fenced, but straight lines will help you to know whether he is moving straight. Markers are also useful to test that your horse is under control, and obedient enough to make transitions or turns at a certain point. If no confined space is available, make use of a suitable fence line, or mark out an area using chalk or tape for clearly defined straight lines.

A standard dressage arena measures 40 x 20m (131 x 66ft) – 60 x 20m (197 x 66ft) is the Olympic size – and is an ideal size for schooling. If it is any smaller it will be difficult for a young horse to negotiate turns without losing his balance and rhythm and may strain him. If it is larger, the horse's balance and agility will not be suitably developed.

Once the horse's balance is good and he can cope with sloping ground, he can be schooled in "natural" surroundings, and taught to adapt to varying terrain, see p. 220.

expected to cope with tight turns or small circles. A circle 20m (66ft) in diameter is a suitable minimum size at the trot; one 15m (49ft) in diameter is suitable at the walk. If at first it is difficult to get him to turn, be careful not to pull back with your inside hand or to cross your hands over his neck. Use an open rein, moving your inside hand wide, to make it obvious in which direction he is to go.

Remember that the aids to make a simple turn are: inside leg – impulsion; outside leg – supporting and preventing the hindquarters from moving outwards; inside hand – direction and bend; outside hand – controlling impulsion and supporting.

Prevent your horse from becoming "rubber-necked" by feeling at least as much with the outside as with the inside hand when turning. If his head and neck bend round, but his shoulder falls outwards, followed by the rest of his body, you have lost control of your horse.

Transitions
In halt to walk, walk to trot transitions, squeeze with your legs and allow your horse to move forward in a straight line, keeping your hands light. Increase the leg

pressure and use your voice, if necessary, and repeat until he responds to the lightest leg aids.

To slow down, from trot to walk and from walk to halt, squeeze slightly with your legs to warn him, and to engage his hindquarters a little, then feel on his mouth with both hands together. Only use your voice if the response is not immediate. Your horse will seek contact and accept the feel of the bit as a result of pressure from your legs, but your hands must remain passive at the first stage.

To help your horse to adjust to your weight, always sit still and upright no matter what he does. Gradually his stride will become longer, steadier and more rhythmic. When this happens he will have recovered his natural balance, and your first goal will have been reached.

Problems of riding "free"

When first riding "free" on your untrained horse, you may find it difficult to keep him

A young horse often wavers off-course, as here, when first learning to go "straight".

on a straight line. He may waver off-course because he lacks balance under your weight, or because he would prefer to go in a different direction. A spirited or disobedient horse might even try "napping" or shying to get his own way.

The most effective way to discipline your horse is to put him on the lunge again or to drive him in long reins until he is completely obedient. Never give him the opportunity to defeat you.

Similarly, if your horse lacks rhythm or impulsion when ridden, or if he rushes, you should return to schooling him from the ground until the problem has been overcome. Then repeat the first steps under saddle, using your voice at first to make simple transitions, followed by simultaneous use of voice and aids, followed by simple aids without the voice.

Most young horses are not well balanced enough to canter with a rider at this stage. Avoid cantering until the horse's balance is more fully developed and concentrate instead on improving his impulsion and rhythm at the walk and trot.

The driving aids

Most horses quickly learn to respond to leg pressure but very tense, over-active horses find it more difficult. If your horse has a tendency to rush off as soon as he feels you move on him, your instinct may be to keep your legs away from his sides. However, until he learns to accept the influence of your legs, his training cannot progress. You must sit deep on this horse: he will eventually get used to the close contact.

To be able to use your legs effectively, you must be able to stop your horse without relying on your hands. Use your legs and seat muscles rather than your hands to slow him down and to induce calmness. Practise halting your horse in an area enclosed with high walls or a fence.

When you can halt the horse by using balance, voice and passive hands, without a fence ahead, ride him on a circle 15–20m (50–66ft) in diameter. Sit very still, and deep in the saddle, and relax your muscles to help him relax in turn. It could take several days of this work before he is calm.

If your horse rushes so much that you have to use half-halts to check his pace and balance, be careful never to prolong the pressure. Your horse will not be ready to ride "normally" on the aids until he accepts your leg pressure without quickening or tensing. Continual circling should help to settle him.

A lazy, unresponsive horse is, in fact, easier to teach. Use your schooling whip rather than incessant kicking to sharpen up his response to your leg aids. A sharp reminder from the whip, repeated if he slows down again, but replaced as soon as possible by only the required light leg aid, will soon effect a cure.

You must dictate the pace of your horse and keep to it, using your back and legs as driving aids.

Flexion to the inside

All horses bend more easily to one side (usually to the left) than to the other, and they find it easier to move with a slight flexion to one side than to move absolutely straight. As a result, flexion to the side (laterally) is a useful exercise to remove tension or resistance in any horse, whether young or old. It can be practised at the halt first.

To flex inwards, feel on the inside rein without pulling back against the horse's mouth. Hold your inside hand slightly wide, to make your intention clear. As soon as your horse's head comes around, release the tension on the inside rein but do not let him straighten up – your outside hand should be giving in order to encourage the bend in his neck. Help your horse to maintain the bend by yielding your inside hand until he remains flexed of his own accord. If the flexion is lost, ask again, and be satisfied

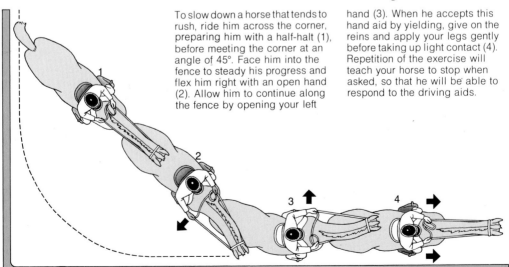

To slow down a horse that tends to rush, ride him across the corner, preparing him with a half-halt (1), before meeting the corner at an angle of 45°. Face him into the fence to steady his progress and flex him right with an open hand (2). Allow him to continue along the fence by opening your left hand (3). When he accepts this hand aid by yielding, give on the reins and apply your legs gently before taking up light contact (4). Repetition of the exercise will teach your horse to stop when asked, so that he will be able to respond to the driving aids.

Left, a young horse on his forehand and, above, a more mature horse whose weight has been brought more over his hindquarters.

with only a small amount of bend at first, provided it is given willingly and in a relaxed manner. Your hands must stay soft to keep the neck relaxed and supple, and therefore able to flex.

Suppling the horse

As already mentioned, before any horse can be ridden "on the aids", he must be taught to stretch his topline by lowering his head, reaching forwards and down with his head and neck. Although it may seem contradictory, this is the method by which the horse's balance is brought off his forehand. It cannot be done by simply raising his head; it must happen as a direct result of bringing his hind legs further underneath him, with his hindquarters lowered down on to his haunches. It will be a gradual process, but, with correct training, the forehand will eventually be raised. The horse's neck should not only be lowered but also stretched longitudinally, to relax his spinal column and to remove the tensions that cause resistance. The more the muscles stretch, the better they contract, and the stronger and more elastic they become, adding greatly to the horse's efficiency. These muscles rarely develop without training, but unfortunately their function is often ignored, and the horse's legs and joints are asked to carry all the strain of

forward propulsion and of carrying the rider's weight. Under pressure, some part of his body is then likely to give out. The development of a strong and supple topline improves a horse's performance in every type of work.

When the horse's muscles are loose and relaxed, you know he is ready to take the bit, and you can prevent him from withdrawing his neck to avoid contact with it. At this point, your horse is ready to work *with* you, rather than against you.

Stretching the neck

Start by riding on a circle to teach your horse to reach downwards and forwards at the walk or trot. Keep your inside hand soft, maintaining slight inside flexion while your outside hand feels gently on his mouth and offers to give if he will stretch down and forwards. Meanwhile, drive your horse forward energetically with your legs to ensure the hindquarters are sufficiently engaged to bear his weight. Your hands must not support him. Do not "ask" for the stretching action with both hands, either alternately or together, but keep his head steady with inside flexion. When your horse yields to slight rein pressure, give both reins instantly. He should reach down to the bit, seeking contact with your hands while you are still pushing him

Points to remember

1 Do not ask your young horse to carry your weight for several circuits on a small circle at the trot as it will cause him unnecessary physical strain. Once he has learned to move to left and right in answer to your leg and hand signals, practise simple transitions – walk-trot-walk-halt-walk.

When these simple exercises are well established, you can practise them along the sides or walls of your schooling, area. Continue to use vocal commands to supplement simple leg and hand aids until your horse has accepted their connection. When you can achieve good forward movement, without using your voice, the first stage of training is completed.

2 Do not pull on your horse's mouth to stop him. Use your voice, and apply your legs, then your hands in a gentle "take-give" motion. Repeat these aids until he responds, then reward by giving the rein and patting him. If you pull hard with either one or both hands you will cause resistance. Your horse is either resisting because he is unbalanced

on his forehand and needs to be given time and help to stop rolling on, or because he lacks training – in which case lunge him until he is more obedient.

3 Do not force your horse into a different "shape" or "outline"; a rounded neck looks nice but is the result of progressive training and development, and should follow naturally at a later stage. Your horse should become fully accustomed to your weight on his back and should be encouraged to go forwards at walk and trot, before being made to use "new" muscles. Too strong a contact is likely to restrict free forward movement, causing resistance. Ride with a light hand on a long rein and be patient. Your first priority is to get him to go forward and straight, both in and out of the schooling area. Do not attempt the next stage of training until this has been established.

4 Never lunge a spirited young horse with a rider on his back. The horse may take fright and unbalance his rider, which could frighten him still more and cause an accident.

forwards with the usual leg and seat aids. Establish this neck-stretching technique on a circle before trying it along a straight track. It should not take long because your horse soon becomes calm and relaxed, and will be willing to comply if your instructions are quite clear. Once on the straight, ask only with one hand while the other remains passive. Do not swing his neck from side to side.

Resist the temptation, when your horse's neck is lowered, to pull back on the reins to find contact if he will not "take" the bit. Instead, press forward more and increase the inward flexion to loosen the neck still more, encouraging him to stretch down further. Remember to reward each step of progress by giving the reins, while still driving him on with your legs. Bear in mind, too, that an older horse, whose muscles have not been trained in this way, will take longer to learn to stretch down on to your hand.

Finding contact

The foundations are now laid to put your horse "on the aids", making the next steps

of his training easier to accomplish successfully. Again work on a circle. Ride forward strongly and take up a gentle feel on the bit, keeping your hands passive. As he is relaxed, your horse has no cause to resist but should enjoy the contact and will "mouth" the bit. His neck is still lowered and loose, and as you take up light contact he will remain relaxed, allowing you to push him up to his bit without changing his rhythm or stride. You are not pulling him back to you, but pushing him forward to feel the bit. You should meet little or no opposition from your horse, either muscular or temperamental.

The energy created by your legs is now more contained, and can be used to improve your horse's balance and strength. He is in a position to accept the aids with increased response and is now ready to work efficiently.

On the aids

By this stage you have gained your horse's confidence with simple but clear instructions. He is able to move quite straight at the walk and trot, balanced over his four legs whether you have rein contact or not. Effectively, your horse is now ready to accept more active influence and to learn to be "on the aids". School your horse in a plain snaffle bridle and use an all-purpose or dressage saddle. This will help you to maintain a secure, balanced seat.

All riding horses should be taught to go "on the aids". This applies both to young horses being trained for the first time, and to older, spoiled or untrained horses. Putting a horse on the aids is the most vital stage of his training, and it is by this process that you train a horse to respond to the rider. Every riding horse, whatever his future, needs this basic education in order to work in close harmony and cooperation with his rider.

Do not attempt this stage of training unless you have already learned how a horse that is properly "on the aids" should feel, and try to have a friend or adviser watching you – some constructive criticism usually helps.

Many horses lack a sound basic training. They usually survive but they and their riders would not only be more comfortable but also safer if they had received better early training for, without a firmly established foundation, real progress cannot ever be made.

A horse that is "on the aids" is willing and able to obey his rider. He is "at attention" but although he is poised for action he is also completely relaxed and without tension. There is no resistance in any part of his body; as a result he can work much more efficiently. He can respond to his rider's influence or aids – legs, reins, seat and back – and perform simple movements in perfect harmony with his rider who, in turn, looks comfortable in the saddle, sitting completely still yet relaxed, and using no visible aids.

In appearance the horse should be calm and supple, showing the following points:
1 Active regular paces at all times.

When turning, he should flex slightly throughout his entire length in the direction of the turn while remaining on the aids and relaxed.

2 A relaxed mouth, neither opening nor moving about, but which is steady and soft in the rider's hands.

3 A steady head and neck carriage, with no break in the slightly rounded outline.

4 A tail carried naturally and still.

All these are obvious signs of the horse being on the rider's aids.

Being on the aids does not mean simply that the horse acquires an attractive head and neck position; he must work as a whole, not in parts. An imposed head-carriage, rather than a gradually acquired self-carriage, is harmful to the horse's proper physical development. Short cuts in training result in wasted time and effort. More seriously, they may easily ruin a potentially good horse.

Putting the horse on the aids

Your young horse may have had a break after his first lessons under saddle. If so, he will first need to be reminded of them calmly and quietly.

The ultimate test. Dressage competitions evaluate the ability of horse and rider to work together harmoniously, the horse responding to the rider's aids without resistance.

Start by lungeing him for a few minutes, using the same vocal commands as before, to remove excess energy. You may need to repeat this process over several days until he is obedient and quiet. But be careful not to tire him; he will be unfit after a break, even if he seems over-active, and your efforts to calm him may strain tired muscles or tendons.

Confirm early lessons off the lunge, replacing voice aids with simple hand and leg signals for turns, changes of pace and transitions. Also test his obedience with frequent halts and transitions made at pre-determined points.

Meanwhile adjust your horse's diet. Avoid overfeeding; if he is either fat or "full of beans" there is greater risk of injury, and progress will be slow. He can be trained off grass at any time of the year, particularly if he tends to be excitable. However, a lazy horse can be stabled and fed a diet higher in protein in order to make him more lively.

In very cold or windy conditions, these preliminary steps may take longer, particularly if your schooling area is not enclosed. At the other extreme, hot summer weather can make a horse lazy and lethargic. If this is the case, feed him extra oats and adapt his work accordingly. Flies irritate horses, so ride early in the day in the summer.

Ideally work your horse on his own so that he can concentrate better and so that

Retraining a spoiled horse

Spoiled, older horses which have missed out on the earlier stages of training, and whose muscular powers are therefore limited, can be retrained. It can be a long, slow process and many horses would actually benefit from starting again at the very beginning, on the lunge. But it is surprising how quickly even a spoiled horse can alter, physically changing shape within a matter of weeks, as a result of systematic retraining.

Your principal task will be to teach the horse to take the rein, and to accept your influence by giving you his full cooperation. This is achieved, as described, by loosening and flexing him on the lunge until he is quite relaxed, and removing all tensions. The process of retraining a horse which has been badly taught or ridden is similar to when training an unspoiled young horse, namely to make him respond to the leg's driving aids; to flex towards the inside; to "stretch the topline"; to seek and find contact with your hands through the reins; and to accept the contact naturally when ridden forwards.

Disobedient horses

The most effective way to cure a disobedient horse which evades the rider's aids, or one which is unwilling to go forwards, is to return to training on the lunge.

Most horses respond to being driven from behind as it is their instinctive reaction to go forward. If a horse is reluctant, the lunge whip can be used as strong forward encouragement.

When the horse is trotting on freely in both directions on the lunge, take him to places where he is likely to revert to his bad habits, such as refusing to leave his friends or veering towards home. When he shows reluctance, drive him forward strongly and reward him when he responds. Continue to give him the opportunity to misbehave, always correcting the tendency firmly and rewarding him when he obeys. He may not be cured at once but this treatment should prove effective if repeated two or three times.

Lazy horses

A lazy horse also benefits from being lunged and, with the help of the whip, can be driven forward effectively. Re-introduce voice aids which will be useful later when you ride him again, too. As you give the commands "walk on", and "trot on", click with your tongue, flicking the lunge whip at the same time.

Excitable horses

A very tense, highly-strung horse can also be retrained on the lunge. As this is usually a problem of temperament, it may take several weeks' consistent work on the lunge to remove tension and settle the horse without the rider's direct interference adding to his anxiety. Be patient and talk to him quietly, using a high fence or wall to slow him down, and frequent transitions back to walk and halt until he is bored, but relaxed. Do this every day, followed by mounted exercises of the same kind when he is more settled.

he receives individual undivided attention. To put a trained horse "on the aids", you simply brace your back and loins then follow instantly with slight leg pressure, using passive hands: the horse should become attentive and ready for action. As yet your young horse has not felt you use your back or your weight, and he must be taught to respond to this new message. Make sure he is thoroughly at ease and calm before this lesson. Sit deeper in your saddle, closer to your horse's back and sides, and use firmer leg contact from now on to increase your influence, and his sensitivity to your leg aids. Make your forward driving aids clear and precise, and if your horse is lazy and unresponsive, he must learn to react more sharply. Support your leg aid with a tap behind the girth from your schooling whip, if necessary, but do not frighten him since calmness is essential. Leg pressure demands forward movement which is not merely an increase in speed but greater impulsion.

Ideally, your horse should be very relaxed so that he can be ridden forward positively at a strong trot with you in control, dictating the pace. Your hands must never restrict his free forward movement. If he rushes, return to the preliminary lessons and, if necessary, to lungeing and long-reining him.

Do not worry yet about his head-carriage; interfering with your horse's bearing at this stage will invite trouble. As his balance improves with the increased engagement of his hindquarters, your horse will become ready for your hand influence, without resistance or evasion: he will find his balance and a good head-carriage, naturally.

Establish a strong regular trot as a basis for further training and before attempting turns and changes of tempo. Do nothing that will interfere with his relaxed rhythm and free forward movement. Always return to this basic working trot if these vital requirements are lost. (It is often possible to cure even the most confirmed bad habits in an older, spoiled horse simply by riding him forward strongly with your legs and seat into passive hands.)

Riding on contact

Now that your young horse has begun to go "on the aids", this education must be fully established in order to prepare him for the next stage of training, and to avoid the risk of his physical development advancing faster than his mental understanding. You must judge and plan your rate of progress according to your horse's nature; the longer you take over his early training, the easier and quicker his progress will be in more advanced work later on.

This progress depends on having your horse working in harmony with you. Whenever he loses that vital looseness and free forward movement, stop whatever you happen to be doing, and work to regain them, with both neck flexions and muscle-stretching exercises. Do not try any new lesson until your horse has regained his natural action with swinging strides and relaxed muscles. Then increase the contact very slightly without pulling back, feeling gently and sustaining light pressure while driving him on with your legs and seat as usual. Your horse should react by yielding willingly, and accepting your hands which must then follow his head movement. If your seat and legs continue to press him forwards, but your hands remain passive and do not allow forward movement (by ceasing to follow his head movement), he will bring his hind legs under him and go into the halt. This is the preliminary stage to achieving collection.

Through systematic riding on the aids, the horse will be able to develop his potential as a riding horse. Gradually his weight will be transferred towards the rear, relieving his over-burdened forehand, and making him a pleasing, well-balanced ride.

Evasions

The common evasions of contact are:

1 The horse raising his head high This is to avoid the action of the bit or to compensate for lack of balance. In both cases, cease the contact and ride forward strongly on a circle until your horse relaxes his muscles and lowers his head and neck, regaining confidence in the bit. Make wide, smooth turns to both left and right. To negotiate

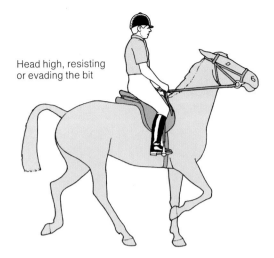

Head high, resisting or evading the bit

of his neck (as he must if he is bending his head to the side), immediately reward him by giving with both hands. Repeat this exercise until he loosens his neck and stretches it out in order to seek contact with your hands.

3 Head and neck are extended, hard and rigid In this case first lunge the horse in side-reins suitably adjusted so that he learns to yield to the bit action while being driven forwards. When normal riding is resumed, ride him forward strongly without allowing him to slacken or deviate when he feels slight pressure on the bit. If you must increase the pressure on his mouth because his response lacks sensitivity, use "sponge-like" hand actions and be sure to keep up even stronger pressure with your legs.

4 Head held low, overbent, and "behind the bit" Do not try to raise his head with

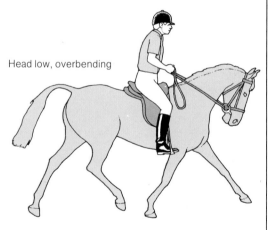

Head low, overbending

them, your horse will have to keep his balance which will help to bring down his head. When you retake a light contact, be very careful to follow his every movement without pulling back, or you will have to start all over again, and keep the contact elastic at all times, always ready to give the rein as encouragement or reward.

2 Head high, tucked in tightly "behind the bit" In this case, do not cease the contact entirely. Instead, ride your horse strongly forward with your legs and, at the slightest hint of his lowering or stretching his neck and head, yield to him with both hands, to give him obvious encouragement and reward. If he does not react further, resume a definite, although light, contact. If his position remains "jammed", feel with one hand more than the other, to produce some movement in his neck. When your horse reacts by stretching the outside line

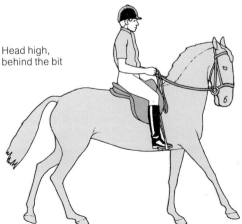

Head high, behind the bit

your hands. Instead maintain a definite light contact and correct the evasion with lateral neck actions as in (2).

5 Head shaking with unrest or irritation This may occur because your hands lack sensitivity. If your arms are truly supple and elastic, you will have the same amount of contact wherever your horse puts his head and he will learn to accept your hands eventually when he realizes that you will not hurt his mouth. Rough, jerky hands will destroy his confidence and trust in you and, perhaps, in all riders, unless you remove his anxiety now. Return to riding on a long rein, on a circle, until his head is perfectly steady. Very carefully take up a light, elastic contact, riding forward strongly and maintaining balance and rhythm as well as possible. Remember it is probably your hands, arms and rigid elbows or shoulders that are responsible for his unrest, so try to correct the fault while riding a school horse. (Also check the condition of the horse's mouth).

6 Head held on one side This is an evasion or an effect of bad training in its earliest stages. It is an easily acquired habit and must be corrected immediately by riding your horse forward and straight. If, when you take up contact, he immediately turns his head, it may be because your hands have an unequal amount of feel, or because he is badly one-sided, or because his mouth is sore on one side.

Always work your horse on both reins equally so that he cannot become one-sided or more muscularly developed on one side than the other. Most riders have one hand stronger than the other and must make a conscious effort to use both equally, to avoid crookedness in their horses.

7 Leaning on the bit This is not strictly an evasion but is still a resistance to the rider's hands. Although a horse can lean on the bit with his head held high, he is more likely, especially when young, to do so with his head low, leaning heavily on his forehand and relying on your hands for a "fifth leg". To correct the fault, ride the horse forwards more strongly than usual, but on a loose rein, so that he has to try to balance himself, and not rely on you to "hold him up". He will feel unsafe at first but will gradually learn to cope with the unaccustomed weight. Lean back slightly to help him to adjust, and when his balance improves, take up contact once more. If he tries to lean again, drop the contact, and ride forward, asking him to carry his own burden. Then try again.

It may be that his mouth is insensitive not through his own fault but as a result of bad training. In this case, increase the pressure on the bit using sponge-like actions. At the same time, use even stronger leg aids to maintain strong forward movement. At the slightest hint of softness and yielding, reward him by giving with your hands. Repeat the process until he is more sensitive to contact, but never pull backwards or his resistance will become even worse. Ask him to yield – never force him.

If your horse leans his head to one side, the cause will probably be one of those mentioned in (6). Examine inside his mouth. If it is in good order, and your hands cannot be blamed, steps must be taken to straighten him. Exercises to supple and loosen him, removing tensions where necessary, cannot be done until he has learned to respond to lateral aids (see page 214) and until his balance and agility have begun to improve.

Rider's faults

1 Forced flexion Riders frequently make the mistake of trying to "flex" their horses by using force. Their hands "saw" at the horse's mouth, either from side to side or up and down, and eventually, after some resistance, the horse has to yield to the pain. The rider then mistakenly assumes that the horse is "on the bit" when, in fact, there is no real contact with or acceptance of the bit. Also the horse is unlikely to *want* contact afterwards and will avoid it by staying behind the bit.

2 Neck stretching without impulsion Once you are riding on contact it is a mistake to start asking the horse to lower and stretch his head and neck at the halt or the walk, if he lacks natural impulsion. Unless you have impulsion to help you, as when trotting, you must create it by encouraging stretching and/or flexion. At the trot it is easier to tell whether *all* the horse's muscles are being used properly, rather than those of his head and neck alone.

3 Pressure on mouth It is a fault to continue pressure on a horse's mouth after he has yielded to you. Unless you reward him the instant he responds, he will not know that he has done the correct thing and will become increasingly tense and anxious. If, when you ask, your horse does not yield immediately, his early training has not yet succeeded. Alternatively, you are not using your back and legs effectively in preparation. Whatever the reason, the horse must be taught to take the rein with confidence before training can progress further.

Signs of successful training

You will know your training has been successful so far when you have achieved the following results:

Relaxation This does not mean "floppiness" (the horse, when ridden must be active) but it does mean complete absence of tension and resistance. Your horse feels relaxed when his paces are free, regular and unhurried, when his mouth and head are steady, and when his back swings freely. In this way he is comfortable to sit to at all paces.

Obedience to back and leg aids Your horse is obedient if he increases pace willingly and immediately when asked with a light back and leg aid.

Test his obedience by asking him to lengthen his stride at the trot. (He should respond to braced back and leg pressure by taking longer, even strides.) Your hands should retain contact but allow him forwards while you drive him on with increased impulsion by the use of your seat and legs.

Test him by going into the halt to see if he is using himself as a whole. First apply your back and legs, with a passive feel on the reins, making a half-halt to prepare him so that he slightly shortens his stride as his hindlegs are engaged, and he "sits up" to halt. The halt is well executed if the horse's quarters lower, his back rounds and his forehand is lightened by the preparatory half-halt. Only the slightest feel on the rein will then be necessary. You should know the difference between bringing up a horse to halt and riding him up to his bit.

He should not be allowed to step backwards in the halt, so keep your hands soft, and be ready to ride forwards.

Test him for lateral obedience by asking him to move away from your leg, sideways. When you apply one leg behind the girth at the trot, walk or halt, he should move away from it. To what extent he does so will depend on the amount of pressure. The movement can be regulated by your outside leg.

Obedience to hand aids your horse cannot obey hand aids alone, they must be combined with the legs. (Remember that the reverse does not always apply.) You can be satisfied with his obedience if he will lower and stretch his topline when asked, both in contact with your hands and without contact. He should be flexible equally to left and right, on a circle or going straight, responding to independent hands. When asking your horse to lengthen his stride, your hands must maintain light contact while allowing him to move forwards.

Improved balance It is your responsibility to help the horse in this task by sitting in the correct position. To adapt to changes of pace and direction, you should be upright and secure over the horse's centre of balance, yet relaxed. When these changes can be performed smoothly at the walk and trot, without loss of rhythm, your horse has good balance. To test this, precede all changes with a mild, preparatory aid to get his attention: brace your back, pressing down on your seatbones. Adjust your hip and shoulder position into the direction you mean to turn and direct your horse with your weight distribution rather than by hand and leg aids alone. Gradually reduce the size of the turns and circles to improve his balance still more, but never sacrifice the true freedom of his paces.

Straightness This is not easily achieved but should always be your aim. Work your horse on both reins equally to supple him both laterally and longitudinally. If he is well suppled and relaxed, he will be much easier to straighten than when tense or stiff. Lateral aids (page 214) will help you to straighten him but the main principle is to ride forward strongly. To walk straight, without the help of much impulsion, is more difficult than to trot straight.

In bad cases of crookedness, first look for the cause and then try to remove it. Concentrate on stretching the muscles along his stiff side, loosening him up until he feels equally supple in either direction.

If you ride on a circle on a freshly marked surface, you can then examine the hoof prints to see if your horse's hind feet follow the exact track of his forefeet.

Schooling exercises

The following exercises are useful for improving your horse's flexion and balance. Use rising trot – sitting trot should only be used for short periods until your young horse has developed stronger back muscles. (The exercises can also be done at the walk, but it is easier to maintain impulsion at the trot.

To improve flexion

Practise extending the neck (see page 202) as a relaxing exercise to loosen first the neck and then the whole body. Then ride a 20m (66ft) circle on both reins, remembering to change diagonals. Ride with contact and on a loose rein alternately, keeping the same pace and rhythm. Flex his neck to the inside while riding on a circle. Practise flexion for a few strides, then straighten and ask him to flex again, and so on. Then ride some turns, going completely straight before changing to the opposite bend.

Serpentine figures will also improve flexion. Practise riding two loops first, then decrease the size so that you can fit in three or four loops within the same area. Do not turn so tightly that your horse loses balance or rhythm, and remember to straighten him for a few strides before changing the bend.

To improve balance

Transitions that are correctly performed will help to develop your horse's muscular power as his back becomes a continuous, active link between hind legs and forehand. Also, the strength in his hindquarters and haunches will increase as they become more engaged, which will help him to balance himself while carrying the weight of a rider. Using the full combination of aids – back, legs, seat, hands – make transitions of pace: halt-walk-trot-walk-halt.

To decrease pace, prepare by bracing your back and seat muscles (as for a half-halt) before feeling on the reins. Repeat, but maintain for longer, before riding forward at a slower pace. To increase pace, apply the normal driving aids – back and legs – giving with the reins when necessary.

Practise halting away from the sides of the schooling area, first from the walk and then from the trot, without using strong hands.

At the trot, make several changes of direction with simple turns, circles and serpentines to improve his equilibrium through changes of bend.

Lateral aids

The lateral aids are used for cantering, straightening the horse, or for increasing or decreasing circles, as well as being useful when opening and closing gates.

On a circle you automatically use a simple form of lateral aids as the horse must bend evenly throughout the length of his body around a central point, which is your inside leg. To prevent his quarters from sliding outwards, your outside leg is held just behind the girth. Your inside hand asks for slight flexion while your outside hand regulates the amount of impulsion and bend, and also controls his straightness.

If you increase the *inside* leg pressure on the girth, while the outside leg is passive, his quarters will move outwards. If you increase *outside* leg pressure behind the girth while your inside leg is passive, his quarters will move inwards.

It is also possible to move his forehand inside or outside the track of the circle, but this is a more advanced movement which requires greater experience and flexibility than a young horse can manage at this point. The smaller the size of the circle, the more obvious the separate influences of each hand and leg. But do not ride on a circle smaller than 15m (49ft) when practising lateral aids and never lose your first priority – to go forward and straight.

Introduction to lateral movements from the halt

Your horse has already learned to move away from your leg when turning. He now needs to be taught to move away from one leg at the halt. This exercise can be taught "in hand" and is similar to asking the horse to "move over" when tied up in the stable. It should be performed calmly so that the horse does not get confused.

When you are riding, to move your horse's quarters to the left (pivoting on his forehand) take your right leg back behind the girth. Use pressure to ask him to move over to the left, so that his off-hind leg crosses in front of his near-hind leg. (You may need to carry a long schooling whip to supplement your right leg aid). Keep your left leg firmly in position to prevent his

Introducing lateral aids from the ground
While an assistant steadies the horse's forehand, the trainer asks the horse to move his inside hind leg forwards across and in front of the outer hind leg, by tapping his quarters with the schooling whip.

Aids to canter

Teaching a horse to canter should be left until he is strong enough to maintain the pace, without strain, as the inside hock bears most of the weight when cantering on a bend. (Working on a circle at the trot will already have strengthened the propelling power of your horse's inside hock.) Cantering is not a naturally straight movement as the horse tends to bend towards his leading leg on a slight curve. To remain cantering you need to maintain the lateral aids, so it is important to know how to use independent leg and rein aids.

Transition to canter

To go into canter, ride on a circle at a trot. Sit to it, and make a half-halt to shorten his stride and engage his hind legs. Then apply your inside leg near the girth while keeping your outside leg further back to control his quarters. Your inside hand should ask for slight flexion while remaining in soft contact, as your outside hand supports and prevents his shoulder from escaping.

If your horse reacts by merely trotting faster, decrease the pace using half-halts. Do not pull at his mouth; instead, make sure he is relaxed and attentive before trying the same aids again more strongly. Remember that it is a bad fault to let your horse trot so fast that he is forced to sprawl headlong into a very unbalanced canter.

On the first occasion do not expect a smooth transition unless your horse is exceptionally well balanced by nature. If he cannot cope with the transition to canter without losing his balance or becoming disunited, you must spend more time practising the lateral aids on a circle and improving his balance with transitions and turns at the slower paces.

Stay on a large circle when teaching the young horse to canter. Always use a bend or corner for your transition as this makes it easier for the horse to engage his inside hock and to strike off on the correct lead. On a straight line, he is likely to run onto his forehand because his hind legs are not sufficiently underneath to support him at this speed and you will then be tempted to use too strong a hand to restrain him.

forehand moving to the left, and to maintain his balance and impulsion. This leg can regulate or stop the motion of the hindquarters at any stage of the exercise. Keep your hands soft and passive, only tightening them if your horse tries to move forwards. Then relax them again immediately.

If your horse is slow to understand or is unresponsive to the lateral aids, dismount and practise from the ground. While an assistant holds his head and forehand steady, ask him to move his quarters sideways by tapping behind the girth or further back on the quarters, until he steps away from you.

Practise this lesson until you can ride a half-turn (or pivot) without resistance or tension. Your horse's neck should remain slightly rounded and relaxed; his tendency as always, must be forwards not backwards, and the steps sideways should be even and unhurried.

Always ride your horse forward if he becomes confused or upset, or loses impulsion when you apply the aids at first. Halt before trying again, making sure his hindlegs are brought up underneath him to allow the "outside" hindleg to cross in front of the "inside" leg.

Cantering on a bend

A young horse loose in the field tends to carry his head and quarters slightly to the right when going into a left canter. This is a natural instinct to allow the leading shoulder plenty of room and to make it easier for the outside hind leg to be nearer his centre of gravity in the first stride. He will probably change onto an inside bend after the transition. Make allowances for this and plan your canter transition to make it as easy as possible for your young horse.

Immediately before applying the lateral aids, allow slight outside flexion to give your horse's inside shoulder maximum freedom. As soon as he is cantering, correct the bend by applying the lateral aids as you would for a circle. As his muscles develop, and can contract and stretch more easily, the correct bend can be held through the transition to canter.

The secret of a good canter transition is in the controlled trot strides that immediately precede it. The strides should shorten but

Faults
The young horse, right, has become unbalanced on a corner and has changed on to the outside (left) lead behind, with the result that he is cantering disunited. When making a transition to canter, the trot strides must be controlled.

The horse, below, is trotting too fast and has too much weight on his forehand to make a good transition. He must be slowed and rebalanced first.

not quicken, and, through the use of half-halt, your horse's centre of gravity must move back towards the propelling hind legs, lightening his forehand.

If you have to teach your horse to canter in an open space rather than in an enclosed or defined area, you will find it easier to strike off on the correct lead if you start by trotting a small circle, to collect impulsion. Then, using an open rein, turn him to the outside, in the opposite direction, while at the same time applying the canter aids. Your horse's outside hind leg on the circle becomes the leading leg when he turns, and is in position to be used under him.

Maintain the aids while cantering on a large circle, encouraging your horse to engage his inside hind leg still more to stay balanced. Do not attempt to go straight until you can keep your horse's balance while maintaining a controlled pace.

Make frequent transitions on either rein but never canter for more than two or three circles at this stage, to avoid tiring or straining him. Most horses find one lead easier than the other and you should work on your horse's "bad" side. To do so, use loosening exercises at the trot and walk, and practise lateral aids.

If you feel when cantering that you are losing the rhythm and balance, or if your horse becomes disunited, move forward into trot, rebalance, and restore a relaxed rhythm. Then prepare with a half-halt to canter again.

If your horse is going too fast or running "downhill" on his forehand, try not to restrain him with tight hands only. Instead, apply a series of half-halts with seat, back and legs, keeping your weight upright or slightly back so that his hindquarters are encouraged to move forward under him. At all paces, it is important that his neck is loose and flexible, both towards and away from his leading leg. In this way your horse can be free of tension, and relax his muscles throughout his body so that his canter is calm and controlled.

Cantering on a circle develops both the longitudinal and lateral flexion in your horse, improving his balance and agility. A well-trained horse can canter a 20m (66ft) circle on a long rein without losing balance. If your horse cannot do this, you will know that your hands have been providing him with a "fifth leg" and you should return to exercises to improve his self-balance. Remember that your hands should only be accessories to your seat and legs – be careful not to overuse them.

Cantering in a straight line

Once your horse can keep his balance easily on a 20m (66ft) circle, try cantering on a straight line. He will tend to lengthen or quicken out of the corner, so make a gradual turn and apply a half-halt to bring greater engagement of the leading hind leg. This will help him to keep his balance while remaining at the same pace as on the circle. If the half-halts and the rein action, in particular, are too strong, or if his hind legs are too weak, he will probably trot or sprawl out instead. If this happens, rebalance, and calm him; then try again. If he is tired, stop cantering, otherwise evasions and resistance will result. As the canter improves, and with it your horse's overall balance, you will find that he becomes much more collected naturally.

Practise lengthening your horse's stride slightly on a straight line, then shortening it again before turning a corner. To decrease pace, use the same aids as for a half-halt (back, legs, and passive hands) but in the lateral position with your outside leg slightly behind the girth to keep your horse straight. Sit square with your weight pressed down over his inside hind leg. His neck and mouth must remain relaxed and soft as he slows.

To lengthen the stride, apply the forward driving aids, giving with your hands and remaining in an upright position to help your horse's balance. This exercise will increase his impulsion and stretch his top-line. Do not try to lengthen the stride around a corner at this stage – your horse would find if very difficult to maintain his equilibrium and rhythm.

When going from canter to trot, to avoid tension against the rein prepare your horse with a half-halt, yielding as soon as he responds to you.

The rein back

In this movement, your horse must learn to step backwards with the diagonal pairs of legs moving in unison. To rein back, your horse is required to round his back and lower himself onto his haunches, without resistance. Although this exercise is comparatively difficult, it can and should be taught as an obedience exercise at an early stage. Your young horse may be reluctant to reverse, particularly as you have always insisted on forward movement.

The exercise should be taught first from the ground. Position your horse alongside a fence or wall to guide him in a straight line. Stand in front of him, slightly to one side so that he cannot knock into you if he becomes agitated. Your position guides his "open" side. Hold the reins in one hand, with a schooling whip in the other.

Tap his knees gently, first one then the other, to ask him to move back, while at the same time saying "back" to him. Do not pull backwards on his mouth. If you force him back with rein pressure, the resistance created will make him fight, so that he will either fail to round his outline and use his back properly, or will sit back on his haunches and move jerkily instead. Let him position his own head and neck, while moving backwards calmly. At first his legs may not move tidily in diagonal pairs, but when he has had more practice and has gained strength in his back and loins, his strides will gradually become longer and more even.

Start with four strides only. Any more would be too much for a young horse and could strain his hocks, hindquarters or back muscles. Always lead your horse forwards on completing a rein back. Your aim is to get him to rein back under saddle with the same balance and impulsion as when he is moving forwards.

Older, spoiled horses can be taught the rein back from the ground, as the horse will submit more easily than when ridden. The rein back is also a useful exercise for levelling up a horse that moves crookedly: this often occurs because the horse has one stiff or lazy hind leg and if so, he will rein back towards that leg. To correct the deviation, line the horse up alongside a fence on his stiff side to help him move back straight. Do not force him: correction must be gradual otherwise he will resent the discomfort and resist.

After the initial training, you should have no problems with the horse under saddle. Your assistant should stand in front of the horse with the schooling whip. As he or she touches the horse on the knee with the whip, you say "back". As before, do not pull on the reins. Your horse will remember what to do, and your only function is to guide him straight with your legs, and to maintain impulsion.

Never pull your horse back, whether on the ground, on long reins, or from the saddle. The neck *must* remain loose and relaxed to allow the back and hindquarters to act freely.

With the horse lined up alongside a guiding fence, stand by his head, slightly to one side, holding the reins in your nearest hand and the whip in the other one. Ask the horse to move backwards by saying "back" and by feeling on the reins, and by tapping him gently on the knees or chest with the schooling whip.

Riding out

You should introduce your young horse to traffic in progressive stages. Obviously it will take longer to train a nervous, highly strung horse to be quiet in traffic but any horse that is not traffic-proof is a liability.

Start by turning him out into a field adjoining a busy road, so that he gets used to seeing traffic. Alternatively, lead him to a place where he can watch it while you stand by his head. Talk soothingly but do not make an issue of the traffic as eventually you want him to ignore it completely. If he has been educated on long reins, you could drive him in them in a field alongside a road, until he is calm enough to go along the road itself. Obviously you must use your discretion to determine at what point in his training this would be safe.

A quiet, reliable older horse is an invaluable calming influence, so if you have the opportunity, let another horse stand with yours as the traffic goes by. Then ride about the field together at the walk and trot before separating and asking your young horse to obey you in some schooling exercises.

Once the horse has been introduced to riding on the road, ride with two experienced horses, one at the front and one at the rear.

On the road

Do not even attempt to go out onto the road until confident that your young horse is calm and under control and that you are sure you know the highway code thoroughly. Choose quiet roads that have a wide shoulder, and which are neither narrow nor high-sided.

You must ensure that any accompanying horse is completely trustworthy. Horses are quick to react to tension and will copy one another. If possible, ride with three experienced horses – one on your outside, one leading, and one at the rear, so that your horse is protected while getting used to unusual sights and sounds. Gradually, as your horse becomes calm, let him share the lead, on the inside. Finally, go in single file, first in front, then at the rear. You will invite disaster if your young horse is too fit or fresh when you introduce him to traffic. How long it will take to reach this stage safely depends very much on the individual horse, his stage of training and your own common sense.

When riding out on the road, never trot downhill – only on level ground or on an uphill slope. Taken gradually, roadwork will help harden up the young horse's legs.

Avoiding danger in traffic

If possible, avoid main roads, however quiet your horse may be. Cars and heavy vehicles may slow down for you but often this is not slow enough. A huge articulated lorry, for example, produces a considerable amount of suction which would frighten a horse of *any* age or experience.

When riding a young horse on the road there is also a danger that he may shy at something which alarms him, and jump sideways into the road in the path of a vehicle. If there is a danger of the horse shying into a hazard, always ride with his head and quarters bent away from it, so that he will find it difficult to jump in that direction. Never relax completely with a young horse, but try to be alert.

Among the hazards that may startle a young horse are machinery (such as tractors, steam rollers, milk vans, motorbikes and road-drills) and bicycles or ladders, or similar objects on the tops of vehicles.

Blind corners on narrow roads are dangerous, so avoid them if you can, or, if you hear a vehicle approaching, stand well back from the bend and wait until it has passed. Alternatively, find a gateway to stand in, with your horse's head facing the oncoming vehicle.

Beware also of bad light with its obvious dangers (see page 65).

The horse shying at a parked lorry. The rider is tightening her outside hand and using her outside leg to control his shoulder, and restrict sideways movement.

In the open

You can introduce your young horse to the "outside world" while he is still in the early stages of his training. Even the dullest horse may "come alive" in the open country-side, especially in company and on inviting stretches of grass. Hacking out keeps him more interested in his school work and helps him to adjust his balance under varying conditions. But the novelty may well go to his head and you may find the excitement makes him increasingly disobedient and inattentive. This can lead to disaster and is also inconsistent with the calmness and obedience you are trying to obtain in the schooling area. By all means let your young horse enjoy himself, but never at your expense. Harmony and cooperation cannot exist if he does not remain "on the aids". As a precaution, ride your young horse in a neckstrap so that you can grab it in an emergency, rather than the reins.

Following a lead horse

Always ride out with a good lead horse and avoid difficult ground and hazards until your young horse can be controlled properly and understands your aids. Following behind a calm, reliable horse, you need not attempt to influence your own horse very much at first. Instead, allow him free use of his head and neck so that he can balance himself on variable ground and slopes. If he stumbles, slip your reins and sit up.

Use rising trot, not sitting, and when crossing rough ground avoid bumping on your horse's back by taking more weight on the stirrups, absorbing the movement through your joints. Remember that your horse is still physically immature. Do not gallop about until he is more developed – it would only damage his bones and tendons. Nothing destroys a horse's legs more rapidly than travelling at speed on rough, uneven ground or on downhill gradients. Ride at a walk until your horse is used to coping with hills and difficult ground. Also avoid deep going, such as ploughed land or mud, which will strain his tendons. Equally, try to avoid very hard ground. If you cannot, ride at a walk or slow trot to avoid jarring.

Taking the lead

As your horse gains in confidence, ride him in front of your companion in preparation for hacking him out alone. This can only be done when he is truly "on the aids". Being in front, he may be inattentive to you and you will have to apply your aids and influence to regain his respect and attention. Without a guide ahead, he may waver off a straight course so your aids must be effective. Keep him between hand and leg so that he is both balanced and more manoeuvrable. You will then have a better chance of controlling the situation if you meet an unexpected hazard.

Hazards

There are many potential hazards in the countryside, including animals such as sheep, cattle, pigs or donkeys, as the general noise and smell could very easily frighten your young horse. If he tries to run away from them or refuses to pass, do not add to his fear by simply thumping with your legs and shouting, but let him stand still and watch until he is more relaxed. If there is

Above, leading a horse correctly by the reins.

Below, in a new situation let the horse stand and watch.

another horse, it should take the lead. Without a companion, if your horse will not move forward from your leg or whip, dismount and lead him past, soothing him with your voice. Without making an issue out of it, you could lead him up and down, letting him stop occasionally to look or even to eat grass until he is quite calm. Then remount and ride him past.

Barbed wire can be a hazard if you have to ride alongside it: keep as far away from it as possible in case your horse shies.

Hacking in the country will test your control and your horse's obedience to the aids. As he gains confidence, your horse may possibly become livelier before you have him truly "on the aids". If he bucks, you will know he is feeling good, but you must suppress it before it becomes a habit. Avoid overfeeding at this stage, and always set off from the stable calmly. Return to the stable at a walk, for at least the last half-mile, keeping the reins relaxed.

Finally, if something does occur to upset your horse so that he bolts or shies, you must try to regain control.

Using natural features

Use natural features to educate your horse and to develop his physical powers. Start by climbing gentle slopes at the walk, then progress to steeper slopes. Always walk downhill straight to prevent straining your horse's hindquarters, joints and muscles: avoid strenuous climbing until he is strong enough to cope with it. You may follow a companion through water and over small ditches and logs, but make sure your horse can cope with them at this stage.

It is also a good idea, occasionally, to find a quiet, flat corner of a field in which to school your horse for a few minutes, asking him to concentrate and to cooperate with you completely. When he submits to a simple exercise, suitable to his level of education, stop and reward him, before continuing on your ride.

Cantering

Although you should not teach your horse to gallop yet, prepare for it by letting him canter in the company of a steady companion. At first your horse will probably lack balance and coordination at this speed, but as he becomes more confident, he may get excited. This will improve his impulsion and his stride but be careful not to let him get out of control.

Opening and closing gates

Sooner or later you will have to open and shut gates when out hacking. At first you will have to dismount but once your horse is obedient to your leg, reins back easily, and is manoeuvrable within a small space, you can practise opening and shutting gates while mounted. It is surprisingly exciting when you perform the whole operation smoothly for the first time, as it is a complex procedure. It involves a very precise halt, immobility, a turn on the forehand or on the haunches, by yielding and lateral movement. These are followed by another carefully positioned halt as you fasten the latch.

Never use both hands to open a gate, leaving your reins dangling loose.

Opening a simple gate

Line up facing the latch, parallel to the gate and stand still. Use one hand to unfasten the latch, holding the reins and whip in the other hand. Be constantly aware of your horse's reactions and prevent him from moving or becoming agitated.

Open the gate to twice the width of your horse to avoid it swinging against him. If your horse hurts himself on a gate post or latch he may subsequently always rush through gateways or stable doorways.

Go through the gate and, if you have to hold the gate open for other riders, position yourself along the far side of the gate to avoid close contact with the other horses.

Push the gate closed with one hand, then line up parallel with it once more. Close the gate with your nearest hand, with your whip and reins held in the other one, controlling your horse.

Retraining

Bad habits and vices must be cured if any horse is to be a safe and enjoyable ride. They arise through ignorant early training or bad handling, or both. You must always examine your own riding first, and if necessary seek advice as to the cause of the problem. If you can identify the reason for the fault, you have a good chance of effecting a complete cure.

Stumbling This has various causes: bad shoeing, or toes that are too long; physical weakness or tiredness; loss of balance; or idleness, particularly if the horse is allowed to go on to his forehand. Stumbling may disappear if you improve the horse's physical condition, but if it does not, it can be cured by transferring your weight and that of the horse back towards the hindquarters so that the forehand is lightened.

Kicking A horse that kicks out at other horses, even under provocation, should be punished immediately. This is best done by using a stern voice and giving the horse a sharp smack on his hindquarters with your whip.

Jogging This is a maddening habit in which the horse takes short running steps when he should be walking. It is often due to excitement and lack of training, in which case the horse will have to be retrained, learning to relax both physically and mentally, and to stretch out using a longer, slower stride.

When he jogs, use half-halts and talk soothingly to your horse. If in company, walk ahead of the other horses or go off in a different direction. If you feel very exasperated with your horse, do not lose your temper, but dismount and lead him until he is more relaxed.

Moving off while mounting If your horse will not stand still when you mount, face him towards a wall or fence and ask someone to hold his head. If you are on your own, turn his head towards the fence and hold the outside rein more tightly. The problem may be caused by discomfort, or a cold back, and if so you should take steps to eradicate the cause.

Bucking Keep your horse's head up and try to anticipate a buck. (His head position

and muscular tension provide warning signs.) If your horse tends to buck, try to keep his head up by raising your hands and driving him forward strongly and fast to ride him out of it. When he is extended, it will be difficult for him to buck, but if he does, put your weight on the stirrups to avoid being catapulted through the air if you hit the saddle hard. Never allow your young horse to buck in play – it can soon become a dangerous habit.

Shying Use your outside rein and outside leg strongly if your horse shies. If he jumps to the right, you must tighten the right rein, turning his head "into the skid". With his shoulder towards the object of alarm (which is often imaginary), your horse will find it more difficult to leap sideways. Try to anticipate shying so you can prevent it.

Pulling This problem is often caused by excitement, particularly when a horse is being ridden with others in the country. It can also be caused by discomfort in the mouth or elsewhere. First discover the cause and then try to remove it. Groundwork to increase his obedience to the aids is often the best solution and can usually overcome one-sidedness or insensitivity which are common characteristics of "pullers". If the pulling continues, however, apply firm half-halts to control the pace, with each momentary resistance followed by a yielding rein to ease pressure and encourage relaxation. Try to relax yourself, no matter how tense you feel.

It will help if you bridge the reins (see below) so that his neck takes most of the strain, rather than your hands. The more you pull on the reins, the more your horse will set his neck and jaw against you. Avoid a battle of strength with your horse as he will probably win. If he does get away from you and ignores your aids, turn him in a

Bridging the reins
If you run each rein through both hands to form a bridge, as shown right, you will be better able to hold a pulling horse. (The cause must be removed with further training.)

diminishing circle, using your voice, being careful not to urge him on by inadvertently gripping with your legs. Do not punish your horse when he does stop, or it is likely to happen again.

Rearing This is a dangerous vice and is difficult to cure. Once your horse is rearing you are powerless, so you must try to anticipate and prevent it. The best way to stop your horse standing up is to ride him forwards very strongly with your legs, and perhaps your whip, at the first hint of trouble. After two or three incidents he is unlikely to repeat the attempt. In a confined space this may not be possible, in which case you should lean forward before your horse gains height and, keeping your balance with one hand, pull his head sideways and down with the other, so that he has to regain his feet to keep his balance. Impose your authority as soon as possible by spinning him in a tight circle, and then ride him forward strongly. In bad cases of persistent rearing, seek veterinary advice.

The rider has little control in this position. If she had pulled her horse's head to one side, before they reached this height, this rear might have been avoided.

Training schedule

While the aims of training should always remain the same (see page 196), training programmes must be adapted to meet the needs of an individual horse. It is impossible to give hard and fast rules about the best age for each stage of training, although, as a general rule, the larger the horse, the later he will mature.

Some tough, native breeds of pony, or the smaller, early-developing types of horse can be backed without damage at two years old, but most horses are best left for another year. For most all-round horses, training for their first three years should be largely confined to handling and some basic commands. A mature two-year old may be lightly lunged but training usually starts in earnest during the fourth year (that is, at three years old) then, by the age of four most young horses are ready to work seriously although their physical maturity and general development will vary. From the age of five most horses are ready to work hard and to compete, having completed a year of basic training.

Some horses need more time. A large thoroughbred type, for example, may not mature until six or seven years old and unless his training is carefully carried out he may be ruined by that age.

While the horse is weak and still growing he can be handled and led. Then at three years he can be lightly lunged on good level ground on a large circle. This will build up muscles, supple him laterally and continue his obedience training until he is strong enough physically and mentally to carry a rider. A nervous or excitable horse equally will need considerably more time.

Lessons should be made as interesting as possible. To prevent boredom and the development of stable vices (see page 257), turn your horse out as much as you can. Ideally, start training your young horse in the summer when he is out to grass. Catch him directly from the field, take him to the stable to prepare him for his lesson, and return him to the field after the lesson.

Warm weather and plenty of grass tend to make a horse fat and lazy and in this "soft" condition he will be easier to train.

Year-by-year programme
Foal Leading; handling; possibly showing; weaning.
Yearling Handling; leading; tying up; foot care; grooming; stable manners.
Two-year old As for yearling; if sufficiently mature, light lungeing for short periods of 10–15 minutes.
Three-year old If mature, well-handled and obedient in hand, start basic education (see programme guidelines); keep lessons short: 20–30 minutes maximum. Avoid over-tiring or straining your horse.
Four-year old Depending on physical maturity and development, either start, continue or complete basic education.
Five-year old If required, competition work; hunting.

Training programme for a mature three-year old
Week 1 Handling in stable; tying up; grooming; stable manners; leading in hand; simple voice aids; bitting; introducing lungeing tack.
Week 2 Lungeing without side-reins; obedience to voice and whip; bitting in stable.
Week 3 Lungeing; obedience lessons.
Week 4 Lungeing with side-reins; loose schooling without jumps.
Weeks 5–8 Lungeing with saddle and bridle; transitions to improve balance; long-reining (if expert available); loose schooling over jumps.
Weeks 8–12 Backing; further lungeing and/or long-reining; introduction to basic aids when led or lunged.
Weeks 12–24 Riding in enclosed area; introduction to leg and hand aids; simple turns and transitions; improving balance with rider; introduction to hacking in countryside and on roads with a "schoolmaster"; loose jumping; some lungeing to improve paces and confirm obedience to voice.
Week 24 onwards Hacking over hills and gradients in company; aids to canter, cantering; rein-back; jumping with a rider – cavalletti, poles, grids; occasional loose schooling and free jumping to improve technique; increasing understanding of the aids; lateral aids; lateral movements, opening and shutting gates; leading off another horse.

Your young horse must be sufficiently mature to begin a concentrated training programme. He must have developed enough strength in his back and hindquarters to carry a rider. This young horse shows good bone and overall conformation, making him suitable for training as a riding horse.

Jumping

It is questionable whether any horse can be said to "love" jumping and many horses find it unnatural and uncomfortable. Only a small minority become "stars" capable of jumping large and difficult obstacles, but most horses can be trained to jump a variety of low fences without difficulty. A horse with only average jumping ability, but which has been skilfully trained to produce his maximum performance will often prove more successful than a less well-schooled, more highly talented one.

A good jumper needs to be athletic, which will depend partly on his physique and natural ability, and partly on correct training. His temperament should be calm yet bold, but this again can be influenced and improved by an expert trainer.

Horses can be trained to jump with or without a rider. When jumping without a rider, a horse may be either "loose" or on the lunge, depending on the trainer's preference, experience and the facilities available. Many people believe in teaching their young horses to jump even before they have been backed.

Some trainers think it wrong to teach a horse to jump without a rider since the horse will first have to learn to jump "naturally" and will afterwards have to adjust his balance and stride to cope with the moving weight of a rider on his back.

There is no one set method of training and it is better to be adaptable to the needs of a particular horse as, although some find jumping fairly easy, others do not. It is the job of the trainer to make jumping as easy as possible for the horse since there are few riders who are capable of being more of a help than a hindrance to the young horse. It is often better to start the horse jumping without a rider, therefore, until he learns to enjoy the experience, without taking too much out of himself.

As a general rule, most horses start by trotting over poles on the ground, progressing to bigger and more varied obstacles. For the best results, the young horse must be taught to jump calmly and confidently at every stage. How far he progresses ultimately will depend on the success of the training methods and on the facilities used, his capabilities, and the ambition and talent of the trainer or rider.

A sample training programme which includes jumping is given on page 225.

Right, a young horse being trained to jump with a rider. He is cantering over a small show jump, having previously tackled similar obstacles successfully at the trot.

Loose jumping

When loose jumping, the horse negotiates obstacles in an enclosed area, without a rider, and is controlled from the ground by a trainer and two carefully positioned, competent assistants.

Loose jumping is an excellent way to teach your young horse to jump, provided that he is sufficiently mature, that there are suitable facilities, and that the trainer is experienced in this skill. Most three-year olds can be taught to jump loose before they have been broken in or ridden, and in many places, such as Ireland, this is general practice. Large, backward horses, however, should be left another year if they obviously lack coordination (see Training schedule, page 224).

Objects of loose jumping

Loose jumping will develop a young horse's muscular strength, impulsion and initiative. Do not be dismayed if your young horse does not show any natural ability to jump at first; many horses are late developers. Nothing will give him a better chance to learn to use himself athletically than a carefully planned training programme that includes two sessions of loose jumping a week to supplement his normal schooling and hacking. Gradually he will learn to concentrate and coordinate both his physical and mental abilities, measuring his approach and sizing up the obstacle in order to jump it accurately, then re-adjusting his balance and stride ready to jump again.

Once he has learned to take small easy obstacles "in his stride", loose jumping can be used to advantage in more advanced training to develop his greater athletic ability, to shorten and lengthen his stride, and to increase his impulsion and boldness of approach. It can also be used to restore lost confidence after a fall, to retrain older spoiled horses and to exercise a horse's muscles when riding time is short or when, for some reason, he cannot wear a saddle.

Finally, loose jumping gives you a chance to observe and study your horse's jumping technique. Often problems can be detected more easily than when you are on his back, and can be cured with training.

It may take several days or even months before your horse learns to jump with economy of effort and fluency. He will also have built up the necessary flexibility, as well as stronger muscles, tendons and

Below, a horse jumping loose over a combination fence under the eye of his trainer.

joints. Once this point is reached, he should have a calm, confident attitude to his jumping, so that when you come to ride him over fences, he is well prepared.

Facilities and equipment

Good facilities are often difficult to find. If possible, you should build your own jumping lane or ring: it is a good investment if you plan to train several horses at some future date.

A jumping lane is built with three to six obstacles in a line. It has the advantage that the young horse does not have to turn, putting strain on the same tendons and joints, but there should be plenty of space in which to stop at the end.

All the jumps should be movable, so that they can be adjusted or removed altogether. If they are permanently fixed, the distance between them may be just "wrong" for a particular horse and if he finds the striding difficult, he will lose confidence and enthusiasm. Also, repeating the same familiar line of jumps is boring for the horse and could encourage rushing.

A jumping ring can be circular or oval-shaped, so that you can direct your horse from the centre. A small circuit of 20m (66ft) diameter is good for loose exercise, but there is a risk of leg and muscle strain if young horses are asked to jump off tight turns before they have developed their strength and self-balance. If you only have access to a small jumping ring use just one small obstacle, and vary its appearance.

A large oval circuit of approximately 20 x 50m (66 x 164ft) is more useful. Again the obstacles should be movable and never placed too near a corner. Corners should be rounded off to encourage the horse to keep moving: a sharp bend might unbalance or even stop him.

A guiding fence of high rails, hurdles or something similar, preferably on both sides of the jumps, is necessary. If the surrounding fence is low, you may have to add higher wings to the approach side of the jumps when the obstacles are raised so that your horse does not jump out over the side of them.

The surface must be even. Rake over take-off and landing areas frequently.

Jumps should be inviting and must always be safe. When planning a free-jumping layout, the distances between jumps should be longer at first, and shortened gradually as the horse learns to balance

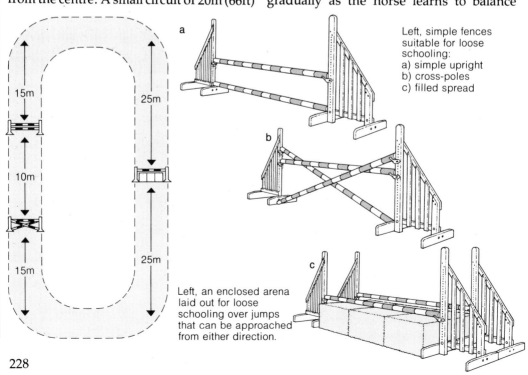

a

Left, simple fences suitable for loose schooling:
a) simple upright
b) cross-poles
c) filled spread

b

c

15m
25m
10m
25m
15m

Left, an enclosed arena laid out for loose schooling over jumps that can be approached from either direction.

himself using a more "collected" stride. If you are short of jumping material, do not be tempted to make do with just a few poles – the horse will jump better over solid-looking obstacles with well-defined ground lines. If the horse makes a mistake, the poles should fall down easily without bringing down the whole construction.

Trainer's assistants should not talk or move about unnecessarily, or do anything that could distract the young horse. If you move ahead of him before he has gone past, you may stop him or slow him up, or he may rush by, anticipating a "move on" instruction. Assistants may carry a lunge whip, either held down or behind their backs unless in use. Only the trainer should speak and then only if absolutely necessary, soothingly to slow the horse down, or briskly clicking the tongue to increase impulsion. The only other instruction to give is "halt" or "whoa" (whichever the horse responds to).

Preparation

Prepare your horse before leading him into the loose-jumping school. He will not need a bridle, but could wear a snaffle without reins if you want him to learn to accept its feel, unimpeded by a rider. For this reason, too, your horse should wear a saddle, but remove the stirrups and tie the saddle flaps down under a surcingle. The girths must not be too tight, so use a breast plate or breast girth to prevent the saddle from slipping. If your horse is not wearing a bridle, leave his halter on so that you can catch him easily. Always protect his legs with boots or bandages.

Before introducing your horse to actual jumps, send him round the jumping track *without* jumps, until he settles down, and is responsive to your voice, trotting round in a relaxed rhythm. A well-balanced mature horse will be able to maintain a canter pace in all but the tightest of arenas, but do not drive your young horse too fast, losing the essential calmness and balance.

Introducing the jumps

To start off, choose the direction your horse finds easiest, and ask him to trot round the

Points to remember

1 Never loose-school unless you have sufficient experience, good facilities and adequate helpers, otherwise you may do more harm than good.

2 Never loose-school your young horse more than twice a week, and keep each session to 20 minutes maximum.

3 Build up the number and size of jumps gradually, and start each lesson with loose schooling "on the flat" on both reins before introducing the first obstacle. If the horse shows a tendency to rush, stop him, calm him, and then lead him quietly to the first obstacle, halt, and send him off slowly.

4 Never overface your horse by making the obstacles too large or too difficult and never site them on bends or at awkward angles.

5 Do not always stop your horse in the same place, otherwise he will anticipate it. He must stop when and where you say.

6 Be adaptable to the needs of a particular horse and adjust the jumps accordingly. If a horse is reluctant to jump or loses confidence, make the obstacles easier until he is jumping well and keenly again.

outside, allowing enough time to settle into an actual rhythm before he meets his first jump. One assistant should stand near the last corner before the jump, in case the horse slows up or needs encouragement. On no account distract the horse by waving the lunge whip, and do not speak unless absolutely necessary, but be prepared to prevent any sudden deviation.

Start with a single, attractive obstacle, such as a small, nicely sloped but *firm* brush fence of approximately 0.6m (2ft). From now on, ask your horse to go in one direction only. This can be reversed for the next lesson but meanwhile there must be continuity; if you stop to change and re-adjust the jumps, your horse will lose concentration. Alternatively, make sure all the jumps can be jumped safely in both directions.

Combination jumps

Once your horse is trotting over the jump happily, add a second jump two canter-strides from the first, that is 10.5–11m (33–36ft) apart. This provides a greater challenge – your horse must remain calm in the

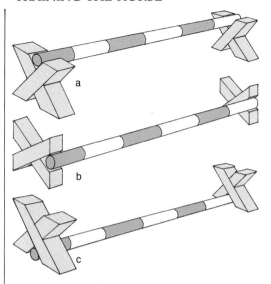

Cavalletti are very useful for training the horse to jump. The cross-pieces at each end can be turned to produce varying heights of jump: a) 50cm (20in); b) 30–35cm (12–14in) and c) 15–20cm (6–8in).

approach, measuring for himself the distance he has to cover in the two intervening strides, and using himself with agility. To make it easier for him, place a large, heavy pole on the ground 2.8m (9ft) in front of the first obstacle. This will ensure that he always meets the first obstacle in the correct place for take-off, and enables him to jump both parts successfully.

The combination can consist of varying types of jump but make sure they are always attractive with large solid-looking poles that "fill the eye" and are not easily dislodged. They should have an encouraging ground-line to help your horse judge his take-off point.

When introducing a spread fence, it is better to guide your horse into it with a small placing fence, correctly positioned, to encourage a "bouncy" stride that will engage his hindquarters and "collect" him.

Cavalletti

A line of cavalletti can also be set up. These are 3m (10ft) long wooden poles supported on cross-bars (above). First you must make sure that your horse is well established in a calm, relaxed trot. Jumping at the trot, he is unlikely to meet the obstacle "wrong";

instead, he will have more time to work out where to put his feet and will jump in a more relaxed manner than at the canter. At the trot the horse has to jump with greater upwards effort off his hocks, rounding his back and thus improving his style. Then introduce them to him one by one and pay great attention to correct distancing (see page 236). Do not discourage him at this stage by setting too daunting a task. The natural length of stride varies from horse to horse; a good jumper can adjust his stride to meet his fences correctly on most occasions and it is your job to teach your horse to do this by making jumping easy for him, while he gradually gains in confidence and physical strength.

Gymnastic combinations

A gymnastic line, based on cavalletti and fences, is the most effective way of developing your horse's jumping ability. Horses usually enjoy the activity (provided the distances are easy and the fences small) because it is rhythmic, interesting and gives confidence. Lines also develop his mental and physical agility and can be used to improve technique. They are usually approached at a trot but thereafter the horse will take "jumping strides".

Nervous horses

A horse which is nervous of jumping, or has learned to dislike it, should always start with loose schooling over poles on the ground. Then, starting with the last obstacle of the line or circuit, you should build up the jumps one by one, keeping the obstacles very small – 60cm (2ft) is high enough. End the schooling session while the horse is still enjoying himself. In the next lesson, start again with poles on the ground, making a little more progress in each session.

Jumping on the lunge

Few people have access to good loose-jumping facilities, and as an alternative the young horse is introduced to jumping on the lunge. Although the latter is easier to organize, it is rarely better than loose jumping. As already mentioned, lungeing is a skilled technique: success will depend largely on your judgment and on the co-ordination of your use of rein, whip and voice. Do not attempt to ask your horse to jump on the lunge until he is attentive and obedient to you on the lunge on the flat, and you are in control of his movements.

Preparation

Prepare your horse for lungeing in the normal way and lunge him in both directions equally for a total of some 20 minutes. The lunge-rein should be attached to the nearest side-ring on the cavesson: if it hangs from the front ring it will jerk un-comfortably on his nose when he jumps. Never attach the lunge-rein directly to the bit – the weight of the rein on his mouth during the jump or any sudden activity will certainly do harm. The head and neck must be left free, so remove the side-reins.

The jump

When your horse is relaxed yet active, and is attentive, introduce one pole on the ground and lunge him over it. Add a second pole, and perhaps a third at random on the circle and let your horse look and learn to judge and adjust his stride – if he shows signs of nervousness, give him plenty of time. Continue until he trots over the poles without difficulty.

Remember that a horse jumps more eas-ily from a straight approach than from a turn. When lungeing him over a jump, always send him over the centre of it, allow-ing at least two strides before and after the obstacle so that he can jump straight.

Always let your horse see any new jump before he attempts to trot over it, or jump it. A simple cavalletti is suitable for the first obstacle, then once he is negotiating it with confidence, introduce another pole in a dif-ferent place. Lunge your horse on an inner circle, then set him in position to approach straight to the jump, always giving him free use of his head and neck. Do not pull your horse round on the circle immediately on landing; let him find his balance without interference. You need to be active enough to follow him, yet quiet enough to allow him to concentrate on his task.

A good demonstration of lungeing a horse over a jump, which has been carefully designed to invite the horse to "round" over it in good style. The lunge rein must be raised, however, to clear the wing, as the trainer is correctly doing here.

Cavalletti

When your horse is jumping small obstacles competently, you can introduce him to a short row of cavalletti. Start with the poles on the ground, and then raise them slightly, one by one. Introduce an inviting single jump, and alternate this with the lines of cavalletti. As he progresses, the single rail can be made into a small spread fence.

Your young horse will tire quickly both physically and mentally. Keep early jumping lessons to approximately 20 minutes each and once he has learned to jump an obstacle well, do not repeat the same one more than twice.

The advantages and disadvantages

If the art of lungeing a horse over jumps is acquired, there are some definite advantages. Jumping on the lunge without a rider can improve a horse's calmness, confidence, style and technique, because he is able to use himself freely, unencumbered by a moving weight over his back. Stiffness in an older, experienced horse should gradually disappear, as the muscles relax, becoming more elastic and useful. For the mature horse of five to six years, jumping off a turn helps the development of new muscles, making him more supple – an advantage later when the horse is asked to turn before or after a jump. Lungeing also develops the horse's physique, particularly the hindquarters and hocks, the shoulder muscles, and the muscles over his loins and along his back and neck. With gradual lessons, his balance, judgment and co-ordination will improve too.

If your horse has not yet learned to canter on the lunge, he could do so while learning to jump. He will approach the pole at a trot but the jump will be an elevated canter stride, and he may continue in canter for a few strides after landing, or until making a turn, which will probably unbalance him so that he returns to the trot. The number of canter strides will increase as he improves his balance, but he should not be pushed on to a longer, flatter stride at this stage as it would unbalance him.

Long-reining over jumps

An officer of the Cadre Noir demonstrating how to long-rein a horse over a large parallel jump. He has full control and is not interfering with the horse's ability to jump freely. Long-reining a horse over jumps is beyond the scope of almost all trainers, however, and should only be practised by a professional and highly skilled trainer.

Lungeing over jumps often re-awakens interest in a bored or sour horse, while for the trainer and rider it emphasizes how important it is not to interfere with the horse's natural jump. Lungeing your horse, you will be able to observe how he moves, how much he uses himself, and where his weaknesses lie, which will help when it comes to riding him over jumps.

Many trainers disapprove of jumping any horse on the lunge, for it can be damaging even in expert hands and ideal conditions. A very young horse should not be asked to jump off a turn, although later on, when he is considerably stronger, it could prove useful.

Another problem is that it is difficult for the trainer to maintain an even contact on the lunge-rein and to control the shape of the circle when the horse is jumping, which, in turn, affects the rhythm and stride, resulting in loss of sensitive communication. If the rein drags or jerks at the horse, particularly in the form of a backward pull, his impulsion, confidence and concentration will all suffer.

Jumping with a rider
Schooling over poles and cavalletti

Cavalletti can be used to develop the horse's athleticism. Energetic walking and trotting over a succession of evenly spaced poles or cavalletti will activate the horse more effectively than lengthy school work on the flat. It promotes the horse's muscular development, strength and flexibility while he learns to adapt his balance so that he can carry a rider.

You will need five or six adjustable cavalletti which must be set up on even ground that is neither too hard nor too heavy. At first they should be spaced to suit the horse's length of stride but later you can position them so that he learns to adjust the length of his stride to negotiate each pole without making mistakes. This not only improves his concentration and judgment but makes him more sure-footed.

As with all stages of training do not force your horse in order to obtain quick results. Remember that before the horse can use his muscles effectively he must be able to relax and stretch them.

You must follow a systematic training programme (see page 225), working towards a definite goal: an active, yet calm and balanced approach to jumping.

Bruce Davidson schooling a young horse at home over a practice cross country jump. Very sensibly, he is wearing a crash helmet, as should all riders in these circumstances.

Correcting a "rushing" horse

To prevent your horse rushing, use a firm half-halt as you approach the cavalletti, but offer him a free rein on reaching the poles, so that he can complete the exercise without interference. Do not restrain the horse so that he stiffens against you, losing his flexibility, rhythm and rounded outline. If he does, settle him by riding on a circle before approaching the cavalletti again. If he is still excited, return to riding on a circle, but include transitions to halt and walk until he is quiet. You may have to reduce the number of cavalletti or use a single one until he is thoroughly relaxed. When he is, you can ask him to trot over three poles on the ground before you return to the raised poles or cavalletti.

Another method of slowing down an excited horse is to ask an assistant to "stand in your way" at or near the end of the row. He or she should move away once you have started down the line. You will still have to work to remove the cause of your horse's rushing, however, by making him calmer, which can only happen when he has learned to extend his topline and relax the tension in his muscles.

The first exercises

Start by walking your horse over a single heavy pole placed on the ground. Allow the horse to lower his neck, so that his back is relaxed, rounded and swinging freely. Then ask him to trot over the pole. You can then arrange a row of evenly spaced poles on the riding track to encourage the horse to keep straight. Once he is walking confidently over them, repeat the exercise at the trot. Then raise the poles slightly or use a line of three cavalletti turned to the lowest height, approximately 1m (3ft 3in) apart. This distance suits the average trot stride of a horse but the cavalletti must be moved closer together or further apart, if necessary. First ask your horse to walk over the raised poles in either direction until he goes straight and confidently without hurrying. His feet must land centrally between the poles. Ride him with a definite rhythm, and light rein contact to encourage a lowered neck and stretched topline. You must stay over your horse's centre of gravity and incline your body slightly forward to avoid getting behind the movement but

Right, trotting over evenly spaced poles, positioned on the ground. Once the horse is trotting over them successfully, the poles can be raised a little from the ground, or cavalletti can be used, turned to their lowest height.

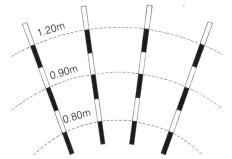

Top, the horse and rider walking over the central route of poles positioned on a circle, spaced as shown above. The outer route can be used to lengthen stride, and the inner route to shorten it.

without leaning so far forward that you throw the horse on to his forehand. Use the rising trot in the approach, keeping your movements to a minimum, and sit lightly, putting more weight than usual on the stirrups (letting your hips, knees and ankles absorb the movement) to allow your horse to relax and extend his back muscles in an easy swinging action.

Your aim is to get your horse to enjoy cavalletti work and to develop a quiet but not lazy attitude to jumping.

When he can perform this first exercise well, increase the number of cavalletti to four, then five, until he trots over them with increasingly elastic, springy and rhythmic steps. Vary the exercise by altering the grouping and spacing between the cavalletti so that your horse has to watch the ground carefully. This should help to improve his judgment.

Once your horse can maintain a level, rhythmic trot throughout these exercises, you can place the cavalletti on a curve, forming part of a 20m (66ft) diameter circle.

When taking a central route through the poles the horse does not alter his stride, but he will have to bend throughout his length, stretching his outside muscles while contracting the inner ones. The inner route of the curve demands more bend, and should not be attempted by an immature horse. With more mature horses the inner and outer routes can be used to teach adjustments of stride.

Canter exercises over cavalletti

Once you can trot successfully over cavalletti, you can ask your horse to canter over them but they must be spaced at 3–3.5m (10–11ft) apart to allow for the increased stride at the canter. A line of three cavalletti can be used, turned to their maximum height of 50cm (20in) so that your horse must make a jump over. Adopt the forward jumping seat to remain over the horse's centre of gravity, and practise maintaining this position at the canter on a circle. Do not attempt to canter over the cavalletti until your horse is calm: an on-going horse should be given the shortest possible approach off the circle so that he has less opportunity to quicken in anticipation.

Jumping a fence

To encourage your horse to enjoy jumping the fences should be attractive and easy: for instance, a simple upright with a good ground-line, or a small spread of ascending height. The former will encourage him to jump upwards off his hocks while the spread demands a wider bascule. Crosspoles (see page 228) are an effective way of making the horse jump through the centre of the fence. The jumps should be approximately 61–75cm (2ft–2ft 6in) high at this stage of training.

Approach the jump at the trot to allow the horse time to coordinate his movements and encourage calmness, thus enabling him to control his balance more easily.

It will help if you place a pole on the ground about 2.7m (9ft) in front of the obstacle. This improves the horse's jumping technique, athletic ability, balance and neatness. Good style is not only attractive to watch but is also the most effective way of clearing an obstacle.

At first the pole may seem a hindrance, as the horse may fumble over it while looking at the jump, but he will soon learn to use it to judge his point of take-off, particularly if it is raised slightly above the ground. This will encourage him to make a canter stride over it, from which he will find it easy to jump the fence. (If the raised pole is placed 5.5m [18ft] from the jump there will be another canter stride before the jump). If you position the pole in the correct place for take-off, the horse gains confidence and is therefore less likely to rush. Later on, when you make the jumps larger or wider, and when you approach at the canter, you will have to adjust the position of the placing pole to give the horse enough space to take off from a comfortable position.

When your horse is approaching both types of jump calmly and confidently, remove the placing pole and jump the fence alone. The transition should be easy.

Jumping several fences

Practise at first trotting over several small jumps using a calm, balanced, straight approach. Return to the rising trot as soon as possible after each jump and reestablish rhythm and calmness before making the next approach.

When he can jump a variety of obstacles (up to 1m [3ft 3in] in height) easily from a trot, he should have developed his technique sufficiently to jump larger, more varied fences at the canter.

Jumping at the canter

Start with a small fence, and place a pole 3.5m (11ft) before the jump once it is raised to over 60cm (2ft 6in) high, increasing this to two strides (10.4m [34ft]), three strides (14m [46ft]) four strides (17.5m [57ft]) and so on. However many young horses tend to lose their balance at first when jumping from a canter, as they are not ready for the degree of collection required; gridwork should help to improve it.

Rushing

Young horses may rush off after jumping either because they are excited or unbalanced. Do not lean forward more than necessary but sit more upright after landing to help the horse to engage his hindquarters and lighten his forehand. If neither sitting more upright, half-halts nor your voice stop him from running on, turn on to a circle of about 20m (66ft) until he is brought under control. Re-establish a relaxed canter before halting quietly.

An older more mature horse with better self-balance can be asked to halt straight on after completing a line of jumps as a discipline to remind him to be attentive to the rider's aids at all times, and to prevent him from getting carried away by the excitement of jumping.

Improving the bascule

Your aim must be to improve your horse's jumping technique so that he rounds or

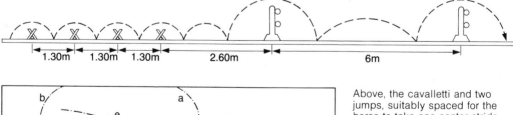

1.30m   1.30m   1.30m   2.60m   6m

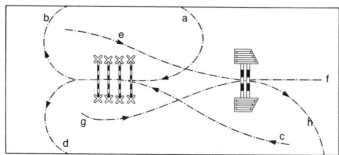

Above, the cavalletti and two jumps, suitably spaced for the horse to take one canter stride after the first jump.

Left, by removing the first jump, you can use the cavalletti and the fence independently, approaching the cavalletti from a circle (a-b) and (c-d) and the fence at an angle (e-f) and (g-h).

A simple grid suitable for a young horse learning to jump. It is composed of ground poles and small uncomplicated jumps and should be approached at the trot to give the horse time to see exactly where he should place his feet.

bascules over the fence using all his muscles effectively. This is probably best done by loose jumping combined with work on the flat to develop the topline, but your horse must still learn to carry his rider easily while jumping.

A placing pole before and after a small jump will encourage your horse to look downwards and lower his head and neck, while the use of parallel bars will encourage him to fold up his forelegs and jump cleanly by developing and improving his agility.

Gridwork

A grid of jumps is a sequence of obstacles, carefully designed to develop the jumping ability of the horse. The easiest grids may consist of a combination of trotting poles and cavalletti, with a small jump at the end. An advanced jumper can improve his technique over difficult grids, such as a succession of three or more parallel bars with one stride between each jump.

To start with, line up poles or cavalletti before a small single jump which is placed 2.7m (9ft) from the last cavalletti or pole.

The jump should be low, as you will be approaching at the trot. As the horse improves, a second obstacle can be added two short strides (9m [31ft]) from the first. This can then be brought in to make one short stride (6m [19ft]). The trotting poles ensure that the horse cannot shorten or lengthen his stride so he must remain balanced. They also prevent an impetuous horse from rushing. Repeat the exercise until the horse is quite calm. If you remove the first jump and leave the trotting poles, you can approach the poles from a circle, in the other direction, and jump the second fence from either side of them. By this time, the horse should jump a single obstacle calmly, with good balance. Trot again as soon as possible after landing and do not repeat the jump until your horse is calm and relaxed. The trotting poles will help to re-establish a good rhythm.

If you set up two parallel bars as shown, you can jump them straight as a double to improve the horse's athletic ability and style, or you can jump each one separately, from an angle, which can be increased as accuracy and confidence improve.

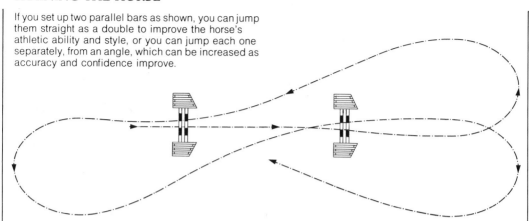

Adjusting the stride

A horse with a long natural stride is more likely to meet a fence "wrong" than a short-striding, bouncy horse. However, work on the ground to shorten and lengthen the stride at trot and then at canter will help you to control and regulate his stride – if you always aim to ride on a medium-length stride you cannot go far wrong.

The long-striding horse should first be allowed to develop his natural jumping ability. Then he can be worked systematically, through cavalletti, grids and combination fences, to gradually shorten his stride by increased activity of the hindquarters without causing tension or resistance. He will then be strong enough to undertake more collected work.

A suitable exercise to shorten the stride is to use a low placing pole in front of the jump. It is then moved in very gradually to encourage a shorter approach stride. Any adjustments to his balance and rhythm should be made at least four strides before take-off.

The short-striding horse may have trouble with spread fences or long distances in combinations. He must be schooled on the flat to extend his stride at trot and canter, to increase the mobility and "reach" of his shoulders and hindquarters, and to stretch his muscles to maximum elasticity.

These problems, however, are more noticeable in advanced jumping. The medium stride can be adopted by nearly every horse and is most effective for show jumping and cross-country fences which are not so difficult that they demand a special approach.

Jumping at an angle

For this exercise the horse has to jump two level parallels (approximately 1m [3ft 3in] high and two strides 10.4m [34ft] apart). The first one can be approached at the trot, with or without trotting poles, to steady and balance the horse. It can then be approached at the canter, with any extra ground poles removed. Jump the parallels from both directions, straight. Then, after landing over the second jump, continue round in a canter (trotting and rebalancing, if necessary) so that you approach the first obstacle from the opposite direction, passing close to the wings of the second. The horse must jump from a slight angle but should go straight over the centre of the jump. Continue and circle back to jump the second oxer from the original direction, again approaching at a slight angle. As your confidence and accuracy improve, the angle can gradually be increased.

Always look ahead in the direction you wish to go, and make sure that your horse follows the exact route. Accuracy is vital otherwise you will frighten the horse.

When intending to turn left on landing, look to the left, your weight in the left stirrup, and give the appropriate lateral aids. Keep equal contact on both reins, although your left hand may move out to the left to indicate the direction.

Retraining

If your horse is jumping badly it may be from one main cause, or for a number of reasons, resulting in such problems as rushing or refusing.

Rushing

Rushing in the approach to a fence has already been mentioned in training the young horse to jump. It is usually caused by an impetuous temperament but it can also be the result of anxiety, fear or pain. You must first discover the cause and then try to overcome it. It may be your riding that is at fault, because you are unbalancing your horse or because your hands are unsympathetic. If your horse anticipates discomfort when he jumps, he cannot relax. In this case, ask a more experienced rider to school him over jumps until he regains his confidence while you improve your own technique by taking lessons.

It may take months to cure a "rusher", but it is well worth the patient effort because good jumping is impossible without a controlled approach. Flat work, free jumping and cavalletti work on a circle, using frequent transitions through walk and halt, are effective measures in most cases. However, if the rider tenses, the horse will sense it, become anxious and start rushing again. Sometimes a line of fences or a grid may encourage rushing as the horse anticipates each one, so avoid this and practise some jumping exercises on a circle instead.

If your horse rushes on landing after a jump, turn in a circle, using half-halts. Alternatively, halt him straight, soon after the jump, and make him stand still, before you reward him. If your horse is allowed to stand and take a mouthful of grass he will be delighted to slow down. He will also be less inclined to rush when jumping *away* from home or the gate.

If the rushing continues, return to trotting over small obstacles, then jump several in succession at the trot, mostly off a turn. Never pull at your horses mouth, as this will only increase tension and resistance, and avoid making strong half-halts immediately before a jump, which will break up the rhythm and throw him off-balance, as well as distract his attention. Instead, check him with a firm but careful half-halt three or four strides before the take-off. After that, sit upright using your weight distribution and quiet seat and hands to help steady him. Practise frequent walk-canter-halt transitions on a circle before and after jumping small obstacles. If your horse is obedient to the aids and does not fight you, he will learn to obey you all the time, and jumping will become easy and incidental for him.

Refusing

Refusals are normally the result of a bad approach to the jump, caused by lack of confidence or communication between horse and rider. A horse ridden "on the aids" and "ahead of the rider's legs" seldom refuses to jump. Since it may take months of careful training to restore loss of confidence (it may never return completely) you cannot afford mistakes.

Start by identifying the cause of the refusals. Having made sure there is no serious underlying problem, always be determined the refusal will not happen again. Approach again from not too far away but allowing enough space to ride at the fence at the correct pace and in balance. If you need to use your whip, make sure you hold

The horse is rushing in the approach to the fence, and needs calming with cavalletti and gridwork.

The horse has approached too fast on his forehand, resulting in a refusal, and the rider is too far forward to improve the horse's balance. More training under supervision is needed for horse and rider.

it on the side where you need it most. If your horse has run out to the left, for example, hold the whip in your left hand and approach at a slight angle from left to right. Approach the jump at a balanced canter or trot, depending on the size of it, making sure that you have enough impulsion. Be ready with legs, and perhaps your whip, to drive your horse on strongly if he hesitates, but do not charge at the jump – controlled power is far more important than speed. Never lose your temper with the horse if he refuses, or he will associate jumping with unpleasantness and refuse still more. Your horse relies on your judgment, skill and experience; if these are lacking, take lessons on a "schoolmaster" before training a young horse to jump.

Physical weakness If your horse is physically weak, he will find jumping strenuous and may develop a dislike for it if you continue to force him. Such a horse must return to training on the flat in order to develop his muscles and to improve his balance. He can then move on to loose jumping, cavalletti and gridwork, progressing gradually over a period of months to jumping small obstacles.

Overfacing You, the rider, must decide whether your horse is physically able to jump a certain fence before you attempt it. Time and again ignorant riders thrash and

spur unfortunate horses into jumps that they cannot cope with. Never ask so much of your horse that he is forced to refuse – it will destroy his confidence. You should not suddenly confront a young horse with an unfamiliar fence; let him see it first, then ride with determination. Once he makes a habit of refusing, it is difficult to eradicate. You will have to start his training again from the beginning, building up his enthusiasm with easy grids and loose jumping, while you increase his physical ability with systematic groundwork.

Falls, injuries and discomfort Any horse which refuses after suffering a fall, even if there is no apparent injury, must be examined by a vet. If his condition is sound, he must have his confidence restored gradually. Other causes of refusals include lameness from injured or bruised feet, legs or tendons, and discomfort from ill-fitting tack. Check that none of the straps on the saddlery, such as the throat lash or breast plate, are too tight.

Insufficient training This is likely to cause refusals. Jumping is not a game of chance and preparation must be thorough to avoid ruining the horse. If your horse does not respond to driving aids, lateral aids or half-halts, then jumping will be hazardous and he must be reschooled.

Unsuitable jumps Other causes of refusals include jumping in bad or very bright light or shadows, difficult take-offs on boggy or undefined ground, or a "scoop" in the ground in front of the jump.

Disobedience Refusals are occasionally caused by disobedience. Some horses are reluctant to leave their friends and will refuse to jump without a "lead". "Nappy" horses will refuse to go in a certain direction while others may dislike water and ditches, for example, and will always try to refuse them. Deal with all such cases by putting the horse firmly "on the aids", by riding forwards strongly, and by taking time to reschool him until he is more obedient.

Keeping a horse

Conformation of the horse

Anyone who looks after a horse, or who intends to buy one, must know something about the horse's conformation. The expression "handsome is as handsome does" is often true: good performers come in all shapes and sizes. Valuable individual qualities such as natural balance, a bold yet calm disposition and flowing paces are more important than a perfect shape. But if he has good conformation, he will not only look attractive, he will be able to perform more easily and undergo more stress and strain, without injury, than a badly made horse can.

The horse should have a fine head, with large bright eyes and an alert expression. He should be well-balanced with his head set well on his neck, which should be longer and more muscled at the top than the bottom. His withers should be level with the croup, and should slope back gently. His back should be strong and fairly short, as a long back tends to be weak. The ribs must be wider and rounder behind the girth, and the hips should be broad. The hindquarters must be rounded, with strong muscular thighs, and with the hocks close to the ground, as a long cannon bone is easily strained. The forelegs must be strong, and straight, perpendicular from the elbow to the fetlock joint. The bones and joints of all four legs must be flat and well-defined. The pasterns should be sloping slightly to absorb the jarring. Good feet are vital: "no foot, no horse". They should match front and back, and should be open, broad and in hard condition, pointing squarely to the front.

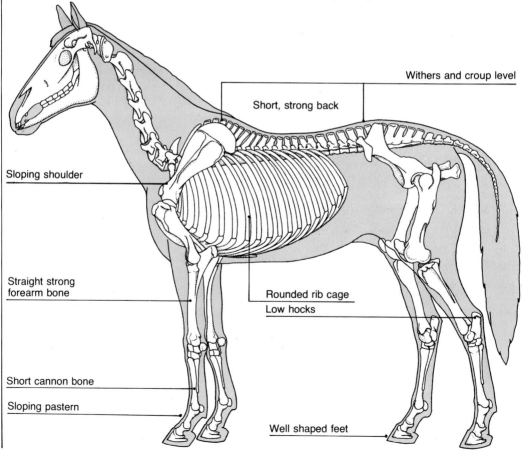

Withers and croup level

Short, strong back

Sloping shoulder

Straight strong forearm bone

Rounded rib cage

Low hocks

Short cannon bone

Sloping pastern

Well shaped feet

Action

The horse must move straight and freely. His action will vary to some extent according to the type and breed (some have a higher, more rounded action than others). All horses should show well-defined paces, however. If you observe the horse from the front, his legs should be put down straight, without deviation to either side.

Common faults are "dishing": when the forelegs swing out in a circular movement; "brushing" when the hoof of one leg hits the fetlock of the other; "going close", often as a result of having too narrow a chest; and "plaiting" when one foot weaves in front of the other.

Breeds

There are over one hundred breeds of horse and pony suitable for riding, and different countries have produced and developed types that are suited to their particular climate and conditions. Nevertheless, many breeds have become popular in countries other than the one of their origin. Among the most popular are the native mountain and moorland pony breeds of the British Isles: the Shetland, Dartmoor, Exmoor, Welsh Mountain, New Forest, Fell, Dales, Connemara and Highland. From these have been developed carefully selected riding horse and ponies, usually as a result of crossing the native pony with larger types

Faults of conformation

Very few horses or ponies have perfect conformation, any more than most people do. Too many faults, however, will make the horse a bad prospect for riding, since the extra weight he has to carry will soon reveal any weaknesses.

A poor or faulty neck and head carriage makes it difficult for the horse to balance, and an enlarged jaw or thick neck restricts flexion. Straight shoulders and upright narrow shoulder blades makes for an uncomfortable ride, and limits movement. Ill-defined, flat withers will cause the saddle to slip forwards or round.

Narrow brittle feet, or small, boxy or contracted ones do not provide sufficient shock absorption. Upright or over-sloping pasterns also invite lameness. Small or rounded joints will not stant up to hard work, nor will a horse with very thin bones below the knee. Bent or bowed forelegs are a serious fault, as are legs which are noticeably splayed or too close together.

Overly sloping quarters with undeveloped thighs should be avoided as the horse will lack strength. Hocks that are thin and too high off the ground are weak, especailly if too bent or too straight.

Poor conformation
The horse, right, shows generally poor conformation with a long, hollow back, a "ewe" neck (stronger at the bottom than on top) and long, weak legs. He also lacks muscle, although this can usually be built up with appropriate exercise and feeding. Weaknesses in conformation, or overwork or strain before the horse's bones are fully mature, can result in a bony enlargement on the legs in the form of a splint, spavin or curb.

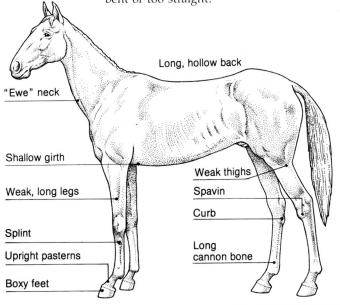

Long, hollow back

"Ewe" neck

Shallow girth

Weak, long legs

Splint

Upright pasterns

Boxy feet

Weak thighs

Spavin

Curb

Long cannon bone

and breeds, particularly the Thoroughbred horse. Among other popular breeds of pony are the Appaloosa of the United States, the Fjord pony of Norway and the Haflinger of Austria. Being smaller than horses, ponies are generally ridden by children.

The cob is a type of pony or small, sturdy horse with a mixture of predominantly Welsh and Hackney blood (the Hackney is a horse or pony with a very high action and is used mainly for driving).

The Thoroughbred, originating in the British Isles, is regarded by many as the finest of all breeds, well-suited to every aspect of the sport. The Thoroughbred is descended from the Arab, a selectively bred, small, spirited horse from the Middle East. The Irish Draught, a heavier horse with strong bone, is often crossed with the

Arab
Above, a splendid example of this breed, showing the typical fine head, arched neck and graceful action.

Thoroughbred
This breed, best known as the "racehorse", has had great influence on breeding world-wide.

Hanoverian
Right, this powerful West German breed is much in demand, and it excels in international dressage and show jumping. The best horses possess superb conformation and balance, and impressive athletic ability.

Morgan
Right, known for their tremendous physical strength and endurance, this breed is equally popular under saddle and in harness.

New Forest pony
Below, this is one of the largest of the native breeds of the British Isles.

Welsh Mountain pony
Below right, this small native breed is predominant in many ponies under 13.2hh.

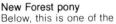

thoroughbred to produce excellent show jumpers and hunters.

Almost every nation of the world where riding is practised has produced its own breeds of horse. Among the best known internationally are the Morgan, Palomino and Quarter Horse of the United States; these are all versatile, all-purpose riding horses. The French Saddle Horse (Selle Francais) is a strong athletic type which is an excellent riding horse. The Lippizaner of Austria and the Andalusian of Spain have found international fame for their superb strength and agility. The Gelderland of Holland is powerful and active, making a good riding horse and show jumper, and the Hanoverian, Trakehner and Holstein of Germany are bred for their strength, good temperament and attractive action, making excellent horses for both show jumping and dressage.

Colours

Horses are often identified and distinguished by their colours.

Bay: brown head and body with black points. The shade of brown hair can vary; making a bright bay horse, or a dark bay or light bay. **Brown:** dark brown almost black coat with similar mane and tail. **Chestnut:** reddish gold coat, mane and tail. The depth of colour can vary to produce light, bright and dark or liver chestnuts. **Dun:** light-toned coat varying in colour from grey-blue (blue dun) to a yellowish hue (yellow dun), and golden dun, with a dark mane and tail. **Grey:** a mixture of white and black hairs, (with varying tail and mane). A horse with mainly white hairs is a light grey. **Black:** black body, mane and tail, possibly with white markings on legs or head. **Piebald:** patches of black and white hair on body, with white or black mane or tail. **Skewbald:** patches of white with any other colour but black. **Roan:** mixture of white and brown hair and a Blue Roan: mixture of white and black hairs. **Appaloosa:** white coat with spots of other colours. **Palomino:** golden body with blond mane and tail.

Buying a horse or pony

Most riders would like to have their own horse, but unless they have sufficient knowledge and experience, and the time and financial means to take full responsibility for it, they should not acquire one.

Before buying a horse or pony, you must consider where you will keep him. If you live in a town, he will have to be stabled. To keep a horse at livery, with someone else looking after him, is expensive, but this could be the best solution for a novice owner as a good stable will not only look after the horse well, but will also teach you the rudiments of horse management.

Another solution is to rent a stable or a field and look after the horse or pony yourself. It is cheapest to keep him at grass, because you only have to supplement his food for part of the year, but you will still have to pay for shoeing and veterinary care, and you will find it time consuming looking after him. Many people keep the horse at grass for part of the year and in the stable for the remainder.

Once you own a horse, his welfare is your responsibility, and must never be neglected. If you are unable to look after the horse yourself for any reason, you must delegate the task to a responsible, knowledgeable person.

Most horses are advertised for sale in the appropriate equestrian magazines and papers. Having picked out a possible horse you should take someone with you to see it

A family pony such as this must be strong, calm dependable and versatile.

Measurement

A horse is classified by breed, type (see pages 243–6) and height. A horse normally stands more than 14.2 hands high at the withers and a pony less than 14.2hh. A hand measures 4in, the measurement deriving from the time when the horse's height was gauged by a man placing one clenched fist on top of the other (the average width of a fist being 4in).

who knows what to look for. He or she is likely to be a better judge than you of what type of horse will be suitable for you. Having made your choice, the horse should be examined thoroughly by a vet, and passed as fit and sound by him.

It is important that the horse is the right size for you, neither too big nor too strong, and that his temperament suits your own. (For example, if you are very excitable, you should choose a placid horse.) He must be completely sound, without serious vices. If you are an inexperienced rider looking for a quiet, reliable hack, do not be tempted by the looks of a flashy hunter.

Every horse owner should know what their liabilities are under the law, with a clear idea of the highway code as it applies to horses. It would be wise to take out some form of insurance, to cover you in case your horse accidentally inflicts injury or damage to a third party or their property.

You should also make sure that you do not contravene any bye-laws in keeping a horse: for example, planning permission is normally required if you wish to erect a stable building.

Condition

The horse must be in good physical and mental condition if he is to be happy. He should have a bold outlook with a calm disposition, and an alert head with bright, wide-open eyes. His ears should flicker, and be warm to the touch. His coat should shine, and the hair must lie close to the skin which should be loose, not stretched tight. His feet and legs should feel cold, and the tendons must be hard and firm, not puffy or swollen. The horse should move freely and easily, with a level action, and he should be neither over-fat nor too thin, and should show well-developed muscles.

In good health, the horse's temperature should be 38°C (100.5°F). His urine should be pale yellow and thickish, normally passed three to four times a day. His bowel movements should occur approximately eight times a day, with rounded firm droppings which break on impact.

To remain in good condition, the horse must be fed regularly and well and worked according to his fitness and condition (see page 259). Since horses dislike being alone, try to provide him with a companion. The horse must be checked daily for injuries, and to ensure that his teeth and feet do not need attention.

If looked after properly, most horses will lead long, fit and happy lives. Like us, they are more prone to injury and disease as they get old and will then need extra care and attention, but never confuse this with spoiling and over-indulgence.

If the horse is incurably sick or very old and weak, he will have to be humanely destroyed. (Some of the complaints affecting horses are given on page 272).

A thin, unhealthy-looking horse with a dull, dry coat, and with his ribs showing.

247

Showing

Show classes are held for all types of horse and pony. They are either shown "under saddle" (ridden) or "in hand" (led), and are judged on their conformation, action, condition, turn-out, manners and temperament. They must also be true to type or to the breed they represent.

In ridden classes the horses are expected to be more than decorative examples of their type: they must go well at all paces and they must be a good ride. In all but the pony classes, the judge may wish to ride the horses.

The four main categories of ridden show classes are for hunters, hacks, cobs and ponies, sub-divided into groups. Show hunters are categorized by the weight they would be expected to carry out hunting, with classes for the heavyweight hunter (suitable to carry 14st 7lb and over); the middleweight, suitable to carry between 13st and 14st 7lb; and the lightweight, suitable to carry up to 13st. There are also classes for the small hunter (up to 15.2hh and suitable to carry at least 12st) and the ladies' hunter which can be of any size but must be suitable to carry a lady either astride or side-saddle. The novice hunter category is for any horse which has not been successful previously at a similar standard of show,

Right, a child's pony of great quality, beautifully turned out, and showing an impressive action at the canter.

Left, the judge examining a working hunter. The saddle has been removed for the purpose, and the horse will be trotted up after to show off his straightness and the freedom of his action.

Above, an elegant turn-out of horse and rider in the hack class. The horse is judged not only on conformation and manners, but also on its ability to provide an excellent ride.

and there is also a class for the four-year old hunter of any weight.

Show hunters must be workmanlike, with good balance, conformation and performance. They are judged as suitable to ride to hounds, although many have never hunted, and perhaps never will, mainly because of the risk of injury. However, a further class exists, the working hunter, in which performance is a more important factor. The horse is expected to jump a short course of rustic or natural-looking obstacles, in "hunting style" which means at a strong pace, yet accurately and safely. The horse will then be judged as for a normal hunter showing class.

Hacks are smaller and more elegant than hunters (they are usually small thoroughbreds) and must have perfect conformation as well as being a comfortable ride. There are large hacks (not exceeding 15.3hh), small hacks (not exceeding 15hh but over

14.2hh) and ladies' hacks, suitable to be ridden side-saddle by a lady.

Cobs are classified as exceeding 14.2hh but not exceeding 15.1hh, and capable of carrying more than 14 stone. They are not a particular breed, but a mixture of several types. (Some ponies are of cob type.) A show cob must be solidly built, but with the ability to move freely and to gallop well. He must have all the attributes of a show hunter, although with less range and scope. (Docking the tails of cobs used to be fashionable but has now been made illegal, thankfully.

Ridden show ponies are usually divided into height classes: up to 14.2hh; up to 13.2hh; and up to 12.2hh – each ridden by children of appropriate age groups. There are also novice pony classes, which may be divided into heights, and a class for a side-saddle pony of any height up to 14.2hh. There is also a category for the family or

Boxing

If you plan to travel your horse over any distance, he will need to be boxed. It is best to use a horse-box or trailer which has both rear and side ramps so that the horse can be led in and out of it forwards. The horse should be rugged up and bandaged (see page 278), and kneecaps used to prevent any injury. It is best to put a bridle on the horse, with a lunge rein attached to it, so that you have better control of him.

With a young or difficult horse, put straw on the ramp of the box to make it look more inviting, and if the trailer has a partition, push it across or take it out until the horse is loading happily. It will help to use some food (nuts, oats or sugar lumps) to entice and reward him, when necessary.

Always load the horse straight, and do not hustle him if he wants to inspect the ramp before stepping on it. Never pull at his head or frighten him in any way. Once he is inside the box reward him. It will also help if you feed the horse in the box, so that he associates it with pleasure.

If the horse is difficult to load, follow the instructions above, but fasten two lunge reins to either side of the box door, with an assistant holding each free end. As the horse is led up to the ramp, the assistants cross the

lunge reins behind him against his hindquarters. The pressure from the reins should urge him up the ramp, without frightening him.

When unloading the horse pause at the top of the ramp and give him time to take a good look, before urging him down it.

Above, horses rugged up and bandaged, having just been boxed to a competition. The horse on the right of the picture is wearing hock boots for extra protection.

utility pony, which is able to carry more weight than the show pony and is more workmanlike. There are also classes for working ponies up to 15hh, which must jump a course in good style, and Show Hunters, which are not required to jump.

Among other classes for showing are those for specific breeds, and a "riding horse", which encompasses any mare or gelding over 15hh, not entitled to show in the hack, hunter or cob classes at the same show. Showing "in hand" is confined to young stock, brood mares, stallions and different breeds.

When a horse or pony is shown "in hand", he is led around the show ring at the walk, while the judges watch from the centre. After several circuits, the judge will choose the order in which the horses or ponies are called in. The judge will then examine the horses one by one at close quarters, and will ask for each to be trotted

up. A preliminary selection will be made, and those selected will walk round once more, while the judges make any final decisions regarding the order of merit.

For both "in hand" and ridden classes the horse or pony must not only look his best but must also be well-schooled. The tack should be of good quality and in impeccable condition. The horse's coat must gleam with health; and as a result of patient attention. The final grooming is done on the morning of the show, and the mane is usually plaited (see page 264), as is the tail, although some people prefer to pull the tail neatly (see page 264). Arabs and native breeds are left unplaited.

The horse will normally need to be boxed to travel to the show (see below).

The rider should be dressed appropriately for the particular show class. For the hunter and cob classes a tweed or dark coat, with a tie or stock, and a bowler or hunting

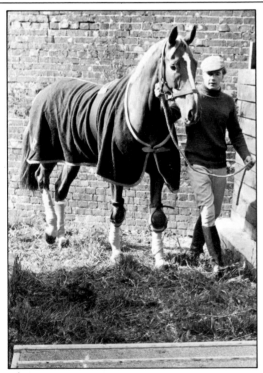

Above and right, when loading and unloading a horse into the box, never hurry him; give him plenty of time to inspect the ramp and lead him up or down it slowly.

cap are normally worn. At bigger shows, a red hunting or dark, cut-away style coat is worn with a top hat. In the hack classes the emphasis is on elegance, and a short top hat and cut-away coat (or a side-saddle habit for the ladies' class) may be worn. For pony classes, children should be neatly dressed: dark coats look elegant, worn with a plain tie, hunting cap, jodhpurs and jodhpur boots.

For showing "in hand", the only rule is that you should be neatly and soberly dressed so that you do not distract attention from your horse's appearance.

Young stock are normally shown in a strong head collar, with a single leading rein. Brood mares and mature horses shown in hand may wear a double or snaffle bridle. In ridden classes, novice horses and ponies should wear a snaffle bridle. A straight-cut show saddle helps show off the horse's sloping shoulder, and a plain leather or string girth looks neat. Boots and bandages are never worn.

The art of showing a horse or pony well is something you will acquire with experience. Compete at small local shows at first, and if you enjoy it and are successful, you can then enter in the larger shows against stronger opposition. Horses that are successful in the show ring can become very valuable, and showing can, therefore, be a cut-throat business. Nevertheless, many owners and breeders enter their stock for the pleasure of showing, win or lose.

A pair of ladies' hacks, ridden side-saddle, awaiting their turn to be judged on their performance, elegance and suitability.

Above, a good-looking cob, capable of carrying a heavy man in comfort. He is showing a fluent, powerful action.

Left, a Welsh pony stallion being trotted up in hand by his handler.

Right, a beautifully proportioned heavyweight hunter, with a bold but calm outlook.

Stable care

The stable

The stable should be solidly constructed on a well-drained site, preferably facing south to give maximum sunshine and shelter from the wind. It must have water, an electricity supply nearby, and an efficient drainage system.

The stable can be built of wood, stone, concrete or brick. Wooden ones are often portable units, and have the advantage of being relatively cheap to put up. However, permanent stone and brick constructions are better insulated against extreme heat or cold. The building may contain one or more loose boxes, each of which should be at least 3.6 × 3.6m (12 × 12ft), to house an average-sized horse, or 3 × 3m (10 × 10ft) for a pony.

Horses are less likely to suffer boredom or the stable vices that result (see page 257) if they are kept in loose boxes opening out on to a yard. The horse will not only find it more interesting, but he will have a ready supply of fresh air, and there is less risk of infection being spread to other horses. The American barn-style of stable block, in which two rows of loose boxes face each other across a wide passageway, is increasingly popular. These stables may also have outside doors and/or windows so

that horses can look out. Large double doors at both ends allow easy access and good ventilation. Fire regulations are strict for this type of stable.

The floors of the stable should be non-slip and hardwearing. Roughened concrete, stable bricks or any hard-packed material all make suitable surfaces, and should be sloped slightly towards the drain, which must be regularly cleaned and disinfected to prevent blockages occurring and to lessen the risks of infection. If moisture is allowed to collect under the bedding diseases such as thrush (see page 272) will develop.

Where several horses are kept, standing stalls are sometimes used: at least two of them can be fitted into the space taken up by a loose box, as they are usually only 1.5m (5ft) wide by 3m (10ft) long. However, the horse has to be tied up and so cannot move about or roll at will, and he is likely to get bored as he will be facing into a wall. On the other hand, stalls are more economical on bedding than loose boxes, and they also take less time to muck out.

The lighting system in the stables must be properly installed and safe, with all switches and wires out of the horse's reach, and with the switches preferably

Features of the stable

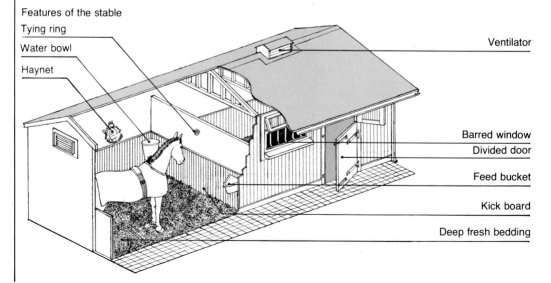

Tying ring
Water bowl
Haynet

Ventilator

Barred window
Divided door
Feed bucket
Kick board
Deep fresh bedding

Stalls are space-saving, but are less comfortable for the horse than a loose box, as he has to be tied up.

positioned outside the loose boxes. The stables must always be well ventilated, and each box should have an opening window, barred over to prevent accidents. Ideally the window should be of the type that slants inwards to open, so that rain is kept out while fresh air can come in.

The door to the box should be divided in two parts, with the top half left open to allow the air to circulate and the horse to look out. It may have to be closed in very cold weather. The window and door should be on the same wall, to prevent draughts.

Any fittings should be well made, with no sharp edges. The door should fasten on the outside at both top and bottom so that if the horse succeeds in undoing the top latch (and many of them do!) he will still be unable to get out. It must also be possible to bolt the door from the inside, but the door should always open outwards so that you can get in and out of the box quickly and easily, and without the risk of injury to the horse.

Rings should be fitted about 1.2–1.5m (4–5ft) up on the wall so that the horse can be tied up while being groomed. If you use

Bedding

The horse must have a comfortable bed in his loose box or stall to encourage him to lie down and to prevent injury when he does so. There are various different types of bedding to choose from (below). Low cost, comfort, lack of absorbency, availability and easy disposal are the main considerations in choosing which material to use.

Straw is the most commonly used bedding, as it is usually available, comparatively cheap and easily disposed of for garden manure. There are three types of straw: wheat, oat and barley. **Wheat straw** is the best as it is the least absorbent and drains well. It is easy to handle, and as it is not palatable the horse is less likely to eat it. **Oat straw** is less satisfactory as it does not drain well and, as it is palatable, horses tend to eat it. **Barley straw**, is very soft and absorbent, and is therefore difficult to muck out. It should be avoided as it is indigestible and can also irritate the horse's skin.

Shredded paper This is one of the most economical forms of bedding, especially if you have your own shredding machine. It has the advantage of being dust free. It must be kept dry and clean or it will be heavy to muck out and will drag on the horse's feet.

Sawdust This is obtainable from saw mills and makes a suitable bed if used plentifully and kept clean. It can be heavy to handle, being very absorbent, and is dusty in poorly ventilated stables. Sawdust cannot be used for manure, nor does it burn well, so disposal may be difficult.

Wood shavings These are usually cleaner and fresher than sawdust. They do not clog up the horse's feet or get into his coat, and they are quicker to muck out, but splinters may occasionally be found amongst hardwood chippings. Used lavishly, wood shavings provide a good, soft bed, but present the same disposal problems that sawdust does.

Peat This makes a good bed but as it has to be well-dug daily with a fork to keep it loose, it is hard work. It can be dusty and tends to get into the horse's coat. It has the advantage of being both unpalatable and easy to dispose of, but it is expensive.

a haynet for feeding the horse, you will need a ring for it, positioned high up on the wall – 1.5–1.8m (5–6ft) – so that when the net is empty, there is no danger of the horse getting his foot caught in it.

Mangers can be fixed or movable, and made from various materials, ranging from stone to plastic. If permanently fixed, they should be positioned about 90cm (3ft) above the ground with the space beneath filled in so that the manger does not jut out from the wall, with the possibility of the horse getting trapped underneath it when lying down or rolling. Movable mangers are easier to clean.

Since the horse needs to drink between 23–68 litres (5–15 gallons) of water a day, and since the stables must be washed out regularly, a handy water supply is essential. Like mangers, all water containers must be carefully positioned, preferably in a corner, to prevent accidents occurring. Some stables have automatic drinking bowls built in, but although they are labour saving it is difficult to know how much the horse is drinking. Whatever type you use, it must be big enough for the horse to get his whole muzzle in, and it should be kept scrupulously clean.

Mucking out
The box should be thoroughly cleaned out every day and the droppings removed more frequently. For this task, you will need a set of tools: a four-pronged fork for shaking up straw bedding and to separate the soiled parts from the clean, and for moving the muck into the barrow; a shovel for picking up droppings; a hard brush for sweeping the floor of the box, and a wheelbarrow for removing the soiled bedding. A skep, or similar container, and a pair of rubber gloves, are useful for removing droppings quickly and easily at other times. The muck heap should be stacked tidily, away from the stable.

Top, picking up the soiled bedding with a fork. The floor should be swept and allowed to dry off before new bedding is shaken out and spread over it, above.

How to muck out
Before mucking out, always tie the horse up (see page 37). Using the fork, toss the dry, clean bedding to the rear and sides of the box. Lift the muck into the barrow with the fork or shovel. Sweep the floor and allow it to air and dry off, before replacing and replenishing the bedding, so that the horse has a deep, comfortable and clean bed to lie on.

Bank the bedding up the walls to help prevent injuries, should the horse roll, or become "cast" (stuck and unable to get up). Keep the bedding deep enough to encourage him to lie down.

At least once a week, remove all the bedding and wash the floor down with disinfectant to keep the stable fresh and to discourage flies and germs. Air it well before remaking the bed in the usual way with fresh bedding.

Stable routine

Plan your stable routine to suit your own convenience and to give your horse the regularity which helps him to eat well and to relax and rest. His well-being and comfort are essential if he is to work well and enjoy being ridden.

In his natural state, a horse eats little and often, mostly feeding early in the morning and late at night. Your stable routine should be built around this principle, always allowing the horse time to digest his food in peace. As he has a small stomach, feed small amounts, three or four times a day, and give the smallest feeds before work, and the largest one at night. Allow at least one hour after a feed before exercising: working on a full stomach is likely to cause colic or indigestion.

Grooming and strapping should be done after exercise, preferably while the horse is still warm, as the pores of his skin will be open, and therefore any dirt will be much easier to remove.

An ideal routine is shown below. You can adapt it to your own needs, bearing in mind the principles above.

Stable routine

7.00 am	Check horse over; straighten rugs; water; feed; remove empty haynet.
8.00 am	Muck out; clean out feed and water containers; brush horse over; pick out and oil feet; tack up.
8.30 am	Exercise.
10.00 am	Groom, strap, rug up horse; give haynet.
12.30 am	Skep out box; straighten rug; feed, water.
4.30 pm	Change rugs, adding extra blankets in cold weather; water; skep out box, refill haynet for night; feed. Clean tack.
9.00 pm	Straighten rugs; water; skep out box; last feed; settle horse for night.

Stable vices

Biting, kicking, or general unruliness in the stable are usually the result of rough handling, but often bad habits are caused by boredom, overfeeding, hunger or spoiling. Some very sensitive horses are irritated by noise or touch. Take time and trouble to find out the cause, and to gain your horse's respect and trust, in and outside the stable.

Be consistent and always make it clear to the horse when his behaviour is unacceptable by speaking sternly and, if necessary, smacking him smartly on his neck, shoulder or hindquarters, as appropriate, but never on the head.

Common bad habits are: –

Crib-biting The horse grabs and bites the edge of the manger, or the top of the door, or some similar protrusion and sucks in air as he does so. It is often incurable because it is deeply rooted and usually caused by boredom when a young, active horse is confined and stabled. Covering all possible surfaces with an anti-cribbing substance such as "Cribox" may cure the habit. To prevent boredom, divide feeds and hay rations into small quantities and give them at frequent intervals so that he has something to eat all the time, and turn him out into a paddock whenever possible.

Wind-sucking As the name suggests, the horse sucks in air with a loud, gulping noise. The habit is catching, so keep an offender away from other horses. In extreme cases, a special anti-windsucking gadget or collar can be worn.

Weaving This habit of rocking sideways, usually in the doorway of the loose box, is also imitated by other horses. It is usually caused by an excitable temperament, coupled with frustration at being confined in a stable. Discourage the habit by installing a vertical bar above the stable door to divide the open area into two. Alternatively you can suspend a log or similar object from the top of the stable door so that every time the horse rocks sideways he touches it; this method is less suitable as it may cause head-shyness.

If you shut your horse in completely, it may make matters worse. He will still continue to weave in the middle of the stable, rocking from one leg to another.

Feeding

The amount and type of feed varies according to the work your horse is doing, his age and size, and his general condition. The sample feed programmes shown opposite provide a general guide, but you will have to adapt the quantity and timing of the feeds to suit your horse. Foals and brood mares, and sick or aged horses, require special feeding and it would be wise to consult your veterinary surgeon for precise instructions. There are certain rules to be followed when feeding the horse.

Water must always be offered to your horse before feeding him, as if he is given water afterwards, the feed will be washed down before it has a chance of being digested. The water must be fresh and clean and all containers scrubbed daily. The horse will drink more in summer than in winter, so make sure an adequate supply is always available to him.

Your horse should always be given the best food available and it must include plenty of bulk to aid digestion, as well as enough variety to keep him interested in it. Never leave stale food in the manger, and

---

Haynets
If you use a haynet, it must be tied securely to a ring positioned high up on the stable wall, so that when the horse empties the net, it doesn't droop down low enough for him to catch a foot in it. The best type of knot to use is the one shown below.

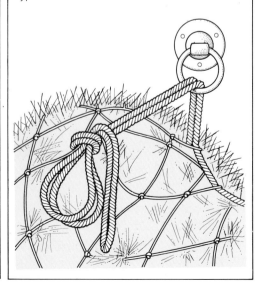

---

always keep the mangers and feed buckets scrupulously clean.

The horse must have adequate time to digest his feed – at least one hour for a small feed, and at least two hours for a large one – before being worked.

Do not feed him hay for at least five hours before a gallop or strenuous work, as a swollen or full stomach restricts lung movement, causing distressed breathing, and could strain his heart. Also, never feed the horse directly after hard work: he could choke or get colic.

Always mix feeds thoroughly, and make sure the food is fresh and of high quality. It should be stored in a dry place.

Types of forage

There are three main categories: low-protein bulk forage, high-protein concentrated feed and supplementary food.

Bulk food

Hay provides bulk for a stabled horse and, being dried grass, is the nearest thing to his natural food. It is at its best from 12–18 months after being cut as it tends to be too rich earlier.

Good hay has a good "nose" – that is, it smells sweet – and it should be light green to light brown. If you are buying several bales, open up some of them to make sure the hay is good all the way through.

There are two main types of hay: meadow or seed. Meadow hay is cut off permanent pasture, and is short, fine and soft, containing some white clover, herbs and vetches. Seed hay is cut from selected, cultivated grasses, and is richer. It may contain red clover, timothy, lucerne and rye grass for example, but has no herbs. Meadow hay, which is wild, may vary in value depending on where it was grown – uplands generally produce better hay.

Hay is fed in either a haynet (see left), which is convenient and economical, or on the ground or in a rack.

It is best to feed a good mixture of seed and meadow hay. Seed hay has a higher nutrient value than meadow hay, but good quality meadow hay is better than poor or mouldy seed hay.

Bran is a by-product of wheat and should be broad, pink-coloured and flaky, not dusty. It must smell sweet. It has bulk value and is easily digested. It can be used wet as a laxative, or dry for the opposite effect. It is much less popular now than in the past.

Chaff Good chaff is good hay, chopped. It adds bulk to feeds – oat straw can be mixed with it – and prevents horses from bolting their food. Mollichaff, or mollichop, is a mixture of chaff and molasses. It makes an excellent bulk additive or appetiser.

Sugarbeet pulp This is fattening, energy producing and easily digestible. It must be soaked for 12 hours before being fed as if it is given dry, followed by a drink, it swells, causing acute and dangerous colic.

Concentrated food

Barley can be fed as hot, boiled feed, and is very nutritious, especially in cold weather, or for building condition and fat. It must be cooked for at least two hours, until the grain has swelled to its maximum extent and is soft – if it swells inside the horse he will suffer. It is often cooked with linseed, or fed in micronised or cooked, flaked form, although it can also be fed uncooked provided it is first rolled or crushed.

Linseed is a high-protein food, and should be fed in small quantities – one handful

Bran mash

A bran mash is particularly good for a horse which is sick or lame, or is unable to be worked because of bad weather. It is also useful after a hard day's work, when the horse needs an easily digestible feed.

To make the bran mash, half-fill a bucket with good quality bran, and add a handful of epsom salts or table salt. If you wish to make the feed more appetizing, you can add a couple of handfuls of oats or a tablespoon of molasses. Pour on just enough boiling water to produce a damp crumbly mixture, after you have stirred it well. Allow it to cool – approximately 20 minutes – before feeding it to the horse.

Scooping the bran into the bucket. (Bran and chaff will both keep fresh longer if stored in a covered container).

Sample feeding programme

	Horse (16hh) in work	Horse (16hh) in light work
Season	Winter	Summer
Kept	Stabled, clipped and rugged	Stabled by day, out at night
Work	Training and competing; show jumper	Schooling, hacking, occasional competition
Feed		
8.00 a.m.	Oats 0.9kg (2lb); handful mollichaff	Oats 0.9kg (2lb); handful bran or mollichaff; flaked maize 0.4kg (1lb)
After work	Hay 2.3kg (5lb)	Hay 1.3kg (3lb)
12 noon	Oats 1.3kg (3lb); 0.2kg (½lb) coarse mix or cubes with carrots, or sugarbeet	Oats 0.9kg (2lb); handful bran and sugarbeet; nuts 0.9kg (2lb)
4.00 p.m.	Oats 1.3kg (3lb); bran 0.4kg (1lb); linseed jelly or boiled barley 0.4kg (1lb). Also salt, cod liver oil	Oats 0.9kg (2lb); handful mollichaff; nuts 0.9kg (2lb)
8.00 p.m.	Oats 1.8kg (4lb); bran 0.4kg (1lb); hay 3.1kg (7lb) – extra nuts can be added for variety	

per feed, per horse. It *must* be fed cooked as it is poisonous raw. It helps to fatten the horse and promotes a shiny coat and healthy skin.

Oats are generally fed lightly rolled, bruised or crushed, as they are easier to digest than when whole. They can also be fed cooked as a light gruel, after hard work.

Maize is fed cooked and flaked to make it more digestible. It is fattening and lies in the stomach for a long time, and should therefore not be fed to horses doing fast or strenuous work, such as racing, hunting or eventing.

Beans are fed cracked, and only to a horse in very hard work, as they are very high in protein and can make the horse too "hot".

Horse nuts are a compound foodstuff, and can include oats, bran, maize, barley, linseed, grass meal, molasses and other nutrients. Some varieties may also contain bonemeal, minerals and vitamins. You must find out what they contain before feeding them, as there is a risk of protein poisoning with some highly concentrated nuts. However, there are special low-protein nuts suitable for bulk feeding.

A coarse mix is a very palatable and nutritious feed combining most of the same ingredients as nuts in a loose, more digestible form. It is convenient, too.

Supplementary food

There are a number of other foods which liven up the horse's palate and provide him with essential vitamins or minerals.

Root vegetables, such as carrots and turnips, can be used in small quantities as an alternative bulk food. Horses love **apples** as an appetizer, and benefit from **cod liver oil** which builds up their resistance to disease. **Glucose** provides energy and helps restore a sick horse; **eggs** are a source of protein – give one or two daily to a horse in hard work if he likes them; **milk powder** fattens and builds up young horses; **bonemeal** or **seaweed** is good for building up young bones; **beer** is an excellent restorative for a convalescent horse; **salt** should be given in a block, as a salt lick to aid digestion and clear the blood, or it can be added in small quantities to the feed.

Exercise and work

Every stabled horse needs regular exercise to keep him in healthy condition. The amount of work done and the nature of the exercise will vary according to the work expected from a particular horse. Regular exercise, mainly walking and trotting without great exertion, is usually enough to keep a horse in active condition for light work. "Work" is normally used to describe any stronger activity such as cantering, jumping and extended periods of schooling or long, energetic rides, which place more strain on the horse. A horse in regular work will need to eat more to keep in condition.

If you are preparing the horse for a competition you must work to a timetable and plan ahead, getting him in peak condition just before the event. The feeding programme should be adapted to his exercise work schedule. Grooming and strapping will also help to condition the horse, by working his muscles without straining him in any way. He must be allowed plenty of rest, as a fit horse may be very tense, and it helps to turn him out in a field to relax for an hour or more each day, if the weather is suitable.

Remember that the horse should never be worked beyond his stage of fitness.

Road exercise, mainly at the walk, is essential in the preliminary stages of getting the horse fit. A horse starting work again after a holiday needs two weeks' walking on the road, as it hardens and strengthens his legs in preparation for jumping and galloping, for example.

Fast trotting on roads should be avoided as it jars the feet and legs unnecessarily. If you must trot on a road, do so for short distances only and never downhill. Find good, level but yielding ground for trotting exercises. Gradually increase the length of time spent trotting, until, after a month, you are trotting for an hour continuously.

Riding up and down hills can be "exercise" or "work", depending on the speed, the terrain and the degree of collection asked. Light hill work (walking and trotting up and down slight inclines) is exercise but it can become work if you ride purposefully and repeat it often. Be careful not to spend more time on hill work than on flat work otherwise you risk straining the horse. Slow work, climbing steep hills, is an efficient way of conditioning the horse as it improves and stimulates the working of his heart, lungs and muscles.

If you ride on flat land, use long, slow cantering twice a week to build up your horse's fitness and stamina. After the early slow work for 5–6 weeks, start with two or three minutes of slow cantering, on either rein, gradually building up to a total of 20–30 minutes at 8–10 weeks of fitness.

If the land is undulating, use the hills to canter up, but do not risk injury by cantering *down* steep slopes.

Long fast gallops are not advisable as they put great stress on the horse's legs, muscles and tendons, and may also strain his heart and lungs. Short, sharp sprints of approximately 400m (450yds) can be used as "pipe openers", when the horse is fit, to clear his wind, stimulate his circulation, and "open him out", especially prior to a race or competition where he is expected to go fast or far. Gallops *must* be on good and even ground, preferably straight to minimise strain, and never downhill.

You should not do "fast work" more often than twice in a week.

All jumping requires exertion and is therefore "work". Cavalletti and grid work are useful to get the horse fit, to supple him, and to help strengthen his muscles and hocks. However it is not essential to include jumping in your conditioning programme, unless the horse is being prepared specifically for show jumping or eventing.

Roughing off

Roughing off a horse that has been in regular hard work over several weeks or months must be a gradual process. After his last day of work, give him bran mashes to clean out his system, and gradually reduce the "hard" food, replacing the protein content with bulk food such as bran and hay, over a period of two to four weeks (depending on how fit he has been).

Cut down his exercise, too, but not suddenly or he may "seize up". After a few days, stop grooming him, except for picking out his feet and seeing that he is comfortable, and remove the rug or blanket, and his shoes (leave his front shoes, if preferred). Then turn him out in a field for short periods at first, when the weather is suitable. See that he does not get cold. His coat will roughen and grow, so that after two to three weeks you may be able to remove his night rug. Gradually turn the horse out for longer periods, but bring him in at night unless the weather is very mild. Continue to feed him, or he will lose condition rapidly, especially if the grass is poor. You must judge how long your particular horse needs before he is completely adjusted to living out, without a rug or supplementary food.

Schedule for a day of hard work
Night before: Do not give boiled food or maize which is too bulky. Feed a normal hay ration.
Morning: Water horse, allowing him to have his fill. Remove water and hay. Feed as usual. Leave bran mash ready mixed for your return; leave grooming and stable equipment ready.

If boxing the horse, prepare him as usual (see page 278). If hacking, ride at a steady jog (4mph) to keep him fresh.
During the day: Make sure that the horse doesn't get cold. Walk him about or cover him as appropriate. Do not let him eat immediately after hard work.

Journey home: Jog home quietly and walk the last mile; you could dismount for the last half mile, leading the horse with a loosened girth. He can be allowed a drink if he is kept on the move afterwards.

If boxing home, tie him up, loosen the girths, lift the saddle to allow air to circulate, and rug him up and bandage him. Then load up, give haynet and drive home.
At home: Prepare hot bran mash. Check the horse is warm enough, unsaddle him and cover him, and give him a short drink. Encourage him to stale. Tie him up, and brush off; rub him dry if he is wet. Rug him up, undo plaits, and check his

ears for warmth. Go over him for injuries, using a torch if necessary. Check him again after an hour to make sure he is not sweating. When dry, rug him up completely. Sponge his eyes, nose and mouth. Feed him the bran mash. Clean tack, and then give him a small dry feed 2½ to 3 hours after the mash. Check that his ears are cool and dry.
Day after: Examine him for injuries and treat if necessary. Trot him up to see if he is sound. If he is stiff, walk him out.

Grooming

A stabled horse should be groomed daily for several reasons: to keep his skin healthy, to improve his circulation, to make his coat shiny and to help prevent the tack, rugs and blankets from getting dirty. A horse at grass should only be dandy-brushed (see page 267).

To groom the horse you will need the grooming equipment shown right, and a box to keep it in, as well as a skep, half a bucketful of water and a head collar.

Tie the horse up by the head collar first and remove any rugs; if it is cold, keep a blanket over his quarters. Start by picking out his feet (below). Then clean the horse's legs with the dandy brush or a handful of straw. Hold the tail to keep it out of the way when working on the hind legs. This will help to stop him moving about or kicking you. Take care with the sensitive parts, such as the inside of his hind legs, where it is better to use a soft brush, or even your hand to groom him.

Using the body brush, separate the hair of the mane, brushing it thoroughly to remove any scurf and grease. Then brush out the tail, standing to the side of the horse so that there is less chance of getting

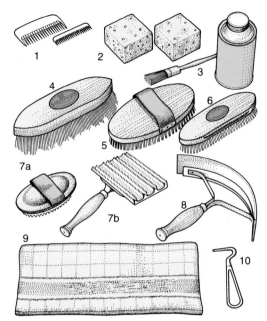

Grooming equipment
1 Mane and tail combs; 2 Sponges (for the eyes and for the dock); 3 Hoof oil and brush; 4 Dandy brush (hard); 5 Body brush (soft); 6 Water brush (soft); 7a Curry comb (rubber), 7b Curry comb (metal); 8 Sweat scraper; 9 Stable rubber; 10 Hoof pick

Cleaning the feet

Pick up each hoof in turn, as shown, and remove any stones and dirt with a hoof-pick, working from the heel down to the toe, to avoid hurting the sensitive frog. Check that the shoes are securely fixed, and that there are no risen clenches (see also page 270).

When grooming the horse with the body brush, keep the curry comb in your right hand and clean off the brush with it after a few strokes

kicked. Separate a few hairs at a time to remove the tangles and straw. Brush the dock vigorously to remove any grease or scurf. Never use a dandy brush on the mane or tail, as it will damage the hairs.

Then, starting on the near side with the body brush in your left hand and the curry comb in your right hand, brush from the top of the neck to the quarters, working with the direction of the horse's hair, in long, smooth, circular movements. Stand well back and put plenty of weight behind the brush to get rid of all the dirt and grease. After three or four strokes, clean the brush on the curry comb, which should be tapped regularly on the ground to remove the dirt. When the near side is complete, repeat the process on the offside, with the body brush in the right hand this time and the curry comb in the left.

Then lay the mane with a damp water-brush, and damp the top of the tail. If the tail is muddy wash it with warm water and soap, rinsing it well afterwards. Put on a tail bandage (see page 278) to keep the hairs of the tail flat. Finally, go over the horse with a damp stable-rubber to remove any dust, and to polish his coat. Then shake out the rugs, if worn, and replace them.

When you have untied the horse and removed the head collar, brush his head with a body brush, being careful not to

Oiling the horse's feet, including the frog, heels and walls of the hoof

bang the bony projections or the sensitive areas. Wipe the eyes, nostrils and muzzle with a damp sponge to refresh the horse, and dry them with a stable rubber.

Oil the feet, including the frog, heel and wall of the hoof up to the coronet, to prevent cracked and brittle hooves.

Strapping

After thorough grooming a horse will benefit from strapping (massaging) to stimulate the circulation. Strapping time can be lengthened each day as the horse becomes accustomed to it. Too much strapping to start with will cause the horse's muscles to become tired and ache.

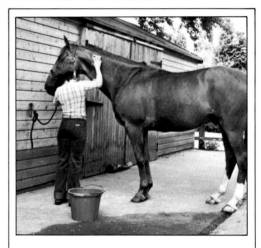

Washing the horse

In hot weather or after hard work, you may need to wash the horse all over to remove the sweat. Always use luke-warm water, and rinse off with cooler water. The excess water should be removed with the sweat scraper, and the horse dried off with stable rubbers or towels, particular attention being paid to the legs, chest, ears and heels.

Walk the horse in hand or let him graze, if it is sunny, until he is completely dry and then strap him to get his circulation going. Never leave the horse unrugged after vigorous grooming, otherwise he will get cold. Finally check that his ears are warm and dry.

It promotes the horse's circulation and tones and massages the muscles, and, therefore, plays an important part in conditioning a horse for hard work.

Untie the horse and hold on to his head collar with your left hand. With the stable rubber in your right, stand well back and bang the muscles on the neck and shoulder, and in front of the saddle area, with the rubber. Then tie him up and bang the muscles on the quarters and thighs, using a follow-through movement. Avoid any sensitive areas, and work with a steady rhythm, giving each muscle time to relax between bangs.

Pulling manes and tails

The hair of the mane and tail can be thinned and shortened by "pulling" it, which gives a neater appearance. Pulling the mane encourages it to lie flat against the horse's neck. It should be done a little at a time over a period of several days to prevent the horse from becoming sore. The hair can be removed more easily after exercise when the skin is warm and the pores are open.

Pulling the mane

Comb the mane well. Then take a small handful of hair and back-comb it until a few hairs stand up from the rest. Wind them around the comb and pull them out *sharply*. (If you do it slowly, it will hurt the horse.) Continue pulling a few hairs at a time, over several days, until the mane is the required length and thickness. Damp the mane afterwards to encourage it to lie flat.

Pulling the tail

Brush out the tail first to remove any tangles. Then pull out a few hairs from either side of the dock, starting at the top and only going halfway down the dock, as if you pull out the lower hairs you will not get such a well-shaped tail. Bandage the tail (see page 278) after it has been pulled, to encourage it to keep its shape.

Plaiting manes and tails

The mane and tail are plaited to give the horse a tidy appearance, and to encourage the mane to lie on the correct side. You will need a strong darning needle, stout thread of a suitable colour, elastic bands, a pair of scissors and a mane comb. You can plait the mane with rubber bands instead of thread.

Plaiting the mane

Damp the mane first and with the comb divide it evenly into the number of plaits that you require – 9 or 11 are suggested – and fasten each section of hair with an elastic band.

Beginning nearest the head, remove the elastic band on the first section and divide it into three equal strands. Plait the hair tightly, securing the end with an elastic band. Repeat for all the sections.

Take a needle and double thread, knotted at the end. Push the needle through the folded end of the plait. Fold the plait

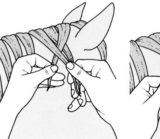

Making the first plait at the top of the neck

Stitching the folded plait together

The finished plaits

up until it lies against the crest and stitch up and down, as shown, pulling the thread tight so that the plait is firm. Finish off securely. Repeat with each section.

Plait the forelock, fold and stitch. It must be straight and should lie flat.

(To undo the plaits, pull gently on the underside until the thread is visible. Snip and cut off the elastic bands).

If securing the plaits with rubber bands, twist the band around the bottom of the plait, double it around the folded plait, and double again over the fold.

Plaiting the tail

Take a section from the sides of the tail alternately with the centre section of the tail, and plait downwards for most of the length of the dock. Plait the ends to form a long pigtail. Secure the plait with an elastic band, turn it up in a loop, and sew up the loop to form a thick double plait. Take care to make the plait even, and not too tight, or the dock will become sore.

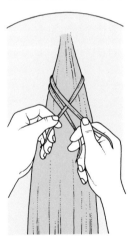
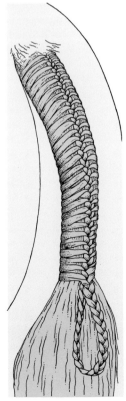

To plait the tail, take sections of hair from either side of the tail alternately, above, and plait down the tail. Secure the end with an elastic band, loop it over and stitch it to form a double plait, right.

Clipping

The horse's winter coat grows from early autumn right through the winter. From autumn onwards, most horses which are working will need to be clipped, to prevent them from sweating too much, thus losing condition. Also, the horse will be easier to groom and keep clean if his coat is short. He will need clipping every few weeks, but the date at which it starts and finishes will depend on how rapidly your horse's coat grows.

If the horse is kept out at night, the first clip of the season should be done early so that the hair has time to grow before bad weather sets in.

It is not easy to clip well, and if you are doubtful of your ability, get an expert to do it for you. Before you clip your horse for the first time, watch it done by an expert so that you have a clear idea how to go about it.

How to clip

You will need good, preferably electric, clippers. There are two main types: those that have a motor in the head of the tool and those that have a separate motor. (The latter type is better if the horse is nervous as it is less noisy.) The clippers must be well looked after and the blades must be sharp. Make sure that you follow the instructions for the use of the clippers and for the fitting of the new blades. They will need regrinding after clipping one horse with a longish coat. While clipping, clean the blades regularly in a little paraffin to prevent them from clogging up with hair.

Clipping the neck

Prepare the horse by making sure that he is clean and dry. Plait the forelock and bandage the tail (see page 278) to keep them out of the way of the clippers. Then mark out the lines of the area to be clipped with damp soap or chalk. Ask an assistant to hold the horse and soothe him, if necessary, while you clip. If the horse shows signs of fear or distress during clipping, stop and try to calm him. If you cannot, take him to an expert who should be able to do the job more quickly and skilfully than you can, thus upsetting him less.

Begin clipping by taking one or two strips off under the stomach to check that the clippers are functioning properly. Move to the rear of the horse and work from the quarters forwards, against the direction of the hair. Work with long systematic strokes, taking care to just overlap the line of the previous stroke, clipping against the line of the hair to avoid unsightly "tramlines". Take care not to clip the roots of the mane or tail. Cover the horse with a rug as you clip to prevent him getting a chill.

When you have clipped one side, repeat the process on the other side. Take care when clipping the sensitive areas, particularly around the head.

When you have finished clipping, check that no patches of hair have been overlooked. Preferably, exercise the horse after clipping. This will bring any scurf or grease to the surface when it can be removed more easily. Brush the horse vigorously to remove the loose hair and dust, and then rug him up. Clean the clippers and oil them before storing them away. Get the blades reground if necessary.

Trimming heels and whiskers

To trim the horse's heels, first clean and dry them thoroughly. Then comb the hair upwards and snip off the ends as the hairs run through the teeth of the comb. Angle the comb so as to get an even cut.

To trim the whiskers you will need a pair of curved scissors. Cut the whiskers as closely as possible, with the curved blades of the scissors held away from the horse, so that there is less chance of accidentally nicking him with them.

Types of clip

There are various types of clip, designed to suit different purposes:

Full clip in which the whole coat is removed. It is used mainly for show horses, or for horses with very woolly legs.

Hunter clip in which the legs and saddle area are left unclipped for extra protection.

Blanket clip in which the hair is removed from the neck and belly. It is useful for horses kept out during the day and in at night.

Trace clip in which the horse is clipped up to the harness trace line (from the days of horse-drawn vehicles). This is also useful for horses and ponies at grass.

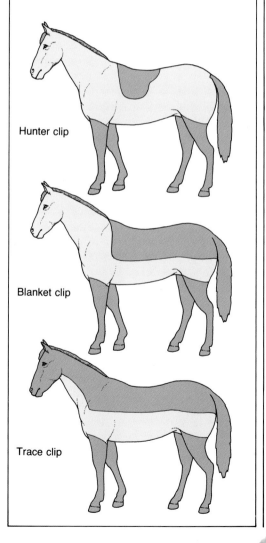

Hunter clip

Blanket clip

Trace clip

Keeping a horse at grass

It is more economical to keep your horse at grass, and often better for him, if there is a suitable field. Horses fed entirely off grass each need at least one acre of good grazing, preferably three. They must have easy access to clean fresh water at all times: a stream or clean pond is ideal (stagnant water must be fenced off), but piped water could be laid on to a trough, which must be sited away from low hanging branches or falling leaves. The trough should be strong and rust-proof, with no sharp projections. The type that refills automatically is best but even then the water should be inspected regularly to make sure it is clean and unpolluted. If there is no existing water supply, fresh water must be carried daily to the field (the horse drinks approximately 8 gallons a day), and put in a heavy container so that it cannot be knocked over.

The field must be strongly fenced, with no gaps through which the horse might escape. Post-and-rail fencing is ideal, as it is safe and durable, provided it is looked after properly. Hedges and walls are also suitable if they are well maintained. Post-and-wire fencing is acceptable, but the wire must be kept taut; the bottom strand should be at least 46cm (18in) high. Barbed or sheep wire should never be used as they are dangerous. Always make sure that there are no nails or sharp protrusions in the fencing.

The gates to the field must open wide and easily, and they should have safe, horse-proof catches. Any gate opening on to a lane or road should be kept locked so that it cannot be inadvertently left open by pedestrians. (It is also a wise precaution against possible theft.)

The field must provide some shelter. Tall hedges or clumps of trees help to protect the horse from cold winds and bad weather, but a suitable building or shed offers better protection, and is also a refuge from flies. It must be safe and large enough to house the horse or horses comfortably and should be inspected and cleaned out regularly. It should have three closed sides with the fourth side open to prevent any horse being trapped by its companions.

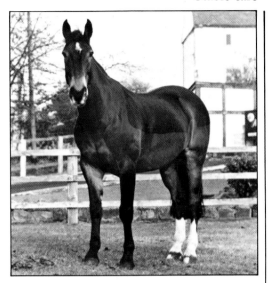

Penwood Forge Mill at grass

The grazing should be suitable for the type of horse: for example, a fat pony with a tendency to laminitis (see page 272) should be kept on poor pasture whereas young stock needs plenty of nutritious grass. (The grass will have to be rested and treated periodically – see overleaf.)

The fields should be inspected regularly before, after and during the time when the horse is turned out to check that they are free of litter and poisonous weeds; any dangerous holes should be filled in straight away to prevent accidents occurring.

Feeding

During the winter, when the grass does not grow, the horse will need supplementary food. Hay and other foods, such as maize, horse nuts and oats, will help to keep the horse warm and in good condition. He should be fed twice daily, at regular times if possible. Hay may be fed in a haynet or loose on the ground but the latter method is less practical as the hay may become wet and soiled, and therefore wasted. Other feed should be put in heavy containers so that the horse cannot kick them over.

Normally, a horse at grass needs no extra food during late spring and summer, but if he is ridden regularly, he should be fed once or twice a day to maintain condition. From November to April, when there is little goodness in the grass, feed him hay daily and other foods twice a day.

Care of the horse

A horse out at grass should be examined daily to ensure that he has suffered no injury. Frequent handling also makes him easier to catch. He should only have the mud removed from his coat with a dandy brush, and a general tidying up before being ridden, as he needs the natural grease in his coat to keep him warm and dry in winter and for protection against flies in summer. However, he will have to be groomed more thoroughly in spring and autumn when changing his coat. His mane and tail can be tidied up, but the tail should not be shortened as he will need it to brush

New Zealand rug

This type of rug is of weatherproof material and is lined with wool, so that it acts as a substitute for the horse's coat (in very cold weather, however, it will not be enough and he will need feeding well to keep warm). It has specially designed straps to prevent it from slipping or flapping if the horse gallops about or rolls. The rug must fit well, and it should be checked daily to make sure that it is not rubbing. It is best to have two rugs, so that the one not in use can be dried and cleaned. The straps must be cleaned frequently to keep them soft and supple.

The rug is useful not only for a horse at grass in cold weather, but also for a stabled, clipped horse that is turned out in winter when he is not being exercised. Extra blankets can be used in very cold weather.

away flies. Never wash the horse's legs and heels when he is out at grass as the protective grease would be removed, and could lead to cracked heels and mud fever. His eyes, nose and dock should be sponged at least once a week. The feet must also be picked out regularly and their condition noted. Look for cracks and bruises, and for signs of thrush (see page 272). Ask the blacksmith to remove the shoes every four to six weeks and trim the feet, before replacing the shoes. His teeth should also be checked for condition (see page 272).

Catching the horse

The horse should normally be easy to catch if you follow the guidelines on pages 36–7, particularly if you feed him after catching him. If your horse is completely unapproachable, and is in the field with others, get help and remove any other horse or horses from the field. Your horse will then be eager to join his companions and will probably come to the gate. If he is on his own, you will have to attempt to corner him as a last resort. Try not to frighten him, and never surprise him from behind. Move quietly, keeping the rope out of sight.

Working a horse off grass

A horse worked off grass will not be as fit as a stabled horse and must be worked accordingly. Regular slow work and good feeding will help to condition him.

Always allow a minimum of one hour's rest after he is fed and before he is ridden. If he is hot and sweating after work, walk him round to cool him down and then turn him out so that he can roll, dry off, and keep warm. The following day, any sweat marks should be rubbed off with straw and he should be inspected for injuries.

A horse being kept at grass needs regular road work to harden his legs, if he will be hunting or competing. He will not be as hard or fit as a stabled horse; his muscles will tire more quickly and he may become stiff from exertion and sweating. Always return home before the horse is over-tired, otherwise injuries may occur.

Before a day of hard work, bring the horse in for the night, if possible, and give him a deep bed, hay and fresh water. At the end of the day's work, check him for any injury, and rub any damp areas with straw, particularly the ears, saddle mark and chest. See that he is cool and dry before putting him out in the field.

A horse being worked off grass should normally be trace-clipped to prevent too much sweating and loss of condition. A New Zealand rug will then be needed at night, or on very cold days.

Turning the horse out
Lead the horse into the field, and turn him round to face the gate before you slip the halter or head collar off. If he kicks out when he gallops off, you can then get out of the way. Never chase a horse away when you turn him out– he may prove difficult to catch next time.

It is best to put two horses out together, for companionship and so that they can whisk flies off each other. If the horses are all of the same sex, there is less risk of quarrelling and kicking. Shod horses should never be turned out together especially if they do not know each other well.

Worms and worming
Worms are often responsible for a horse's loss of condition. The types of worm commonly found in horses are: red, round, lung, pin and tape worms. You can recognize a horse that is worm-infested by its pot belly, visible ribs, harsh, staring coat, anaemia, loose smelly droppings (containing worms), coughing and tail rubbing.

All horses have some worms, and even regular worming cannot eliminate all of them. Regular doses of worm treatment are needed to keep them under control.

Before worming a horse, get a worm count taken by sending a sample of his droppings for a laboratory analysis. This will reveal the number of eggs per gram of dropping, for each worm group. Less than 100 eggs per gram means the horse is relatively worm free, and regular worming thereafter, every two or three months, should keep the worms under control. A horse coming from grass after a rest should be wormed immediately. There are various worm treatments on the market, to combat different types of worm, and to suit different horses, so seek veterinary advice.

Care of grassland

Grassland must be well looked after to ensure that it has sufficient food value. Horses will ruin a field if allowed to graze it continuously, as they tend to pick out the best grass, leaving the unpalatable coarse or weedy parts and, understandably, will not eat any soiled patches. Droppings should be removed regularly to counteract this problem and to avoid worm infestation.

The field should be rested before it becomes horse-sick (patchy and uneven) and ideally it should be grazed for a while by cattle, which will level off the grass and then by sheep which will crop it close so that it regrows evenly.

The grass must be fertilized regularly, but never with stable manure if it is to be grazed by horses within six months, as worms may be passed back into the soil. A soil analysis will tell you what deficiencies must be made up, by the addition of nitrogen, lime, phosphate or potash.

Weeds compete with grass and take away nourishment from the soil. Docks must be pulled up. Poisonous plants, such as ragwort or hemlock for example, should be removed and burned.

The field should be well-drained, as good grasses will not grow where water is lying.

Harrowing and rolling
Regular chain harrowing and rolling are important to keep the field in good condition. Harrowing loosens and aereates soil, drags out the old grass, and spreads the droppings over the field, if they are not removed by hand. Harrowing should be done without fail in March, before the grass grows, and whenever possible throughout the summer. The field should be left unstocked for two to three days afterwards to allow the grass to recover. If you cannot buy or borrow a chain harrow, you will have to maintain the grassland with a fork and rake.

Shoeing

Working on hard surfaces wears down the horse's feet faster than they can grow so he will need to be shod. Shoes can also improve the horse's action and help to correct any faults of conformation, if carefully designed and applied. Horses at grass are best left unshod or shod with grass tips, as the feet remain healthier, and the horses are less likely to injure one another.

Unshod feet must be trimmed regularly to prevent pieces of foot splitting and breaking off. All shoeing must be done by a qualified blacksmith, as it requires considerable skill. However, you should know how to remove a shoe yourself, in case your horse spreads a shoe at any time. Ask your farrier to show you exactly how to do it, and then practise under his supervision. You will need the equipment shown below.

A set of shoes should last from four to six weeks before needing to be removed and replaced. The type of shoes used will depend on the work your horse is doing and on whether he has any foot problems that require "special" shoes (see right).

If the horse is doing a lot of roadwork he may need to be reshod every two to three weeks. Between shoeing, inspect his feet regularly; if the foot is growing out over the shoe you will need the farrier. If the horse loses a shoe, check the foot over to make sure that there are no nails left behind, and that the tender area has not been bruised or cut. If it has, swab the foot well and pour iodine on the wound to prevent it becoming infected.

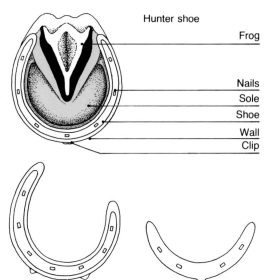

Hunter shoe — Frog, Nails, Sole, Shoe, Wall, Clip

Three-quarter shoe   Grass tip

Types of shoe

The simplest type of shoe has an iron "web" with holes for the nails drilled at intervals along it, and a toe clip which stops the shoe from moving backwards. Quarter clips are usually fitted instead on the hind shoes so that the horse does less damage to himself if he over-reaches. For most riding horses, the hunter shoe is most suitable. It

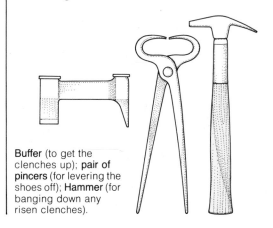

Buffer (to get the clenches up); **pair of pincers** (for levering the shoes off); **Hammer** (for banging down any risen clenches).

Signs of correct shoeing

When a horse is correctly shod:

. the type and weight of shoe will be suitable for the work to be done and for the size of his foot.

. the shoes will fit the feet, and not vice versa: if the wall and toe are rasped back to meet the shoe, the horn will be exposed, and will split and crack, causing lameness.

. the frog will be in contact with the ground, otherwise it will shrink and become useless.

. the clenches will be in a line about 2.5cm (1in) from the ground.

. there will be no daylight between the shoe and foot.

. the heels of the shoe will neither be too long nor too short.

. the toe clip will be fitted properly.

. the nails will be of the right size and in a sufficient number; three on the inside and four on the outside are normally used for an average-sized shoe.

creates less suction in heavy going than an ordinary shoe because its lower surface is grooved ("fullered") not flat and is "concave". The nail heads fit into the grooves. Grass tips are used when the horse is turned out, to protect the toe while allowing the frog and heel contact with the ground, which helps to keep the foot healthy. There are also various types of "orthopaedic" shoes to counteract particular ailments or faults of conformation. For example, a three-quarter shoe can be fitted if the horse tends to have corns. Special lightweight shoes are used for racing.

Studs

Studs can be inserted into the shoe to prevent the horse slipping. There are two types: permanent ones attached by the farrier when the horse is shod, and which are used for horses doing heavy road work or crossing rough terrain; and those that can be screwed in as a temporary measure to provide extra grip when jumping or schooling, for example. If you use temporary studs, always remove them immediately after use, before the horse is stabled, as he may cut himself with them if he lies down or rolls.

Fitting a shoe
Above, the farrier has sized the shoe and is now fitting it with new nails. Accuracy is vital as each nail passes through the wall of the hoof.
Right, when all the nails are hammered home, the projecting clenches are bent over, cut flush and rasped smooth.

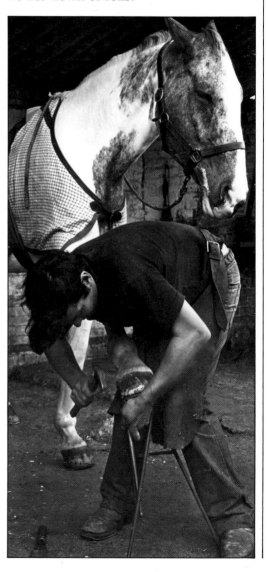

Veterinary notes

If you own or look after a horse you must have a sound basic knowledge concerning its general condition, so that you can recognize simple ailments and the symptoms of ill-health. You will need at least one good veterinary manual, and you should keep a stock of the most essential medical equipment (see below). Your horse will also need regular protection against tetanus and influenza. Following the initial course of two injections, an annual booster is required. At least once a year, his teeth and gums should be inspected and the teeth rasped, if sharp in places. He will also need regular worm analysis and treatment (see page 269).

Your horse will need veterinary attention when he has a high temperature (above 39.5ºC [103ºF]), abnormal pulse rate or breathing (see opposite), lost appetite, stomach or kidney disorders (abnormal bowel or urinary behaviour), colic, heat swelling or pain in any part of the body (usually the legs), persistent coughing, lameness, or severe bleeding, usually from a wound in need of stitching.

It is more practical and less expensive to learn how to treat any of the more common *minor* ailments and injuries yourself. However, if in any doubt about your horse's condition, seek veterinary advice.

To treat any superficial grazes and cuts, usually on the horse's legs, apply a cold compress to the wound to stop any bleeding. Then clean the wound thoroughly using cold water and a mild antiseptic, clipping the hair round it if necessary. Dress the wound using antiseptic powder or cream to encourage healing. Minor wounds should not need bandaging.

Strains to the muscles or tendons are also quite common. Once diagnosed, they can be treated by hosing the painful, swollen area with cold water, or by using a cold compress, alternating the cold treatment with the application of a hot poultice. If the symptoms persist, or if the horse goes lame, call the vet. Bruising can be alleviated by applying witch hazel and a cold compress to the affected area.

Girth galls or sores may occur as a result of the saddlery rubbing (through negligence) and should be treated with salt and water, or with surgical spirit, to harden the skin. If the horse gets a sore mouth from the bit rubbing (usually from rough hands or an ill-fitting or worn bit), rub vaseline or healing cream into the corners of the mouth (it also helps prevent soreness and cracks), and remove the cause of the trouble.

Thrush is a foot condition in which the frog area becomes spongy and foul-smelling. It is usually the result of standing on soiled and soggy bedding, and can be cured by keeping the stable dry and clean, and by treating the horse's feet with Stockholm tar.

More serious ailments

Strangles This is a contagious and dangerous infection, causing inflammation and abscesses around the throat area. It is spread by direct contact, or via contaminated food or water. Young horses are more susceptible to it than older ones, and it is prevalent in a damp, cold climate. Antibiotics usually cure this painful complaint.
Ringworm This is a very contagious, fungal disease, of which there are several types. The symptoms are raised circular spots on the skin, varying in size, Eventually patches of hair come off, leaving a dry, scaly surface. It will have a debilitating effect on the horse. There are several types of skin disease and the vet will diagnose the appropriate treatment.
Laminitis This condition usually affects the front feet (mainly of ponies) with the result that the pony stands back on his heels with his hind legs tucked beneath his body.

Contents of veterinary chest
Thermometer, scissors, small surgical dish, gamgee tissue, cotton wool, assortment of bandages, surgical gauze, witch hazel, boracic powder, Animalintex/kaolin poultice, colic drench, antiseptic cream/powder liniment, common/epsom salts, surgical spirit, iodine, Cornucrescine, Stockholm tar.

There is heat in the foot, especially at the front and toe region, and the horse moves forward with reluctance with short "pottery" steps. He will be unwilling to put weight onto the affected foot or feet and his temperature may rise, and his pulse and respiration rate increase.

There are two types of laminitis: acute (in which sudden pain and lameness occurs, and chronic (in which the sole eventually drops as the pedal bone is affected due to pressure within the hoof), and rings form on the wall of the hoof. The condition is often incurable, and the horse may have to be put down.

Colic The horse suffers abdominal pain and is restless, and he will look round and kick at his belly, paw the ground and may lie down and roll in an attempt to escape the pain. His temperature may rise and his pulse and respiration rate increase. He will also sweat or break out in patches. You *must* walk the horse round at the first signs of colic, and call the vet immediately.

Azoturia This usually occurs when a horse in hard work has had a rest day without having had his corn sufficiently reduced and a laxative mash the day before. The onset of azoturia is rapid. The horse may seem normal but suddenly, at exercise, will roll and stagger behind and go lame. He may collapse if made to continue. The muscles over the loins harden, his temperature will be high and he will sweat and blow. *Never* try to walk him or ride him home; transport him in a box, or leave him where he is. Call the vet immediately.

Lymphangitis This may be caused as above, or by germs entering an infected wound. It normally affects one hind leg which will be very swollen and painful from the coronet up to his stifle, and the horse will be lame. The vet will prescribe suitable treatment, according to the cause.

Destroying the horse

If the horse is so ill that the vet decides he must be humanely destroyed, you should ask him to do it on your own premises. It is kinder to the horse, although not pleasant for you.

General health care

Although much of the veterinary care of the horse is skilled, the following basic tasks can be learned quickly so that you can establish whether the horse is healthy or not, and attend to him if he is sick. For detailed information on the care of the horse, consult your veterinary surgeon and/or a good veterinary manual.

To take the horse's temperature

Smear vaseline on the thermometer and stand to the side of his hindquarters and grasp his tail. Hold it upwards, and insert the bulb of the thermometer into the horse's rectum. Keep it in for approximately two minutes before removing it and taking the reading. If it is over 39.5°C (103°F), call the vet immediately. The normal adult temperature should be between 37.5–38°C (100°–100.5°F). A foal's temperature may be slightly higher.

To take the horse's pulse

There is usually a clear pulse on either side of the horse's jaw where the artery passes under and inside the jawbone or in the middle of the inside of the forearm, level with the elbow. When the horse is resting, his pulse should be 35–40 beats a minute.

Checking respiration

Watch the horse's flanks and time the visible movements of his ribs. There should be 8 to 15 breaths a minute when he is resting.

Administering medicine

Pills and powders are best given in a small feed or mash, with black treacle or something similar to disguise any unpleasant taste, if necessary. Drenching and tubing should be left to a vet, as it is a skilled job, and an unskilled person could cause damage.

Applying a poultice

There are two main types of poultice, which are usually applied to the legs. A kaolin poultice reduces swelling and inflammation. It is heated until "hand hot", pasted thickly over the injury and covered with insulating, moisture-proof wrapping, and finally bandaged in place (see page 278). Animalintex is a pre-prepared antiseptic poultice which can be applied directly to a wound, to draw out infection and ease bruising. Cut it to the appropriate size to cover the injury, wet it with hot water, and bandage it in place.

Saddlery and equipment

Saddles

The purpose of the saddle is to help the rider to keep his balance and adjust it smoothly while allowing the horse to change his balance, without interference, whenever he starts, stops or jumps a fence. A correctly fitting saddle is essential to protect the horse's back. The rider's weight should be placed as closely as possible over the horse's centre of gravity.

Saddles differ in design to allow the appropriate weight distribution for every equestrian activity and style. Some must be specially adapted to suit the conformation of a particular horse.

The foundation of a saddle is the "tree" which is usually made of light wood or fibreglass, reinforced with metal. The stirrup bars are attached to the tree and have hinged safety catches which should release the leathers and irons automatically when they are under pressure. They should be kept in the "open" position when the horse is ridden.

The rider's legs rest on the outer leather flaps which cover the panels. The principal types of saddle are: the general purpose, which is popular as it is versatile enough to be used for most types of riding; the dressage saddle (see page 119), which has a deeper seat and straight-cut flaps, the jumping saddle (page 148), which is forward-cut with knee rolls; the show saddle, which is a flatter version with straight, neat flaps; and the racing saddle: a lightweight and exaggerated form of the jumping saddle. Side-saddles and Western saddles are specially designed to suit these forms of riding.

If the saddle is to fit correctly, the front arch must rise high enough above the horse's withers to avoid pinching them, and to allow the shoulder blades to move freely. The back arch (cantle) is flatter and wider, and is joined by shaped and padded panels to keep the rider's weight evenly distributed over the horse's back without pressing on the spine or loins. The entire framework is covered with leather which will require working in when new.

A numnah (see page 35) is often placed under the saddle to protect the horse's back. It should never be used to correct an ill-fitting saddle.

Breastplate and breast girth

The breastplate is a strap attached to the front arch (D-rings) of the saddle, on either side of the withers. It runs down from the chest, between the horse's forelegs, to the girth. It is used as a precaution when the girth alone is not sufficient to keep the saddle firmly in place, particularly for hunting, cross country riding and racing. It should be loose enough for you to be able to slip your hand between it and the horse's chest. The breast girth runs across the chest only, attached to the girth straps.

Martingales

A martingale may be used to help to prevent the horse raising his head above the angle of control. There are two principle types. The running martingale, right, acts indirectly on the bit when the reins are pulled. It must have stops on the reins to prevent the rings getting caught on rein buckles or the bit. The standing martingale joins the girth directly to the back of the cavesson noseband. It should not be fas-

Bits and bridles

There are many different types of bits and bridles. those shown below and below right are a selection of the most commonly used. Others are shown on page 35.

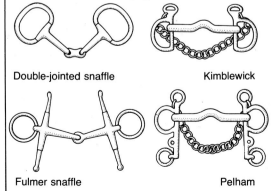

Double-jointed snaffle

Kimblewick

Fulmer snaffle

Pelham

Running martingale

work with maximum efficiency. The bit rests on the smooth bars of the mouth, between the canine teeth and the grinders. You should use a mild bit, if possible; stronger, more severe bits must only be used by expert riders, and even then with great sensitivity and caution. If the horse fails to go well or becomes out of control in one of the milder bits, below, you should try to establish the reasons for this, rather than attempt to cure the problem by using a stronger bit. Most faults can, and should, be overcome by retraining.

In general, the thicker the bit, the more gentle its action on the bars of the mouth, with the pressure distributed more widely. Bits are usually made of stainless steel, but the mouthpiece can be covered in rubber or vulcanite to make it kinder.

The simple-jointed snaffle bit (see page 35) exerts pressure on the corners of the horse's mouth and the tongue. A Fulmer snaffle can be used to prevent the bit from slipping through the horse's mouth; a double-jointed snaffle acts on the tongue and the corners of the mouth.

tened too tightly, and should never be used with a drop noseband, which could restrict the horse's breathing. When correctly fitted, the martingale should reach into the horse's gullet when pulled taut.

Bridles and bits

The bit provides the principle means of communication with your horse, and helps to encourage the correct head carriage and overall balance which will enable him to

A double bridle consists of two bits on separate pairs of reins, the snaffle (or bridoon) combined with a curb bit and curb chain attached, which makes it more severe than the snaffle. This bridle should only be used by a very experienced rider and will

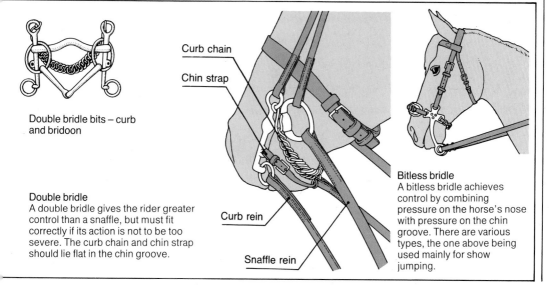

Double bridle bits – curb and bridoon

Curb chain

Chin strap

Curb rein

Snaffle rein

Double bridle
A double bridle gives the rider greater control than a snaffle, but must fit correctly if its action is not to be too severe. The curb chain and chin strap should lie flat in the chin groove.

Bitless bridle
A bitless bridle achieves control by combining pressure on the horse's nose with pressure on the chin groove. There are various types, the one above being used mainly for show jumping.

vary in severity, depending on the leverage produced by the length of the side-pieces of the curb bit. The Pelham is a combination of a straight-bar snaffle and curb in one bit, and has an uncompromising action. A bit-less bridle is a variation used principally in Western riding (see page 83) and by show jumpers. It has no mouthpiece and the pressure is on the horse's nose and chin instead. It can be very severe, and should only be used by expert riders.

Whatever type of bridle is used, it must fit correctly. The bit must be neither too wide nor too narrow – the mouthpiece should be half-an-inch wider in total than the horse's jaw. When the bridle is done up, the bit should just wrinkle the corners of the horse's mouth.

The throat lash must be loose enough to allow the horse to flex without hindrance, and the noseband (in its various forms) should be correctly fitted, neither too low over the nostrils, nor too high, rubbing on the cheekbones.

It is a false economy to buy cheap saddlery. It is essential for the safety of horse and rider that they do not break, causing an accident, so invest in good equipment.

Cleaning and storing tack

All tack must be cleaned regularly to help preserve the leather and stitching, and should be checked often for signs of wear, particularly around the buckle areas.

Leather needs regular feeding with glycerine or a good saddle soap to keep it supple, otherwise it will become brittle and cracked.

For tack cleaning you will need rough cloths or sponges for washing off the tack, saddle soap or glycerine with a separate sponge for putting it on, metal polish and cloths to apply it, and a duster to shine the metal. If the leather has become stiff or very dry, it may need treating with special leather preservative.

It is useful to have a wooden horse to put the saddle on while cleaning it. Your tack room should have hooks on which to hang the bridle, stirrup leathers and girth, both while cleaning them and for storing them away, and saddle brackets on which to hang the saddle.

Cleaning the bridle

Remove the bit from the bridle and soak it in warm clean water. Undo all the straps from their keepers, without unbuckling them (about once a week undo all pieces, and clean them thoroughly). Using a damp cloth or sponge, wipe all the leather thoroughly to remove any grease and dirt. Allow it to dry off. Lightly dampen the soap-sponge and apply the saddle soap to all the leather pieces, on both sides. Dry the bit, and polish it, then put it back on the bridle. To hang it up, loop the reins through the throat lash and fasten it. Fasten the noseband around the outside and hang up on the bridle hook.

Cleaning the saddle

Remove the girth and stirrup leathers. Soak the stirrup irons in cool water, if very dirty. Wash, dry and soap all the leather, as for the bridle, and be careful not to oversoap the seat of the saddle or it will be sticky to sit on, and the soap will stain the rider's breeches. Do not neglect the underside of the saddle. Clean and polish the stirrups, replace them on their leathers and reattach them to the saddle. Finally hang up the saddle, preferably in a cool dry place, and cover it with a stable cloth to keep it dust-free. The girths should also be cleaned daily, and the numnah, if used, washed or brushed, as appropriate.

Non-leather girths may need washing when very dirty but mud will brush off.

Bridle correctly hung

Rugs and horse clothing

Rugs are used for keeping a horse warm, especially if he is clipped, or sick. They also help to keep the horse clean.

It is very important that a rug fits securely, otherwise it will rub or give the horse sore withers or shoulders, or it may slip, possibly causing him to panic if it twists right underneath him. If the rug is too loose and flaps around his neck, it will work back uncomfortably behind his withers. If it is too small, it will restrict his chest movement when he walks or puts his head down, and he may burst open the buckle. The sides of the rug should reach down to just below the stomach line, and as far back as the tail, as shown.

Above, a cotton mesh sweat sheet. It can be used to cool an over-heated horse or under a night rug, if the horse sweats.

Among the many types of rug are: summer sheets (usually made of cotton and used to protect the horse from flies or from stable soiling); mesh sweat sheets; night or day rugs (of varying thicknesses and warmth) and waterproof exercise sheets (for outdoor use). Lightweight rugs, particularly those used outside, usually have a fillet string attached, which lies loosely under the horse's tail, below the hindquarters, to prevent the rug from flying about in very windy weather.

Most rugs have to be held in place with either a padded roller or a surcingle sewn into the rug. A New Zealand rug is used to protect horses from bad weather when out at grass (see page 268). In very cold weather a blanket or blankets may also be needed.

When putting a blanket on the horse, throw it up well forward on his neck and then pull it back to cover the loins – never pull it against the lie of the horse's coat. It must be smoothed out before the rug is put on, and can be turned back at the neck over the rug to prevent it slipping. Secure the breast-strap or buckle of the rug, and fasten the roller firmly, but not so tightly that it presses on the horse's spine.

Rugs should be aired as often as possible and cleaned regularly, so you will need spare ones. When not in use, they should be stored in a mothproof chest or cupboard.

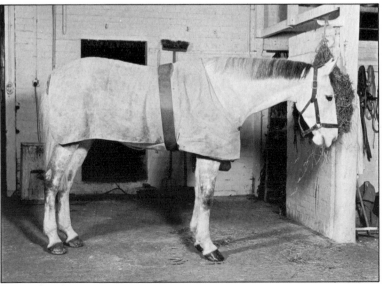

Right, a wool-lined jute night rug, used to keep the horse warm.

Boots

Various types of boot are used to protect the horse's legs, especially when jumping, schooling or galloping. The main ones are shown below. **Brushing** boots guard the legs against knocks. **Tendon** boots give the back of the leg extra protection against over-reaching, or similar blows. **Fetlock** boots protect the hind fetlock joints from brushing, if the horse tends to move "close" behind. **Over-reach** boots prevent the horse from stepping with his hind foot on the heel of his forefoot.

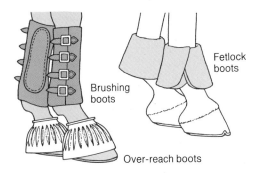

Brushing boots

Fetlock boots

Over-reach boots

Kneecaps

Kneecaps protect the horse's knees when exercising on slippery or rough ground. A padded version is normally used for protection while travelling the horse. The top strap of the kneecap should be done up tightly enough to prevent it slipping, while the bottom strap should be loose enough to allow the joint to bend.

Bandages

Bandages are normally of wool, stretch or adhesive fabric, or crepe, and may be used for leg protection when travelling, exercising or in the stable, or to keep the tail neat and tidy when travelling. They can also be used to keep a poultice or dressing in place on an injured leg.

All leg bandages should be applied over a soft form of padding, which must lie flat against the leg. Cotton gamgee tissue is ideal, but fur fabric or thin pieces of foam are also suitable. Woollen bandages are normally used for the stable or travelling, stretch fabric or crepe for exercise, and crepe for the tail.

Support bandages should be applied in a figure of eight, over gamgee tissue, to give greater support and more evenly applied pressure. They must not be so tight that they prevent proper circulation.

When rolling up a bandage after use, fold the tapes inside and roll the bandage over the tapes tightly. Brush any mud off the bandage after use, and clean them regularly.

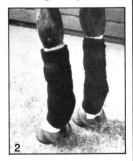

Putting on a stable bandage
Always put the bandage on over gamgee tissue, which should protrude above and below the bandage so that the edge does not cut into the horse's leg. Roll the bandage in the same direction as the gamgee so that it does not bulge or wrinkle. Start unrolling the bandage below the upper joint at an angle so that there is no hard edge. (1) Continue down to the coronet, before rolling it up towards the knee or hock. The tapes must always be tied on the inside or outside of the leg (2), otherwise the knot may press on the tendon. After removing bandages, rub the horse's legs to get the circulation going.

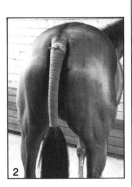

Putting on a tail bandage
Damp the tail well and start bandaging at the top of the dock. Work downwards, rolling the bandage quite firmly around the first two-thirds of the dock (1), and then more loosely towards the end, so that the circulation is not impeded. Tie the tape on the outside and bend the dock slightly inwards so that it lies naturally (2). (Never leave a tail bandage on overnight as the dock will become sore.) To remove the bandage, slide it gently off from the top. If the tail is plaited, however, unwind the bandage carefully.

Appendix

Rider's fitness

Although physical strength is not vital for riding, overall fitness will improve your ability to ride well. The exercises on these pages are for increasing muscular strength and suppleness. Build a programme of exercise, aiming to do a few repetitions of each to start with, gradually building up your schedule to the maximum number of repetitions suggested for each one. If you are very unfit, or elderly, consult your doctor before embarking on any fitness programme.

For legs

Step-up
Step up onto a block about 30cm (12 in) high, first with your left foot and then with your right foot.
Repeat 25 times.

Swinging one leg
Stand straight, resting your hand on the back of a chair for support. Swing one leg back and forth 15 times, then repeat 15 times with the other leg.

Knee bend
Stand with your back against a wall. Hold your arms outstretched in front of you and bend your knees so that you slide slowly to the ground. Rise and repeat 8 times.

For hips

Pelvis rotating
Stand with your legs slightly apart, your hands on your hips. Pull in your stomach and rotate your pelvis, first in one direction, then in the opposite one. Repeat 50 times.

Bouncing
Sit on the floor with your legs bent and your weight to one side as shown. Stretch your arms in front of you and keep your back straight. Bounce from right to left and left to right, 10 times.

Leg circling
Lie flat on the floor, your arms at your sides. Raise one leg in the air, and circle it 20 times. Repeat with the other leg.

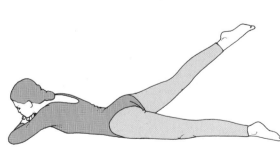

Loosening joints

Rotating
Swing your arms freely from the shoulders and rotate your head, wrists and ankles to loosen and supple your joints.

General muscle toning

Stretching
Stretch up, standing straight, with your legs together, and swing your arms up and over your head to clap your hands. Repeat 30 times.

Bicycling
Lie flat on your back, with your arms by your sides. Pedal with your legs, alternating fast and slow movements. Repeat 50 times.

General fitness

Running on spot
Run on the spot, up to 50 steps, lifting your arms high as you do so.

Skipping
Skip on the spot, up to 50 times.

Crouch jumps
Bend your knees and crouch, and then spring up in the air, raising your arms above your head as you do so. Repeat 20 times.

281

Glossary

A

Above the bit Said of a horse which is evading rein contact by bringing his nose in front of the vertical and carrying his head too high.

Aids The means by which the rider communicates his intentions to the horse. The natural aids are the use of hands, legs, body and voice. The artificial aids are the use of spurs, whips, martingales and/or other gadgets.

B

Bearing The horse's general carriage and balance.

Behind the bit Said of a horse which is evading rein contact by drawing his head in, with his nose coming behind the vertical.

"Between hand and leg" see "On the aids"

"Blind" obstacle One in which the horse cannot see the landing side when taking off.

Brushing When the inner side of one of the horse's hooves strikes the opposite leg, usually on the fetlock joint.

Buffer Tool used in shoeing to withdraw nails from the shoe.

C

Cadence Quality of the horse's pace, showing rhythm, energy and springy steps.

Capriole High school movement in which the horse springs from his hocks and, with his forelegs raised, kicks his hind legs out before landing square.

Cast (1) When a horse is stuck on the ground, and cannot get up into a standing position; (2) to "lose" a shoe.

Cavalletti Poles 3m (10ft) long supported on cross-pieces.

Change of hand (also known as change of rein) A change of direction.

Change of lead A change of the horse's leading leg when cantering or galloping.

Chestnut A corny growth on the inside of the horse's legs.

Collection The term used to describe a horse whose outline has shortened and rounded up, as his hind legs have moved further under his body, thus improving his balance.

Combination A jump made up of more than one part or element. It may take the form of a double (two elements), a treble (three elements) or more.

Compulsory halt The 10-minute break taken between phases of the Speed and Endurance test in a three-day event.

Conformation The physical structure of the horse.

Contact The amount of feel on the reins linking the rider's hands to the bit.

D

Disunited Said of a horse which is cantering with a diagonal pair of legs leading instead of the near or offside pair.

Driving aids The means by which the horse is ridden forward – usually a combination of seat and leg aids, but supplemented if necessary by the whip. It is not effective unless the horse accepts the bit.

E

Emergency grip When the side-saddle rider clamps both legs tightly into the pommels to secure her position. It is used mainly for jumping.

Engagement Term used to describe the action whereby the horse's hind legs are brought further underneath his body.

Ergot A horny substance found in the fetlock.

"Ewe" neck When the horse's neck is longer and more developed in the lower line than the top line, giving it a concave bend with the crest sloping inwards.

Extension The lengthening of stride at the walk, trot or canter. The horse should show equal extension in both hind and fore legs.

F

FEI *Fédération Equestre Internationale*. The governing body for officially recognized equestrian competitions.

Flexion The rounding of the neck in answer to the aids.

Flexion, lateral The suppleness and muscular development of the horse which allows him to bend on a circle throughout the length of his spine.

Forward seat

Forward seat The position adopted by the rider for jumping or galloping, in which the stirrups are shortened and the rider's weight is brought further forward to allow him to stay over the centre of gravity more easily.

G

Ground-line The projecting base of a jump used by the horse to judge its take-off point.

H

Half-halt A bracing of the rider's back which acts as a warning signal to the horse before any alteration of pace, balance or direction.

Hunting seat The traditional seat (once very common in the hunting field but no longer considered correct) where the rider sits well back in the saddle with feet and legs thrust forward, particularly when jumping.

I

Impulsion The energy generated by the activity of the horse's hindquarters. (Do *not* confuse it with speed.)

In-hand When the horse is led from the ground, rather than ridden.

J

Jump off The deciding phase of a show jumping competition in which all riders who have completed a clear round jump again, usually over slightly raised obstacles and a shortened course, to decide the winner. It is often timed.

L

Leaning on the bit When the horse appears to balance himself by leaning against the rider's hands for support.

Levade A high school movement in which the horse lowers himself on his haunches, and raises his forelegs in the air. The longer the levade is held, the more difficult it is to perform.

Long rein, on a When the reins are as long as possible without the rider losing contact with the bit, but allowing the horse to stretch its neck freely (*not* a "loose" rein, however).

N

Napping Any type of resistance from the horse. It may take various forms, including rearing or bucking.

Near side The left side of the horse.

Neck-reining Method of turning the horse by rein contact alone, used in Western-style riding.

Numnah A saddle-shaped pad of soft material used under the saddle to absorb any sweat, and minimize any discomfort thus caused. It should not be used to "correct" an ill-fitting saddle.

O

Off side The right side of the horse.

On the aids The term used to describe a horse which is attentive and responsive to the rider's actions (seat, legs, hands), ready to perform any movement required of him.

On the bit When the horse carries himself easily, with good balance and impulsion, without any form of resistance to the bit when the aids are correctly applied.

One-sidedness A tendency on the part of the horse to work more efficiently in one direction than the other, usually because his muscles are more developed on one side than on the other.

Optimum take-off zone The ideal zone within which a horse must take off to clear a jump successfully. It will vary according to the height and type of jump.

Overbent When the nose of the horse comes behind the vertical, usually with an exaggerated bend of the neck, with the result that the head is drawn in close to the chest.

Overfacing Presenting the horse at an obstacle which is too large or too difficult for it to jump.

Over-reaching When the toe of the horse's hind foot strikes the heel of the forefoot.

Oxer A form of parallel fence (composed of a spread) with more than one plank or pole at the front, and a single pole at the rear, usually with a lower brush placed between the two parts of the fence.

P

"Pipe-opener" The term used to describe a short, sharp gallop in which the horse's lungs are cleared, and its circulatory system stimulated, usually before fast or extended work.

Pivot A turn performed on the spot, either on the haunches or the forehand.

Position, to (left or right). To flex or bend the horse to left or right before asking for lateral movement.

Presentation The manner in which the rider puts his horse at a jump.

R

Running "downhill" Said of a horse which is taking quick, hurried strides, with too much weight on its forehand.

Running out Veering off to the side of a jump so that the horse fails to jump the obstacle: a form of refusal.

S

Schoolmaster An experienced, well-trained horse.

Slip rein A method of securing a rein to an object, such as a head collar, so that it can be released quickly by letting go of one end.

Slip the reins Allowing the reins to slide out through the fingers to their maximum length, if necessary, to let the horse use his head and neck to recover after an awkward landing or stumble.

Spanish walk An exaggerated and elevation form of walk, when the forelegs show much greater activity and extension than the hind legs.

Spread (1) A jump which is wide as well as high; (2) term used to describe a shoe which has shifted out of position.

T

Track The path taken by the horse's fore and hind legs; **on two tracks** – when the forefeet and hind feet move along two parallel tracks, as in the lateral movements.

Tracking up When the horse's hind feet overlap the imprints of its forefeet.

W

Weaving A stable vice in which the horse rocks from side to side in his box or stall, usually as a result of boredom.

Weight cloth A cloth carried by riders in competitions where there is a minimum weight requirement, and where the rider is under that weight. The cloth is weighted with pockets of lead.

Index

Acknowledgments

Photographic sources

T = top, C = centre, B = bottom, L = left, R = right

All Sport, 161 TL
Sally Anne Thompson and R. Willbie (Animal Photography Ltd), 11, 27L, 56, 73B, 75B1, 80, 98, 99, 143T, 145, 146B, 147, 151T, 172B, 178B, 187, 190, 199, 206L, 245T, 247, 250, 256, 262R, 264, 265, 268, 277
Andrew de Lory, 15, 42TR, BR, 53, 76, 79, 82, 83, 84, 85, 88, 91, 93, 96, 97, 103, 104, 122B, 136, 137, 138, 139B, 143B, 206R, 221T, 251R, 278, 279
Bob Gordon, 119, 125, 135, 136BL, BR, 198, 202, 216, 218, 220
Clive Hiles, 18, 108, 122T, 124, 130, 139T, 181T, CL, CR, 182, 183, 184TL, TC, TR, 251L
Kit Houghton, 4/5, 6/7, 10, 12/13, 16TR, BR, 17, 19, 21, 22/23, 25, 27R, 29, 36L, 41BR, 42L, 43, 55, 58, 59, 61, 63, 66, 68C, B, 71, 72, 73TL, BL, 75TL, TR, BR, 78, 100, 105, 111, 113, 117, 150, 151B, 155, 158, 161TR, B, 164, 168, 170, 171, 172T, 173, 174, 176, 178T, 184B, 185, 186, 189, 200/201, 204, 219, 221B, 227, 231, 232, 233, 235, 244, 245C, BL, 246, 248, 249, 252, 253, 262L, 267
Bob Langrish, 2/3, 24, 60, 107, 109, 114, 146T, 154B, 159, 165, 169, 181B, 208, 224, 245BR
Observer, The, 65
Mike Roberts, 12
Chris Smith, 16L
Vision International Ltd, Elisabeth Weiland, 14, 64, 68, 77, 115, 116, 118, 120, 132/133, 144
Steven Wooster, 20, 36TR, BR, 37, 38, 39, 40, 41T, BL, 46, 48, 49, 52, 54, 166, 226, 234, 237, 239, 240, 241, 263, 271, 288

In addition, valuable help in the preparation of this edition has been given by the following.
Alison Melvin; Helen Douglas-Cooper; Lee Griffiths; Jenny Speller.

Mary Gordon-Watson and Dorling Kindersley Ltd would like to thank the following people and organizations for their cooperation.

Julia Baxter
Candy Dean
David Hunt
Debra Lee
Priscilla Leigh
Sharon Leonard
Jennie and Anne
 Loriston-Clarke
Miranda Morley
Moss Bros Ltd
G. W. Parker and Sons
Sandy Pflueger
Maureen van der Wyck
Colin Wares
Col. Frank Weldon
Lavinia Winch

Horses featured
Badger
Borodino
Cornishman
Fuzzypeg
Magnifique
Marco Polo
Omega
Sharjah
Sporting print

Main illustrations by
David Ashby

Other illustrations by
Hayward and Martin
Carol Johnson
Jim Robbins
Lorna Turpin
Venner Artists Ltd

Photographic services
Ron Bagley
Negs Ltd

Reproduction
Llovet S.A., Barcelona

Typesetting
D.P. Media Ltd, Hitchin